MEDITERRANEAN COOKBOOK WITH HEALTHY SLIMMER DIET RECIPES

A Massive Collection Of Over 100 Top Nutritious Meals To Make Adapting To This Aegean Lifestyle Quick And Easy For You As A Beginner

By

Lauren M. Angelo

Table Of Contents

Discover the Mediterranean Magic - A Journey to Health and Flavor

Welcome to a culinary adventure that promises to transform the way you eat and embrace a lifestyle that exudes vibrancy and vitality. The Mediterranean Diet, a time-honored tradition dating back centuries, has enchanted generations with its captivating flavors, colorful ingredients, and remarkable health benefits. As you embark on this journey to a healthier and more joyful way of living, we invite you to savor the abundance of tastes, textures, and aromas that this bountiful region has to offer.

In the pages ahead, you will find an array of delectable recipes crafted for beginners eager to dip their toes into the Mediterranean culinary waters. This cookbook didn't just jump into recipes, it gives you enough details as a beginner to start this awesome journey. Each recipe provides additional data like utensils needed, nutritional value, and vital tips about each recipe.

Whether you're a seasoned foodie or someone discovering the joys of cooking for the first time, this recipe book is your gateway to exploring the sun-kissed flavors of the Mediterranean.

Beyond its reputation for mouthwatering meals, the Mediterranean Diet is renowned for its positive impact on overall well-being. From reducing the risk of chronic diseases to enhancing cognitive function and promoting longevity, the Mediterranean way of eating has been scientifically proven to unlock the secrets of a healthier and happier life. But this is not just another diet – it is a celebration of life, a philosophy of balance and pleasure that embraces fresh, whole foods, and nourishing traditions.

Imagine your taste buds dancing with delight as you indulge in succulent olive oil drizzled over vibrant salads, the melody of herbs and spices that weave their way into every dish, and the rich, velvety texture of creamy hummus. Picture yourself savoring the simplicity of a Mediterranean table, where meals are savored slowly, and conversations linger long after the plates are cleared. This is not a diet of deprivation; it is an invitation to savor life's abundance.

In this recipe book, you'll find recipes that are both approachable and inspiring. Each dish is lovingly crafted to capture the essence of Mediterranean cuisine while keeping the cooking process simple and accessible. We understand that the journey to a healthier lifestyle can be daunting, but with these recipes as your guide, you'll find that cooking and eating the Mediterranean way is not only nourishing but also remarkably enjoyable.

From the sun-drenched coasts of Greece to the rustic villages of Italy and the bustling markets of Morocco, the Mediterranean region is a treasure trove of culinary wonders. We've handpicked a selection of recipes that showcase the diversity and cultural richness of this remarkable die

As you embark on this voyage of flavors, we encourage you to embrace the Mediterranean way of life beyond the plate. Take time to savor meals with loved ones, indulge in regular physical activity, and prioritize self-care. Beyond the kitchen, the Mediterranean Diet teaches us to connect with nature, honor the seasons, and celebrate the simple pleasures of life. Welcome to the Mediterranean magic – let's begin!

Benefits Of The Mediterranean Diet - Unlock the Secrets of the Mediterranean Diet: A Pathway to Health and Longevity

In a world where fad diets come and go, the Mediterranean Diet stands tall as a timeless treasure, celebrated for its exceptional health benefits and delectable flavors. Originating from the sun-soaked shores of the Mediterranean region, this time-honored way of eating has captured the hearts and taste buds of millions around the globe. So, what makes the Mediterranean Diet so special? Let's delve into its captivating benefits and discover why it's more than just a diet – it's a lifestyle.

1. Heart Health – A Love Story with Your Heart

At the core of the Mediterranean Diet is a profound love affair with heart health. Packed with heart-friendly monounsaturated fats from olive oil, nuts, and avocados, this diet works wonders in reducing LDL cholesterol levels while elevating HDL cholesterol, the good kind. The abundance of antioxidants in fruits and vegetables, coupled with omega-3 fatty acids from fish, offers a protective shield against cardiovascular diseases, lowering the risk of heart attacks and strokes. With every bite, you nurture your heart, promoting its vitality and longevity.

2. Longevity – Savor the Sweetness of Life

Mediterranean dwellers have long been revered for their vibrant and fulfilling lives, often reaching centenarian status with grace. Embracing this diet opens the gateway to a longer, healthier life. Research indicates that adherence to the Mediterranean Diet is associated with a reduced risk of premature death and age-related illnesses. The magic lies in the diet's ability to curb inflammation and oxidative stress, promoting cellular health and resilience.

3. Brain Power – Nourish Your Mind

As we age, maintaining cognitive function becomes paramount. The Mediterranean Diet comes to the rescue with its potent brain-boosting nutrients. The generous intake of fruits, vegetables, and whole grains provides essential vitamins and minerals that fortify memory and cognitive agility. Moreover, the healthy fats found in fish, nuts, and olive oil fuel the brain, enhancing focus and protecting against neurodegenerative conditions like Alzheimer's disease.

4. Weight Management – Shed Pounds with Pleasure

Unlike restrictive and short-lived diets, the Mediterranean Diet doesn't demand sacrifice or deprivation. By emphasizing nutrient-dense, whole foods, and portion control, this diet supports sustainable weight loss and weight maintenance. The combination of fiber-rich foods and satisfying proteins keeps hunger at bay, preventing overeating and promoting a sense of satiety. With the Mediterranean Diet, you'll embark on a culinary adventure that doesn't compromise on taste or waistline.

5. Diabetes Management – A Balanced Plate for Balanced Blood Sugar

For those grappling with diabetes or insulin resistance, the Mediterranean Diet offers a glimmer of hope. Its focus on low-glycemic index foods helps stabilize blood sugar levels, reducing the risk of sudden spikes and crashes. The presence of healthy fats also aids in improving insulin sensitivity, supporting better diabetes management and reducing complications associated with the condition.

6. Anti-Inflammatory Power – A Shield Against Diseases

Chronic inflammation lies at the root of many diseases, including arthritis, cancer, and heart disease. The Mediterranean Diet, rich in antioxidants and anti-inflammatory compounds, acts as a formidable shield against these ailments. The colorful array of fruits and vegetables, complemented by herbs and spices, helps combat inflammation and reinforces the body's natural defense system.

7. Gut Health – Nourish Your Microbiome

The health of our gut microbiome plays a pivotal role in our overall well-being. The Mediterranean Diet, abundant in fiber and fermented foods like yogurt, nurtures a diverse and thriving gut microbiota. A healthy gut is associated with improved digestion, enhanced immune function, and even mental well-being.

The Mediterranean Diet is not merely a diet but a transformational journey to optimal health and vitality. Embrace this time-tested way of eating, and you'll unlock a world of delicious flavors and incredible benefits. From the shores of Greece to the hills of Italy, the Mediterranean Diet has woven a tapestry of health and happiness that transcends time and borders. Let this dietary adventure be your gateway to a life filled with abundant health, savoring the richness of life and cuisine.

Unveiling The Do's And Don'ts Of A Wholesome Lifestyle For The Mediterranean Diet

The Mediterranean Diet, with its tantalizing flavors and life-enhancing benefits, has captured the hearts of many seeking a healthier and more enjoyable way of life. Rooted in the rich culinary traditions of countries bordering the Mediterranean Sea, this diet emphasizes fresh, whole foods that nourish both body and soul. To fully embrace the magic of the Mediterranean Diet, it's essential to understand the do's and don'ts that will guide you on this savory journey.

The Do's:

1. Savor the Bounty of Fruits and Vegetables:

Let the vibrant colors and refreshing tastes of fruits and vegetables grace your plate. These nutritional powerhouses are packed with essential vitamins, minerals, and antioxidants, making them the cornerstone of the Mediterranean Diet. Aim to fill at least half your plate with a rainbow of produce at every meal.

2. Embrace Healthy Fats:

Bid adieu to unhealthy saturated and trans fats and welcome the heart-healthy monounsaturated fats found in olive oil, avocados, and nuts. These fats not only promote cardiovascular health but also add a rich and satisfying flavor to your meals.

3. Make Friends with Whole Grains:

Whole grains like quinoa, brown rice, and whole wheat pasta are a fundamental part of the Mediterranean Diet. Their high fiber content helps regulate blood sugar levels, aids digestion, and keeps you feeling fuller for longer.

4. Indulge in Seafood:

The Mediterranean Diet places seafood at the center of the plate. Fish, especially fatty varieties like salmon and mackerel, provide a potent dose of omega-3 fatty acids that benefit heart and brain health.

5. Cultivate a Love for Legumes:

Beans, lentils, and chickpeas are a treasure trove of plant-based protein and fiber. Incorporate them into soups, salads, and stews for a satisfying and nourishing meal.

6. Relish in Fresh Herbs and Spices:

Herbs and spices like basil, oregano, garlic, and cumin are the secret to the Mediterranean Diet's delightful flavors. They add depth to your dishes without relying on excessive salt or unhealthy condiments.

The Don'ts:
1. Avoid Processed and Sugary Foods:

Bid farewell to processed and sugary foods that offer little nutritional value and contribute to inflammation and chronic diseases. Steer clear of sugary beverages, refined grains, and packaged snacks.

2. Limit Red Meat Consumption:

While the Mediterranean Diet celebrates lean poultry and fish, it advises limiting red meat consumption. When enjoying red meat, opt for lean cuts and consider it an occasional treat rather than a staple.

3. Say "No" to Refined Oils:

Refined oils lack the nutritional value of extra virgin olive oil and can undermine the health benefits of the Mediterranean Diet. Avoid using refined vegetable oils like soybean, corn, or sunflower oil in your cooking.

4. Beware of Excessive Dairy:

Although dairy products are not entirely excluded from the Mediterranean Diet, it's essential to moderate your intake. Opt for low-fat or Greek yogurt and cheese in smaller portions.

5. Don't Rush Your Meals:

The Mediterranean Diet is not just about what you eat, but how you eat. Slow down, savor each bite, and enjoy meals in the company of loved ones. Avoid mindless eating in front of screens or on the go.

6. Avoid Excessive Alcohol Consumption:

While moderate alcohol consumption, especially red wine, is a part of the Mediterranean lifestyle, excessive drinking can be detrimental to your health. Stick to the recommended guidelines and savor your beverage with meals.

Embracing the Mediterranean Diet is about nourishing your body, mind, and soul with the goodness of nature. By following the do's and avoiding the don'ts, you can unlock the secrets of this wholesome lifestyle and experience its remarkable benefits. The Mediterranean Diet isn't a restrictive regimen; it's an invitation to savor life's abundance and celebrate the joy of wholesome, flavorful eating. So, relish the journey, and let the Mediterranean Diet be your pathway to a healthier, happier, and more vibrant you.

Unveiling the Mediterranean Secret to a Slimmer You: Embrace the Wholesome Path to Weight Loss

In a world obsessed with quick fixes and fad diets, the Mediterranean Diet stands tall as a beacon of balance and sustainability. Its time-tested principles and mouthwatering flavors have charmed countless individuals seeking a slimmer, healthier physique. If you're looking to shed those extra pounds while relishing delicious meals, the Mediterranean Diet is your ultimate guide to a fulfilling weight loss journey.

1. Savor Nutrient-Dense Foods:
One of the key aspects of the Mediterranean Diet is the focus on nutrient-dense, whole foods. Instead of empty calories from processed snacks and sugary treats, indulge in the abundance of fresh fruits, vegetables, and whole grains. These satisfying and nourishing foods will keep you fuller for longer, reducing the urge to overeat and helping you manage your calorie intake effortlessly.

2. Embrace the Power of Healthy Fats:
Contrary to popular belief, fats are not your enemy when it comes to weight loss. The Mediterranean Diet emphasizes the consumption of heart-healthy monounsaturated fats found in olive oil, nuts, and avocados. These fats not only add richness to your meals but also promote satiety, reducing the likelihood of unhealthy snacking between meals.

3. Choose Lean Proteins:
Protein plays a vital role in weight loss, as it helps preserve lean muscle mass while promoting fat burning. Opt for lean sources of protein like fish, poultry, legumes, and Greek yogurt. These

protein-rich foods will keep you feeling full and satisfied, curbing your appetite and supporting your weight loss efforts.

4. Practice Portion Control:
In the Mediterranean culture, meals are savored and enjoyed, but portion sizes are modest. Avoid overindulging by using smaller plates and savoring your food slowly. When you eat mindfully and pay attention to your body's hunger cues, you'll naturally consume fewer calories and feel more satisfied.

5. Say "Yes" to Regular Physical Activity:
The Mediterranean Diet is not just about what you eat; it also emphasizes the importance of an active lifestyle. Engage in regular physical activity, whether it's brisk walking, swimming, cycling, or dancing. Find activities that you enjoy, and make them a part of your daily routine. Exercise not only aids in weight loss but also contributes to overall well-being and stress reduction.

6. Limit Processed Foods and Sugary Treats:
To achieve weight loss success on the Mediterranean Diet, it's crucial to minimize processed foods and sugary treats. These calorie-dense foods offer little nutritional value and can hinder your weight loss efforts. Instead, focus on wholesome, real foods that nourish your body and support your health goals.

7. Hydration is Key:
Staying hydrated is often overlooked but plays a significant role in weight loss. Drinking enough water throughout the day helps control your appetite, boosts metabolism, and supports proper digestion. Additionally, drinking water can often be mistaken for hunger, so staying hydrated can help you avoid unnecessary snacking.

8. Prioritize Sleep and Manage Stress:
Restorative sleep and stress management are essential components of a successful weight loss journey. Lack of sleep can disrupt your hormones, leading to increased appetite and cravings for unhealthy foods. Practice relaxation techniques, such as yoga or meditation, to manage stress and emotional eating.

9. Seek Support and Accountability:
Embarking on a weight loss journey can be challenging, but you don't have to do it alone. Seek support from friends, family, or a weight loss group. Having a support system can keep you motivated, accountable, and inspired to stay on track with your Mediterranean Diet lifestyle.

The Mediterranean Diet offers a holistic approach to weight loss, emphasizing nourishment, balance, and joy in eating. By savoring nutrient-dense foods, embracing healthy fats, practicing portion control, staying active, and prioritizing overall well-being, you can achieve your weight loss goals and cultivate a lifelong commitment to a slimmer, healthier you. So, embark on this exciting journey, and let the Mediterranean Diet be your gateway to a more vibrant and fulfilling life. Now, let' start making Mediterranean meals!

Mediterranean Side Dishes

Roasted Mediterranean Vegetables

Preparation Time: 20 minutes **Cooking Time:** 30 minutes **Total Time:** 50 minutes **Servings:** 4

Ingredients:
- 2 medium zucchinis, sliced into 1/2-inch rounds
- 1 large red bell pepper, cut into bite-sized chunks
- 1 large yellow bell pepper, cut into bite-sized chunks
- 1 medium eggplant, cut into bite-sized chunks
- 1 cup cherry tomatoes
- 1 red onion, cut into thin wedges
- 4 garlic cloves, minced
- 3 tablespoons extra-virgin olive oil
- 1 tablespoon balsamic vinegar
- 1 teaspoon dried oregano
- 1 teaspoon dried thyme
- 1/2 teaspoon dried rosemary
- 1/2 teaspoon dried basil
- Salt and black pepper, to taste
- Fresh basil leaves (for garnish)

Utensils Needed:
- Large mixing bowl
- Baking sheet or roasting pan
- Parchment paper or aluminum foil (optional, for easy cleanup)
- Cutting board and knife
- Measuring spoons
- Wooden spoon or spatula

Recipe:
1. Preheat your oven to 220°C (425°F).

2. In a large mixing bowl, combine the sliced zucchinis, red and yellow bell pepper chunks, eggplant chunks, cherry tomatoes, red onion wedges, and minced garlic.

3. In a separate small bowl, whisk together the extra-virgin olive oil, balsamic vinegar, dried oregano, dried thyme, dried rosemary, dried basil, salt, and black pepper.

4. Pour the olive oil mixture over the vegetables in the large mixing bowl. Toss the vegetables gently to ensure they are coated evenly with the seasoned oil.

5. Prepare a baking sheet or roasting pan by lining it with parchment paper or aluminum foil for easier cleanup.

6. Spread the seasoned vegetables evenly on the prepared baking sheet or roasting pan in a single layer. Avoid overcrowding the vegetables to allow them to roast properly.

7. Place the baking sheet or roasting pan in the preheated oven and roast the vegetables for about 25-30 minutes, or until

they are tender and slightly caramelized. You can stir the vegetables once or twice during the roasting process to ensure even cooking.

8. Once the vegetables are roasted to perfection, remove them from the oven and transfer them to a serving dish.

9. Garnish with fresh basil leaves for added freshness and flavor.

Nutritional Information (per serving):
(Note: Nutritional values are approximate and may vary based on specific ingredients used):
- Calories: 180 kcal
- Carbohydrates: 20g
- Protein: 4g
- Fat: 11g
- Saturated Fat: 2g
- Fiber: 7g
- Sugar: 10g
- Sodium: 20mg
- Vitamin C: 100mg
- Potassium: 700mg

Recipe Notes:

- *You can customize this recipe by adding other Mediterranean vegetables such as artichoke hearts, sliced mushrooms, or roasted red peppers.*
- *Feel free to adjust the seasoning according to your taste preferences. You can add a pinch of red pepper flakes for a bit of heat or a squeeze of lemon juice for extra brightness.*
- *Leftovers can be stored in an airtight container in the refrigerator for up to 3 days. These roasted vegetables are delicious on their own, but you can also use them as a topping for salads, pasta, or sandwiches.*

Enjoy your Roasted Mediterranean Vegetables as a delicious and nutritious side dish or a light and flavorful main course!

Lemon Garlic Roasted Potatoes

Preparation Time: 15 minutes **Cooking Time**: 30-35 minutes **Total Time**: 45-50 minutes **Servings**: 4

Ingredients:
- 1.5 lbs (680g) baby potatoes, halved (if they are larger, quarter them)
- 4 tablespoons olive oil
- 4 garlic cloves, minced
- Zest of 1 lemon
- 2 tablespoons freshly squeezed lemon juice
- 1 teaspoon dried oregano
- 1/2 teaspoon dried thyme
- 1/2 teaspoon dried rosemary
- 1/2 teaspoon paprika
- Salt and black pepper, to taste
- Fresh parsley, chopped (for garnish)

Utensils Needed:
- Large mixing bowl
- Baking sheet or roasting pan
- Parchment paper or aluminum foil (optional, for easy cleanup)
- Cutting board and knife
- Small bowl for mixing the dressing
- Whisk or fork for mixing the dressing
- Wooden spoon or spatula

Recipe:
1. Preheat your oven to 220°C (425°F).

2. Wash the baby potatoes thoroughly and halve them (or quarter them if they are larger) so that they are roughly the same size. This ensures even cooking.

3. In a large mixing bowl, combine the halved potatoes, minced garlic, lemon zest, freshly squeezed lemon juice, olive oil, dried oregano, dried thyme, dried rosemary, paprika, salt, and black pepper.

4. Toss the potatoes gently in the lemon-garlic mixture to ensure they are evenly coated.

5. Prepare a baking sheet or roasting pan by lining it with parchment paper or aluminum foil for easier cleanup.

6. Spread the coated potatoes evenly on the prepared baking sheet or roasting pan in a single layer.

7. Place the baking sheet or roasting pan in the preheated oven and roast the potatoes for about 30-35 minutes or until they are golden brown and crispy on the outside, and tender on the inside. You can stir the potatoes once or twice during the roasting process to ensure even cooking.

8. Once the potatoes are roasted to perfection, remove them from the oven and transfer them to a serving dish.

9. Garnish with chopped fresh parsley for added color and freshness.

Nutritional Information (per serving):

(Note: Nutritional values are approximate and may vary based on specific ingredients used)

- Calories: 280 kcal
- Carbohydrates: 35g
- Protein: 4g
- Fat: 14g
- Saturated Fat: 2g
- Fiber: 4g
- Sugar: 2g
- Sodium: 160mg
- Vitamin C: 30mg
- Potassium: 650mg

Recipe Notes:

- For added flavor, you can toss in some sliced red onions or cherry tomatoes with the potatoes before roasting.

- You can adjust the seasoning to your taste. Feel free to add more lemon juice or garlic if you prefer a stronger lemon-garlic flavor.

- This recipe works well with various types of potatoes, such as Yukon Gold or red potatoes.

- Leftover roasted potatoes can be stored in an airtight container in the refrigerator for up to 3 days. To reheat, you can use a microwave or oven until they are warm and crispy again.

Enjoy your Lemon Garlic Roasted Potatoes as a delightful side dish or a flavorful addition to any meal!

Herbed Quinoa Pilaf

Preparation Time: 10 minutes **Cooking Time**: 20 minutes **Total Time**: 30 minutes **Servings**: 4

Ingredients:
- 1 cup quinoa, rinsed and drained
- 2 cups vegetable broth or water
- 1 tablespoon olive oil
- 1 small onion, finely chopped
- 2 garlic cloves, minced
- 1 teaspoon dried thyme
- 1 teaspoon dried rosemary
- 1/2 teaspoon dried oregano
- 1/2 teaspoon dried sage
- 1/2 cup chopped parsley
- 1/4 cup chopped fresh basil
- 1/4 cup chopped fresh chives
- 1/4 cup toasted pine nuts (optional)
- Salt and black pepper, to taste
- Lemon wedges (for serving)

Utensils Needed:
- Medium-sized saucepan with a lid
- Fine mesh strainer (for rinsing quinoa)
- Cutting board and knife
- Wooden spoon or spatula

Recipe:
1. Rinse the quinoa in a fine mesh strainer under cold running water. This helps remove any bitterness or residue from the quinoa.

2. In a medium-sized saucepan, heat the olive oil over medium heat. Add the chopped onion and sauté for about 3 minutes until softened and translucent.

3. Add the minced garlic, dried thyme, dried rosemary, dried oregano, and dried sage to the saucepan. Stir and cook for another 1-2 minutes until the herbs become fragrant.

4. Add the rinsed quinoa to the saucepan and stir to coat it with the herbs and onions.

5. Pour in the vegetable broth or water, and add a pinch of salt and black pepper. Stir briefly.

6. Bring the mixture to a boil, then reduce the heat to low, cover the saucepan with a lid, and let the quinoa simmer for about 15 minutes or until the liquid is fully absorbed and the quinoa is fluffy.

7. Once the quinoa is cooked, remove the saucepan from the heat and let it sit, covered, for 5 minutes. This helps the quinoa to steam and become even fluffier.

8. In the meantime, chop the fresh parsley, basil, and chives. You can also toast the pine nuts in a dry skillet over

medium heat until lightly browned, if using.

9. Fluff the quinoa with a fork, and then stir in the chopped parsley, basil, and chives. If using, sprinkle the toasted pine nuts on top for added crunch and flavor.

10. Adjust the seasoning with salt and pepper, if needed.

11. Serve the herbed quinoa pilaf hot with lemon wedges on the side. The lemon juice adds a bright, citrusy kick to the dish.

Nutritional Information (per serving):

(*Note: Nutritional values are approximate and may vary based on specific ingredients used*)
- Calories: 230 kcal
- Carbohydrates: 32g
- Protein: 7g
- Fat: 9g
- Saturated Fat: 1g
- Fiber: 5g
- Sugar: 2g
- Sodium: 350mg
- Vitamin C: 15mg
- Iron: 3mg
- Calcium: 70mg

Recipe Notes:
- *You can customize this pilaf by adding other vegetables such as sautéed mushrooms, roasted bell peppers, or cooked peas.*
- *If you prefer a richer flavor, you can substitute vegetable broth with chicken broth.*
- *To make it vegan, use vegetable broth and omit the optional pine nuts or replace them with toasted almonds or walnuts.*
- *Leftover quinoa pilaf can be stored in an airtight container in the refrigerator for up to 4 days. It's a great option for meal prep or quick lunches.*
- *This versatile dish pairs well with grilled chicken, roasted vegetables, or a fresh green salad.*

Enjoy your delicious and nutritious Herbed Quinoa Pilaf!

Couscous with Dried Fruits and Nuts

Preparation Time: 10 minutes **Cooking Time**: 15 minutes **Total Time**: 25 minutes **Servings**: 4

Ingredients:
- 1 cup couscous
- 1 1/4 cups vegetable broth or water
- 2 tablespoons olive oil
- 1/2 cup dried apricots, chopped
- 1/2 cup dried cranberries or raisins
- 1/4 cup chopped almonds or pistachios
- 2 green onions, thinly sliced
- 1/4 cup chopped fresh mint leaves
- 1/4 cup chopped fresh cilantro or parsley
- Zest of 1 lemon
- Juice of 1 lemon
- Salt and black pepper, to taste

Utensils Needed:
- Medium-sized saucepan with a lid
- Fine mesh strainer (optional, for rinsing couscous)
- Cutting board and knife
- Large mixing bowl
- Fork for fluffing couscous

Recipe:
1. If your couscous requires rinsing, place it in a fine mesh strainer and rinse it under cold running water. This step helps prevent clumping during cooking.

2. In a medium-sized saucepan, bring the vegetable broth or water to a boil. Once it's boiling, add the couscous and a pinch of salt. Stir briefly, cover the saucepan with a lid, and remove it from the heat.

3. Let the couscous sit in the hot liquid for about 5 minutes. During this time, the couscous will absorb the liquid and become tender.

4. While the couscous is steaming, heat the olive oil in a separate skillet over medium heat. Add the chopped dried apricots and cranberries (or raisins) to the skillet. Sauté them for 2-3 minutes until they plump up slightly.

5. Add the chopped almonds (or pistachios) to the skillet and continue sautéing for another 2 minutes until the nuts are lightly toasted.

6. Once the couscous has steamed for 5 minutes, fluff it with a fork to separate the grains.

7. In a large mixing bowl, combine the fluffed couscous with the sautéed dried fruits and nuts.

8. Add the thinly sliced green onions, chopped fresh mint leaves,

chopped fresh cilantro (or parsley), lemon zest, and lemon juice to the bowl. Mix everything together gently.

9. Season the couscous with salt and black pepper to taste. Adjust the lemon juice or other seasonings if needed.

10. Serve the Couscous with Dried Fruits and Nuts warm or at room temperature.
Nutritional Information (per serving):
(Note: Nutritional values are approximate and may vary based on specific ingredients used)

- Calories: 330 kcal
- Carbohydrates: 53g
- Protein: 8g
- Fat: 11g
- Saturated Fat: 1g
- Fiber: 6g
- Sugar: 18g
- Sodium: 300mg
- Vitamin C: 10mg
- Iron: 2mg
- Calcium: 70mg

Recipe Notes:

- Feel free to customize this couscous dish by adding other dried fruits like chopped dates, figs, or currants.
- Nuts can also be substituted or combined according to your preference. Try using walnuts, pecans, or cashews for variation.
- This dish can be served as a light and flavorful main course or as a side dish with grilled chicken, roasted vegetables, or lamb.
- If you prefer a vegan version, use vegetable broth instead of water.
- Leftovers can be stored in an airtight container in the refrigerator for up to 3 days. You can enjoy them cold or reheat gently in the microwave or on the stovetop with a splash of water or broth to maintain moisture.

Enjoy this delightful Couscous with Dried Fruits and Nuts as a healthy and satisfying meal option!

Sauteed Greens with Garlic and Lemon

Preparation Time: 10 minutes **Cooking Time**: 10 minutes **Total Time**: 20 minutes **Servings**: 4

Ingredients:
- 1 bunch of leafy greens (spinach, kale, Swiss chard, or collard greens), washed and roughly chopped
- 2 tablespoons olive oil
- 4 garlic cloves, thinly sliced
- Zest of 1 lemon
- 2 tablespoons freshly squeezed lemon juice
- Salt and black pepper, to taste
- Red pepper flakes (optional, for added heat)

Utensils Needed:
- Large skillet or sauté pan
- Cutting board and knife
- Microplane or zester (for lemon zest)
- Wooden spoon or spatula

Recipe:
1. Wash the leafy greens thoroughly under cold running water. Remove any tough stems and roughly chop the leaves into bite-sized pieces.

2. In a large skillet or sauté pan, heat the olive oil over medium heat.

3. Add the thinly sliced garlic to the pan and sauté for about 1 minute, or until the garlic becomes fragrant and lightly golden. Be careful not to burn the garlic.

4. Add the chopped leafy greens to the pan. Use tongs or a wooden spoon to toss the greens in the garlicky oil, ensuring they are evenly coated.

5. Continue to sauté the greens for 4-5 minutes, or until they wilt down and become tender. The cooking time may vary depending on the type of greens used.

6. Once the greens are cooked to your desired tenderness, remove the pan from the heat.

7. Sprinkle the lemon zest over the sautéed greens and drizzle the freshly squeezed lemon juice on top. Toss the greens gently to distribute the lemony flavors.

8. Season the sautéed greens with salt and black pepper to taste. If you like a bit of heat, add a pinch of red pepper flakes as well.

9. Transfer the Sauteed Greens with Garlic and Lemon to a serving dish and serve immediately while still warm.

Nutritional Information (per serving):
(Note: Nutritional values are approximate and

may vary based on specific ingredients used)
- Calories: 80 kcal
- Carbohydrates: 5g
- Protein: 2g
- Fat: 6g
- Saturated Fat: 1g
- Fiber: 2g
- Sugar: 1g
- Sodium: 150mg
- Vitamin C: 25mg
- Iron: 1mg
- Calcium: 80mg

Recipe Notes:
- *You can use a combination of different leafy greens to create a mix of flavors and textures.*
- *For extra richness, you can add a small pat of butter or a splash of balsamic vinegar to the greens before serving.*
- *This dish pairs well with grilled chicken, fish, or tofu. It also works as a side dish alongside roasted vegetables or pasta.*
- *If you prefer a vegan version, ensure you use olive oil instead of butter.*
- *Leftovers can be stored in an airtight container in the refrigerator for up to 2 days. Reheat gently on the stovetop or in the microwave when ready to eat.*

Enjoy this healthy and delicious Sauteed Greens with Garlic and Lemon as a nutritious addition to your meals!

Grilled Eggplant with Tahini Sauce

Preparation Time: 20 minutes **Cooking Time:** 15 minutes **Total Time:** 35 minutes **Servings:** 4

Ingredients:
- 2 large eggplants, sliced into 1/2-inch thick rounds
- 2 tablespoons olive oil
- Salt and black pepper, to taste
- 1/4 cup tahini (sesame seed paste)
- 2 tablespoons lemon juice
- 2 garlic cloves, minced
- 2-4 tablespoons water
- 1 tablespoon chopped fresh parsley (for garnish)
- 1 tablespoon toasted sesame seeds (for garnish)

Utensils Needed:
- Grill or grill pan
- Basting brush or spoon
- Mixing bowl
- Whisk or fork (for mixing tahini sauce)
- Serving dish or platter

Recipe:
1. Preheat the grill or grill pan over medium-high heat.

2. While the grill is heating up, prepare the eggplants. Slice them into 1/2-inch thick rounds. If you prefer, you can also cut them lengthwise into planks. Brush both sides of the eggplant slices with olive oil and season with salt and black pepper.

3. Once the grill is hot, place the eggplant slices on it. Grill each side for about 3-4 minutes, or until they are tender and have distinct grill marks. Remove the grilled eggplant from the heat and set aside.

4. In a mixing bowl, combine the tahini, lemon juice, minced garlic, and a pinch of salt. Whisk the mixture until it forms a smooth sauce. If the sauce is too thick, gradually add 2-4 tablespoons of water to achieve your desired consistency. The tahini sauce should be pourable but not too runny.

5. Arrange the grilled eggplant slices on a serving dish or platter.

6. Drizzle the tahini sauce generously over the grilled eggplant slices.

7. Garnish the dish with chopped fresh parsley and toasted sesame seeds for added flavor and presentation.

Nutritional Information (per serving):

(Note: Nutritional values are approximate and may vary based on specific ingredients used)
- Calories: 180 kcal
- Carbohydrates: 12g
- Protein: 4g
- Fat: 15g
- Saturated Fat: 2g
- Fiber: 5g
- Sugar: 6g
- Sodium: 15mg
- Vitamin C: 10mg
- Iron: 1mg
- Calcium: 50mg

Recipe Notes:
- *For a smokier flavor, you can add a pinch of smoked paprika or ground cumin to the tahini sauce.*
- *Grilled eggplant with tahini sauce can be served as a delicious appetizer, side dish, or part of a Mediterranean-inspired meal.*
- *You can also serve the grilled eggplant with pita bread or as a topping for salads.*
- *This dish is best when served fresh and warm from the grill. However, leftover eggplant can be stored in the refrigerator for up to 2 days and reheated before serving.*
- *If you don't have a grill or grill pan, you can achieve similar results by roasting the eggplant slices in the oven at 200°C (400°F) for about 15-20 minutes.*

Enjoy your Grilled Eggplant with Tahini Sauce as a flavorful and healthy addition to your meals!

Baked Stuffed Tomatoes with Rice and Herbs

Preparation Time: 25 minutes **Cooking Time**: 50 minutes **Total Time**: 1 hour 15 minutes **Servings**: 4

Ingredients:
- 4 large ripe tomatoes
- 1 cup long-grain white rice
- 2 cups vegetable broth or water
- 2 tablespoons olive oil
- 1 small onion, finely chopped
- 2 garlic cloves, minced
- 1/2 cup chopped fresh parsley
- 1/4 cup chopped fresh mint
- 1/4 cup chopped fresh dill
- 1/4 cup chopped fresh basil
- Salt and black pepper, to taste

Utensils Needed:
- Baking dish
- Medium-sized saucepan with a lid
- Cutting board and knife
- Mixing bowl
- Spoon for stuffing tomatoes

Recipe:

1. Preheat your oven to 180°C (350°F).

2. Cut the tops off the tomatoes and set them aside. Gently scoop out the seeds and pulp from the tomatoes, being careful not to damage the walls. Reserve the pulp in a bowl for later use.

3. In a medium-sized saucepan, heat 1 tablespoon of olive oil over medium heat. Add the finely chopped onion and sauté for about 3 minutes until it becomes translucent.

4. Add the minced garlic to the saucepan and cook for another minute until it becomes fragrant.

5. Stir in the rice and sauté for a couple of minutes until it's lightly toasted.

6. Add the vegetable broth or water to the saucepan, along with the reserved tomato pulp. Season with salt and black pepper. Bring the mixture to a boil, then reduce the heat to low, cover the saucepan with a lid, and let the rice simmer for about 15 minutes or until it's fully cooked and the liquid is absorbed.

7. While the rice is cooking, prepare the herb mixture. In a mixing bowl, combine the chopped fresh parsley, mint, dill, basil, and 1 tablespoon of olive oil. Season with salt and black pepper to taste.

8. Once the rice is cooked, remove the saucepan from the heat and let it sit, covered, for 5 minutes. Then, fluff the rice with a fork.

9. Gently mix the herb mixture into the cooked rice until it's well combined.

10. Stuff each hollowed-out tomato with the herbed rice mixture, pressing it down slightly to fill the tomatoes evenly.

11. Place the stuffed tomatoes in a baking dish. Put the tomato tops back on.

12. Drizzle the stuffed tomatoes with the remaining olive oil.

13. Bake the stuffed tomatoes in the preheated oven for about 25-30 minutes, or until the tomatoes are tender and the tops are lightly browned.

14. Once the Baked Stuffed Tomatoes with Rice and Herbs are done, remove them from the oven and let them cool slightly before serving.

Nutritional Information (per serving):

(Note: Nutritional values are approximate and may vary based on specific ingredients used)
- Calories: 290 kcal
- Carbohydrates: 47g
- Protein: 6g
- Fat: 8g
- Saturated Fat: 1g
- Fiber: 4g
- Sugar: 6g
- Sodium: 600mg
- Vitamin C: 40mg
- Iron: 2mg
- Calcium: 70mg

Recipe Notes:

- You can customize the herb mixture by adding other fresh herbs like cilantro, chives, or thyme.
- For added richness, you can sprinkle some grated Parmesan or feta cheese on top of the stuffed tomatoes before baking.
- This dish can be served as a delightful appetizer or a light main course. It pairs well with a fresh green salad and crusty bread.
- Leftovers can be stored in an airtight container in the refrigerator for up to 2 days. Reheat gently in the oven or microwave before serving.

Enjoy your Baked Stuffed Tomatoes with Rice and Herbs as a flavorful and wholesome dish!

Greek Gigantes Plaki

Preparation Time: 12 hours (for soaking beans) **Cooking Time:** 2 hours **Total Time:** 14 hours **Servings:** 6-8

Ingredients:
- 2 cups dried gigantes beans (or large white beans), soaked overnight
- 1 large onion, finely chopped
- 4 garlic cloves, minced
- 2 large carrots, diced
- 2 celery stalks, diced
- 1 can (400g) crushed tomatoes
- 1/4 cup tomato paste
- 1/4 cup extra-virgin olive oil
- 2 tablespoons fresh lemon juice
- 2 teaspoons dried oregano
- 1 teaspoon dried thyme
- 1 teaspoon smoked paprika (optional, for added depth)
- Salt and black pepper, to taste
- Fresh parsley or dill (for garnish)

Utensils Needed:
- Large pot or Dutch oven
- Colander or strainer (for draining soaked beans)
- Cutting board and knife
- Wooden spoon or spatula
- Baking dish or casserole dish

Recipe:
1. Rinse the dried gigantes beans thoroughly under cold running water and then place them in a large bowl. Cover the beans with plenty of water and let them soak overnight or for at least 12 hours.

2. After soaking, drain and rinse the beans again.

3. In a large pot or Dutch oven, heat the extra-virgin olive oil over medium heat.

4. Add the chopped onion, minced garlic, diced carrots, and diced celery to the pot. Sauté the vegetables for about 5 minutes until they start to soften and become fragrant.

5. Stir in the crushed tomatoes, tomato paste, dried oregano, dried thyme, smoked paprika (if using), and a pinch of salt and black pepper.

6. Add the soaked and drained gigantes beans to the pot and mix everything together.

7. Pour enough water into the pot to cover the beans by about an inch.

8. Bring the mixture to a boil, then reduce the heat to low, cover the pot with a lid, and let the gigantes plaki simmer for about 1.5 to 2 hours or until the

beans are tender and fully cooked. Check the water level occasionally and add more if needed to keep the beans covered.

9. Once the beans are tender, add the fresh lemon juice and adjust the seasoning with more salt and pepper if desired.

10. Preheat your oven to 180°C (350°F).

11. Transfer the gigantes plaki from the stovetop to a baking dish or casserole dish.

12. Bake the gigantes plaki in the preheated oven for an additional 15-20 minutes to allow the flavors to meld and the sauce to thicken.

13. Once it's done, remove the dish from the oven and let it cool slightly before serving.

14. Garnish the Greek Gigantes Plaki with fresh parsley or dill before serving.

Nutritional Information (per serving, assuming 6 servings):

(Note: Nutritional values are approximate and may vary based on specific ingredients used)
- Calories: 350 kcal
- Carbohydrates: 51g
- Protein: 15g
- Fat: 10g
- Saturated Fat: 1.5g
- Fiber: 13g
- Sugar: 7g
- Sodium: 350mg
- Vitamin C: 10mg
- Iron: 4mg
- Calcium: 150mg

Recipe Notes:
- Gigantes Plaki is traditionally served as a main course or as a side dish in Greek cuisine.
- This dish is best served warm or at room temperature and pairs well with crusty bread or a simple green salad.
- You can customize the flavors by adding other herbs like rosemary or bay leaves, or by using a combination of different beans.
- Leftovers can be stored in an airtight container in the refrigerator for up to 3 days. Reheat gently on the stovetop before serving.

Enjoy this hearty and delicious Greek Gigantes Plaki, rich with Mediterranean flavors!

Moroccan Carrot Salad with Cumin

Preparation Time: 15 minutes **Cooking Time:** 10 minute **Total Time:** 25 minutes **Servings:** 4

Ingredients:
- 1 lb (450g) carrots, peeled and grated
- 2 tablespoons olive oil
- 1 teaspoon ground cumin
- 1/2 teaspoon ground coriander
- 1/4 teaspoon ground cinnamon
- 1/4 teaspoon ground ginger
- 1/4 cup chopped fresh cilantro
- 1/4 cup chopped fresh parsley
- 1/4 cup raisins or chopped dried apricots (optional, for sweetness)
- Juice of 1 lemon
- Salt and black pepper, to taste
- Toasted sesame seeds (for garnish, optional)

Utensils Needed:
- Large mixing bowl
- Grater (if not using pre-grated carrots)
- Small skillet or saucepan
- Wooden spoon or spatula
- Serving dish

Recipe:
1. If you're using whole carrots, peel and grate them using a grater. If you prefer, you can purchase pre-grated carrots to save time.

2. In a small skillet or saucepan, heat the olive oil over medium-low heat.

3. Add the ground cumin, ground coriander, ground cinnamon, and ground ginger to the skillet. Stir the spices in the oil and cook for about 1-2 minutes until they become fragrant. Be careful not to burn the spices.

4. Pour the spiced oil over the grated carrots in a large mixing bowl.

5. Add the chopped fresh cilantro and chopped fresh parsley to the bowl.

6. If you want to add some sweetness to the salad, toss in the raisins or chopped dried apricots.

7. Squeeze the juice of one lemon over the mixture to add a refreshing tanginess.

8. Season the Moroccan Carrot Salad with salt and black pepper to taste. Mix all the ingredients together thoroughly until well combined.

9. Transfer the salad to a serving dish.

10. If desired, sprinkle some toasted sesame seeds on top for added crunch and nuttiness.

Nutritional Information (per serving, assuming 4 servings):
(*Note: Nutritional values are approximate and may vary based on specific ingredients used*)
- Calories: 150 kcal
- Carbohydrates: 18g
- Protein: 2g
- Fat: 8g
- Saturated Fat: 1g
- Fiber: 4g
- Sugar: 9g
- Sodium: 110mg
- Vitamin C: 7mg
- Iron: 1mg
- Calcium: 50mg

Recipe Notes:
- This Moroccan Carrot Salad with Cumin can be served as a side dish or a light and refreshing appetizer.
- For a spicier version, you can add a pinch of cayenne pepper or a dash of hot sauce.
- The salad tastes even better when allowed to marinate in the refrigerator for a few hours before serving, as the flavors will meld together.
- Leftovers can be stored in an airtight container in the refrigerator for up to 3 days.

Enjoy this vibrant and flavorful Moroccan Carrot Salad with Cumin as a healthy and delightful addition to your meals!

Italian Grilled Polenta with Tomato Sauce

Preparation Time: 10 minutes **Cooking Time:** 30 minutes **Total Time:** 40 minutes **Servings:** 4-6

Ingredients:
- 1 cup instant polenta (yellow cornmeal)
- 4 cups water
- 1 teaspoon salt
- 2 tablespoons unsalted butter (optional, for added richness)
- 1/2 cup grated Parmesan cheese (optional, for added flavor)
- 2 cups tomato sauce (homemade or store-bought)
- 2 tablespoons olive oil
- 2 garlic cloves, minced
- 1/2 teaspoon dried oregano
- 1/2 teaspoon dried basil
- Salt and black pepper, to taste
- Fresh basil leaves (for garnish)

Utensils Needed:
- Medium-sized saucepan
- Whisk or wooden spoon for stirring polenta
- 9x13-inch baking dish or pan
- Grill pan or outdoor grill
- Small saucepan for tomato sauce
- Cutting board and knife
- Spoon for serving

Recipe:
1. In a medium-sized saucepan, bring 4 cups of water and 1 teaspoon of salt to a boil.

2. Gradually whisk in the instant polenta, stirring constantly to prevent lumps from forming.

3. Reduce the heat to low and continue to cook the polenta for about 5 minutes, stirring frequently until it thickens and pulls away from the sides of the pan.

4. If using, stir in the unsalted butter and grated Parmesan cheese until well combined. This step is optional but adds creaminess and flavor to the polenta.

5. Remove the polenta from the heat and pour it into a greased 9x13-inch baking dish or pan.

6. Spread the polenta evenly in the dish and let it cool and set for about 15-20 minutes.

7. While the polenta is cooling, prepare the tomato sauce. In a small saucepan, heat the olive oil over medium heat.

8. Add the minced garlic, dried oregano, and dried basil to the saucepan. Cook for

about 1 minute until the garlic becomes fragrant.

9. Pour in the tomato sauce and season with salt and black pepper to taste.

10. Simmer the tomato sauce over low heat for about 10 minutes to allow the flavors to meld.

11. Preheat your grill pan or outdoor grill over medium-high heat.

12. Once the polenta has set, cut it into squares or rectangles for grilling.

13. Grill the polenta pieces for about 3-4 minutes per side or until they have grill marks and are heated through.

14. Serve the Italian Grilled Polenta with Tomato Sauce by topping the grilled polenta with the warm tomato sauce.

15. Garnish with fresh basil leaves for added freshness and color.

Nutritional Information (*per serving, assuming 6 servings, without optional ingredients*):
(Note: Nutritional values are approximate and may vary based on specific ingredients used)
- Calories: 250 kcal
- Carbohydrates: 37g
- Protein: 5g
- Fat: 8g
- Saturated Fat: 1.5g
- Fiber: 2g
- Sugar: 4g
- Sodium: 580mg
- Vitamin C: 10mg
- Iron: 1mg
- Calcium: 60mg

Recipe Notes:
- *If you prefer a smoother polenta, you can use regular cornmeal and cook it according to the package instructions for a longer time, stirring continuously to avoid lumps.*
- *You can adjust the seasoning of the tomato sauce to your taste by adding herbs like fresh basil or thyme.*
- *This dish can be served as an appetizer or a side dish, and it pairs well with grilled vegetables, sautéed greens, or a fresh green salad.*
- *Leftover polenta can be stored in an airtight container in the refrigerator for up to 3 days. To reheat, you can grill it again or warm it in the microwave or oven.*

Enjoy your Italian Grilled Polenta with Tomato Sauce as a tasty and comforting dish with Mediterranean flavors!

Mediterranean Seafood Recipes

Grilled Mediterranean Shrimp Skewers

Preparation Time: 30 minutes **Marinating Time:** 1-2 hours **Cooking Time:** 8-10 minutes **Total Time:** 2 hours (including marinating time)

Ingredients:
- 1 lb (450g) large shrimp, peeled and deveined
- 2 tablespoons olive oil
- 2 tablespoons lemon juice
- 2 cloves garlic, minced
- 1 teaspoon dried oregano
- 1 teaspoon dried basil
- 1/2 teaspoon dried thyme
- 1/2 teaspoon paprika
- 1/4 teaspoon red pepper flakes (adjust to your spice preference)
- Salt and black pepper to taste
- 1 medium red bell pepper, cut into chunks
- 1 medium yellow bell pepper, cut into chunks
- 1 medium red onion, cut into chunks
- 1 cup cherry tomatoes
- Lemon wedges and fresh parsley for garnish (optional)

Utensils Needed:
1. Medium-sized mixing bowl
2. Whisk
3. Wooden or metal skewers
4. Grill or grill pan
5. Basting brush

Instructions:
1. In a medium-sized mixing bowl, whisk together the olive oil, lemon juice, minced garlic, dried oregano, dried basil, dried thyme, paprika, red pepper flakes, salt, and black pepper.

2. Add the peeled and deveined shrimp to the marinade, making sure they are well-coated. Cover the bowl with plastic wrap and refrigerate for 1 to 2 hours, allowing the flavors to meld and the shrimp to absorb the marinade.

3. Prepare your grill or preheat a grill pan over medium-high heat.

4. While the grill is heating, assemble the skewers. Thread the marinated shrimp, alternating with chunks of red and yellow bell peppers, red onions, and cherry tomatoes onto the skewers.

5. Lightly brush the grill grates with oil to

prevent sticking. Place the assembled shrimp skewers on the grill and cook for 4-5 minutes on each side, or until the shrimp turn opaque and are cooked through. Baste the skewers with any remaining marinade during grilling.

6. Once the shrimp are cooked, remove the skewers from the grill and transfer them to a serving plate.

7. Garnish with lemon wedges and fresh parsley if desired, and serve hot.

Enjoy your delicious Grilled Mediterranean Shrimp Skewers with your favorite side dishes or a fresh salad!

Optional Serving Suggestion:

Serve the skewers with a side of lemon garlic butter sauce. To make the sauce, melt 4 tablespoons of butter in a small saucepan over low heat. Add 2 minced garlic cloves and cook for a minute until fragrant. Remove from heat, and stir in 1 tablespoon of lemon juice, a pinch of salt, and chopped fresh parsley. Drizzle the sauce over the grilled shrimp skewers before serving.

Nutritional Information (per serving - serves 4):
- Calories: 250 kcal
- Protein: 30g
- Carbohydrates: 8g
- Fat: 10g
- Saturated Fat: 1.5g
- Cholesterol: 240mg
- Sodium: 280mg
- Fiber: 2g
- Sugar: 4g

Recipe Notes:
- *You can use fresh or frozen shrimp for this recipe. If using frozen shrimp, ensure they are fully thawed before marinating.*
- *Soak wooden skewers in water for about 30 minutes before using to prevent them from burning during grilling.*
- *You can customize the vegetable selection to your preference. Zucchini, mushrooms, or cherry tomatoes work well too.*

Baked Lemon Garlic Salmon

Preparation Time: 15 minutes **Marinating Time:** 30 minutes (optional) **Cooking Time:** 15-20 minutes **Total Time:** 1 hour (including marinating time, if applicable)

Ingredients:

- 4 salmon fillets (about 6 ounces each), skin-on or skinless
- 3 tablespoons olive oil
- 3 tablespoons lemon juice
- 4 cloves garlic, minced
- 1 teaspoon lemon zest (optional, for extra lemon flavor)
- 1 teaspoon dried oregano
- 1 teaspoon dried thyme
- 1/2 teaspoon salt
- 1/4 teaspoon black pepper
- Lemon slices for garnish
- Fresh parsley, chopped, for garnish (optional)

Utensils Needed:

1. Baking dish (9x13 inches)
2. Aluminum foil (optional, for easy cleanup)
3. Small mixing bowl
4. Whisk or fork
5. Basting brush or spoon

Instructions:

1. Preheat your oven to 400°F (200°C). Grease the baking dish with a little olive oil or line it with aluminum foil for easy cleanup.

2. In a small mixing bowl, whisk together the olive oil, lemon juice, minced garlic, lemon zest (if using), dried oregano, dried thyme, salt, and black pepper to make the lemon garlic marinade.

3. Place the salmon fillets in the prepared baking dish, skin-side down if using skin-on fillets.

4. Pour the lemon garlic marinade over the salmon, making sure each fillet is coated. If marinating, cover the dish with plastic wrap and refrigerate for 30 minutes.

5. Once marinated (if applicable), remove the plastic wrap and place the baking dish in the preheated oven.

6. Bake the salmon for 15-20 minutes or until the salmon is cooked through and flakes easily with a fork. The cooking time may vary depending on the thickness of the fillets.

7. During baking, you can baste the salmon with some of the marinade or drizzle it over the fillets a couple of times to keep them moist.

8. Once the salmon is cooked, remove the baking dish from the oven. Carefully transfer the salmon fillets to individual plates or a serving platter.

9. Garnish the salmon with lemon slices and chopped fresh parsley, if desired.

10. Serve the Baked Lemon Garlic Salmon hot with your favorite side dishes like roasted vegetables, quinoa, or a fresh green salad.

Enjoy this delicious and nutritious Baked Lemon Garlic Salmon with your family and friends!

Optional Serving Suggestion:
For added freshness, serve the salmon with a side of cucumber and dill yogurt sauce. Simply mix together 1 cup of plain Greek yogurt, 1/2 cup diced cucumber, 1 tablespoon chopped fresh dill, 1 tablespoon lemon juice, a pinch of salt, and a dash of black pepper. Serve the sauce alongside the salmon for a delightful complement to the dish.

Nutritional Information (per serving - serves 4):
- Calories: 350 kcal
- Protein: 34g
- Carbohydrates: 1g
- Fat: 24g
- Saturated Fat: 4g
- Cholesterol: 90mg
- Sodium: 350mg
- Fiber: 0g
- Sugar: 0g

Recipe Notes:
- *You can use fresh or frozen salmon fillets for this recipe. If using frozen salmon, ensure they are fully thawed before marinating or baking.*
- *For extra flavor, you can marinate the salmon fillets in the lemon garlic mixture for 30 minutes before baking. While optional, marinating enhances the taste of the salmon.*
- *Adjust the cooking time based on the thickness of your salmon fillets. Thicker fillets may require a few more minutes in the oven.*

Sicilian-style Tuna Steak

Preparation Time: 15 minutes **Marinating Time:** 30 minutes (optional) **Cooking Time:** 10-12 minutes **Total Time:** 1 hour (including marinating time, if applicable)

Ingredients:
- 4 tuna steaks (about 6 ounces each)
- 1/4 cup olive oil
- 2 tablespoons lemon juice
- 2 cloves garlic, minced
- 2 tablespoons fresh parsley, chopped
- 1 tablespoon capers, drained and chopped
- 1 tablespoon black olives, pitted and chopped
- 1 teaspoon dried oregano
- 1/2 teaspoon red pepper flakes (adjust to your spice preference)
- Salt and black pepper to taste
- Lemon wedges and additional chopped parsley for garnish (optional)

Utensils Needed:
1. Mixing bowl
2. Whisk
3. Large non-stick skillet or grill pan
4. Tongs or spatula

Instructions:
1. In a mixing bowl, whisk together the olive oil, lemon juice, minced garlic, chopped parsley, capers, black olives, dried oregano, red pepper flakes, salt, and black pepper to make the Sicilian-style marinade.

2. If marinating the tuna, place the tuna steaks in a shallow dish and pour the marinade over them. Coat each steak evenly with the marinade, cover the dish with plastic wrap, and refrigerate for 30 minutes.

3. Heat a large non-stick skillet or grill pan over medium-high heat.

4. If you marinated the tuna, remove the steaks from the marinade and discard the marinade.

5. Place the tuna steaks in the preheated skillet or grill pan. Cook the tuna for 2-3 minutes per side, depending on the thickness of the steaks, until they are seared on the outside and slightly pink in the center for medium-rare. Adjust the cooking time if you prefer your tuna more or less cooked.

6. Use tongs or a spatula to carefully flip the tuna steaks to sear the other side.

7. Once the tuna is cooked to your desired level, remove the steaks from the pan and transfer them to a serving plate.

8. Garnish the Sicilian-style Tuna Steaks with lemon wedges and additional chopped parsley, if desired.

9. Serve the tuna steaks immediately with your choice of side dishes like roasted vegetables, couscous, or a fresh green salad.

Enjoy the delicious and vibrant flavors of this Sicilian-style Tuna Steak for a memorable meal!

Optional Serving Suggestion:
For a complete Sicilian-inspired meal, serve the tuna steaks with a side of traditional Sicilian caponata, a sweet and sour eggplant relish. It complements the tuna beautifully and adds a burst of flavor to the dish.

Nutritional Information (per serving - serves 4):
- Calories: 320 kcal
- Protein: 40g
- Carbohydrates: 2g
- Fat: 16g
- Saturated Fat: 2.5g
- Cholesterol: 80mg
- Sodium: 300mg
- Fiber: 0.5g
- Sugar: 0g

Recipe Notes:
- Ensure the tuna steaks are of high quality and fresh for the best results.
- Tuna cooks quickly, so be careful not to overcook it to avoid dryness.
- You can marinate the tuna steaks in the olive oil, lemon juice, garlic, parsley, capers, olives, oregano, red pepper flakes, salt, and black pepper for 30 minutes before cooking to enhance the flavors. However, if you're short on time, you can skip the marinating step.
- The cooking time may vary depending on the thickness of your tuna steaks and your preferred level of doneness.

Moroccan Spiced Cod

Preparation Time: 15 minutes **Marinating Time:** 30 minutes (optional) **Cooking Time:** 12-15 minutes **Total Time:** 1 hour (including marinating time, if applicable)

Ingredients:
- 4 cod fillets (about 6 ounces each)
- 3 tablespoons olive oil
- 2 tablespoons lemon juice
- 2 cloves garlic, minced
- 1 teaspoon ground cumin
- 1 teaspoon ground coriander
- 1 teaspoon paprika
- 1/2 teaspoon ground cinnamon
- 1/2 teaspoon ground ginger
- 1/4 teaspoon ground turmeric
- 1/4 teaspoon cayenne pepper (adjust to your spice preference)
- Salt and black pepper to taste
- Fresh cilantro or parsley, chopped, for garnish (optional)
- Lemon wedges for serving

Utensils Needed:
1. Mixing bowl
2. Whisk
3. Baking dish (9x13 inches)
4. Aluminum foil (optional, for easy cleanup)
5. Basting brush or spoon

Instructions:

1. Preheat your oven to 400°F (200°C). Grease the baking dish with a little olive oil or line it with aluminum foil for easy cleanup.

2. In a mixing bowl, whisk together the olive oil, lemon juice, minced garlic, ground cumin, ground coriander, paprika, ground cinnamon, ground ginger, ground turmeric, cayenne pepper, salt, and black pepper to make the Moroccan spice marinade.

3. Place the cod fillets in the prepared baking dish.

4. Pour the Moroccan spice marinade over the cod, making sure each fillet is coated. If marinating, cover the dish with plastic wrap and refrigerate for 30 minutes.

5. Once marinated (if applicable), remove the plastic wrap and place the baking dish in the preheated oven.

6. Bake the cod for 12-15 minutes or until the fish is cooked through and flakes easily with a fork. The cooking time

may vary depending on the thickness of the fillets.

7. During baking, you can baste the cod with some of the marinade or drizzle it over the fillets a couple of times to keep them moist.

8. Once the cod is cooked, remove the baking dish from the oven. Carefully transfer the cod fillets to individual plates or a serving platter.

9. Garnish the Moroccan Spiced Cod with chopped fresh cilantro or parsley, if desired.

10. Serve the cod hot with lemon wedges on the side for an extra burst of citrus flavor.

Enjoy the rich and aromatic Moroccan flavors of this spiced cod dish!

Optional Serving Suggestion:
For a complete Moroccan-inspired meal, serve the cod with a side of couscous or quinoa, and some roasted vegetables or a refreshing cucumber and tomato salad dressed with lemon juice and olive oil. The combination will make for a delightful and well-rounded meal.

Nutritional Information (per serving - serves 4):
- Calories: 220 kcal
- Protein: 23g
- Carbohydrates: 2g
- Fat: 13g
- Saturated Fat: 2g
- Cholesterol: 60mg
- Sodium: 200mg
- Fiber: 0.5g
- Sugar: 0g

Recipe Notes:
- *You can use fresh or frozen cod fillets for this recipe. If using frozen cod, ensure they are fully thawed before marinating or baking.*
- *Adjust the level of spices and cayenne pepper based on your preference for spiciness.*
- *Marinating the cod is optional, but it adds more depth to the flavors. If marinating, cover the baking dish with plastic wrap and refrigerate for 30 minutes.*

Shrimp and Vegetable Paella

Preparation Time: 20 minutes **Cooking Time:** 40 minutes **Total Time:** 1 hour

Ingredients:
- 1 lb (450g) large shrimp, peeled and deveined
- 1 1/2 cups Arborio rice or Spanish short-grain rice
- 4 cups chicken or vegetable broth (warm)
- 1/4 cup olive oil
- 1 onion, finely chopped
- 1 red bell pepper, diced
- 1 yellow bell pepper, diced
- 1 cup frozen green peas
- 3 cloves garlic, minced
- 1 teaspoon smoked paprika
- 1/2 teaspoon saffron threads (optional but highly recommended for authentic flavor)
- 1/4 teaspoon cayenne pepper (adjust to your spice preference)
- 1 lemon, cut into wedges for serving
- Fresh parsley, chopped, for garnish
- Salt and black pepper to taste

Utensils Needed:
1. Large paella pan or a wide, shallow skillet (12 inches in diameter)
2. Wooden spoon or spatula
3. Cutting board
4. Chef's knife
5. Measuring cups and spoons

Instructions:
1. In the paella pan or wide skillet, heat the olive oil over medium heat.

2. Add the chopped onion and sauté for 2-3 minutes until softened.

3. Stir in the diced red and yellow bell peppers and cook for an additional 3-4 minutes until they start to become tender.

4. Add the minced garlic and smoked paprika, and cook for another minute, stirring constantly to prevent burning.

5. Pour in the Arborio rice and stir well, ensuring that the rice is coated with the aromatic mixture.

6. If using saffron, add the saffron-infused broth to the pan and mix thoroughly.

7. Gradually add the warm chicken or vegetable broth, one cup at a time, stirring constantly. Allow the liquid to be absorbed

before adding the next cup. This process will take about 15-20 minutes.

8. Add the frozen green peas and continue to cook until the rice is almost fully cooked and has a creamy consistency. The rice should still have a slight bite to it.

9. Season the paella with salt, black pepper, and cayenne pepper to your taste preference.

10. Gently nestle the peeled and deveined shrimp into the partially cooked rice. Cook for about 5-6 minutes or until the shrimp turn pink and are fully cooked through.

11. Once the shrimp are cooked, remove the paella from the heat. Cover the pan with a clean kitchen towel and let it rest for a few minutes to allow the flavors to meld.

12. Garnish the Shrimp and Vegetable Paella with chopped fresh parsley and serve it with lemon wedges on the side.

13. Enjoy the flavorful and colorful paella with your family and friends!

Optional Serving Suggestion:
Pair the paella with a side of garlicky aioli or a fresh green salad for a well-rounded and satisfying meal. Also, you can serve some crusty bread on the side to soak up the delicious juices from the paella.

Nutritional Information (per serving - serves 4):
- Calories: 520 kcal
- Protein: 31g
- Carbohydrates: 64g
- Fat: 14g
- Saturated Fat: 2g
- Cholesterol: 220mg
- Sodium: 980mg
- Fiber: 4g
- Sugar: 6g

Recipe Notes:
- *Paella traditionally includes saffron for its distinctive flavor and vibrant yellow color. If using saffron, steep it in a few tablespoons of warm broth for 10 minutes before adding to the paella.*
- *You can customize this paella by adding other vegetables such as artichoke hearts, asparagus, or cherry tomatoes.*
- *Make sure to use a pan or skillet with a wide surface area to ensure even cooking and a desirable crispy bottom layer of rice called "socarrat."*

Grilled Octopus with Lemon and Herbs

Preparation Time: 20 minutes **Cooking Time:** 45 minutes **Total Time:** 1 hour and 5 minutes

Ingredients:
- 2 lbs (900g) octopus, cleaned and tentacles separated
- 1/4 cup olive oil
- 1/4 cup lemon juice
- 3 cloves garlic, minced
- 1 tablespoon fresh parsley, finely chopped
- 1 tablespoon fresh oregano, finely chopped
- 1 teaspoon lemon zest
- 1/2 teaspoon red pepper flakes (adjust to your spice preference)
- Salt and black pepper to taste
- Lemon wedges for serving
- Fresh parsley and oregano leaves for garnish

Utensils Needed:
1. Large pot or Dutch oven
2. Grill or grill pan
3. Tongs
4. Cutting board
5. Chef's knife
6. Whisk or fork
7. Basting brush

Instructions:
1. In a large pot or Dutch oven, bring water to a boil. Add the cleaned octopus and reduce the heat to a simmer. Cook the octopus for about 30-40 minutes or until it becomes tender. You can test the tenderness by inserting a fork into the thickest part of the tentacles; it should go through easily.

2. While the octopus is cooking, prepare the marinade. In a bowl, whisk together the olive oil, lemon juice, minced garlic, chopped parsley, chopped oregano, lemon zest, red pepper flakes, salt, and black pepper.

3. Once the octopus is tender, remove it from the pot and let it cool slightly. Cut the octopus tentacles into manageable pieces for grilling.

4. Place the octopus pieces in a shallow dish and pour the marinade over them. Ensure all the pieces are well-coated. Cover the dish with plastic wrap and let the octopus marinate for about 15-20 minutes.

5. Preheat your grill or grill pan over medium-high heat. Brush the grates with a little oil to prevent sticking.

6. Remove the octopus from the marinade

and place it on the preheated grill. Grill the octopus for about 2-3 minutes per side or until it gets charred grill marks and develops a smoky flavor.

7. While grilling, you can baste the octopus with the remaining marinade using a basting brush.

8. Once the octopus is grilled to your desired level, remove it from the grill and transfer it to a serving platter.

9. Garnish the Grilled Octopus with Lemon and Herbs with fresh parsley and oregano leaves.

10. Serve the grilled octopus hot, with lemon wedges on the side for an extra zesty kick.

Enjoy the succulent and flavorful Grilled Octopus with Lemon and Herbs as a delightful appetizer or main dish!

Optional Serving Suggestion:
Pair the grilled octopus with a simple side salad dressed with lemon vinaigrette or serve it with a side of sautéed vegetables and crusty bread to create a satisfying meal.

Nutritional Information (per serving - serves 4):
- Calories: 250 kcal
- Protein: 30g
- Carbohydrates: 4g
- Fat: 12g
- Saturated Fat: 2g
- Cholesterol: 150mg
- Sodium: 450mg
- Fiber: 0.5g
- Sugar: 1g

Recipe Notes:
- *Octopus can be tough, so it's best to tenderize it before grilling. You can do this by freezing the octopus for a day or two before cooking or by gently pounding the tentacles with a meat mallet.*
- *Fresh herbs are recommended for the best flavor, but you can use dried herbs if fresh ones are not available.*
- *Be careful not to overcook the octopus, as it can become rubbery. Cooking time may vary depending on the size and tenderness of the octopus.*

Greek Baked Fish with Vegetables

Preparation Time: 20 minutes **Cooking Time:** 30 minutes **Total Time:** 50 minutes

Ingredients:
- 4 fish fillets (such as cod, haddock, or sea bass), about 6 ounces each
- 2 large tomatoes, sliced
- 1 large red bell pepper, sliced
- 1 large yellow bell pepper, sliced
- 1 red onion, thinly sliced
- 1/4 cup pitted Kalamata olives
- 1/4 cup extra-virgin olive oil
- 2 tablespoons lemon juice
- 3 cloves garlic, minced
- 1 tablespoon fresh oregano, chopped (or 1 teaspoon dried oregano)
- 1 tablespoon fresh thyme, chopped (or 1 teaspoon dried thyme)
- 1 teaspoon ground coriander
- Salt and black pepper to taste
- Lemon wedges and fresh parsley for garnish (optional)

Utensils Needed:
1. Baking dish (9x13 inches)
2. Aluminum foil (optional, for easy cleanup)
3. Large mixing bowl
4. Whisk or fork
5. Cutting board
6. Chef's knife

Instructions:
1. Preheat your oven to 400°F (200°C). Grease the baking dish with a little olive oil or line it with aluminum foil for easy cleanup.

2. In a large mixing bowl, whisk together the olive oil, lemon juice, minced garlic, chopped oregano, chopped thyme, ground coriander, salt, and black pepper to make the Greek marinade.

3. Place the fish fillets in the prepared baking dish.

4. Pour the Greek marinade over the fish fillets, ensuring that each fillet is coated with the flavorful mixture.

5. Arrange the sliced tomatoes, red bell pepper, yellow bell pepper, red onion, and Kalamata olives around and over the fish fillets in the baking dish.

6. Drizzle any remaining marinade over the vegetables.

7. Cover the baking dish with aluminum

foil, ensuring it's not touching the fish or vegetables. This will help create steam and keep the fish moist while baking.

8. Bake the Greek Baked Fish with Vegetables in the preheated oven for about 25-30 minutes or until the fish is cooked through and easily flakes with a fork. The baking time may vary depending on the thickness of the fillets.

9. Once the fish is cooked, remove the foil and broil the dish for an additional 1-2 minutes to lightly brown the top.

10. Carefully remove the baking dish from the oven and let it rest for a couple of minutes.

11. Garnish with lemon wedges and fresh parsley, if desired.

12. Serve the Greek Baked Fish with Vegetables hot, with the flavorful vegetables and juices spooned over the fish.

Enjoy this delicious and nutritious Greek Baked Fish with Vegetables with your loved ones for a delightful Mediterranean-inspired meal!

Optional Serving Suggestion:
Serve the dish with a side of lemon-herb rice or quinoa for a complete and satisfying meal. The rice or quinoa will soak up the delicious juices from the fish and vegetables, adding extra flavor to the meal.

Nutritional Information (per serving - serves 4):
- Calories: 320 kcal
- Protein: 30g
- Carbohydrates: 12g
- Fat: 17g
- Saturated Fat: 2.5g
- Cholesterol: 70mg
- Sodium: 480mg
- Fiber: 4g
- Sugar: 6g

Recipe Notes:
- *You can use any firm, white fish fillets for this recipe. Adjust the baking time based on the thickness of the fillets.*
- *Feel free to add or substitute vegetables according to your preference. Zucchini, eggplant, or artichoke hearts work well too.*
- *Fresh herbs are recommended for the best flavor, but you can use dried herbs if fresh ones are not available.*

Stuffed Calamari with Herbs and Rice

Preparation Time: 30 minutes **Cooking Time:** 1 hour **Total Time:** 1 hour and 30 minutes

Ingredients:
- 8 large calamari tubes (cleaned and tentacles separated)
- 1 cup Arborio rice or short-grain rice
- 2 cups fish or vegetable broth
- 1/4 cup olive oil
- 1 large onion, finely chopped
- 3 cloves garlic, minced
- 1/4 cup fresh parsley, chopped
- 2 tablespoons fresh dill, chopped
- 2 tablespoons fresh mint, chopped
- 1/4 cup white wine (optional)
- 1 lemon (zest and juice)
- Salt and black pepper to taste
- Toothpicks or kitchen twine
- Lemon wedges and additional fresh herbs for garnish

Utensils Needed:

1. Large pot or Dutch oven
2. Medium saucepan
3. Baking dish (9x13 inches)
4. Cutting board
5. Chef's knife
6. Wooden spoon or spatula

Instructions:

1. In a medium saucepan, bring the fish or vegetable broth to a boil. Add the rice and simmer, covered, for about 15 minutes or until the rice is cooked and has absorbed the liquid. Remove from heat and let it cool slightly.

2. In a large pot or Dutch oven, heat 2 tablespoons of olive oil over medium heat. Add the chopped onion and sauté for 3-4 minutes until softened.

3. Stir in the minced garlic and cook for an additional minute until fragrant.

4. Add the cooked rice to the onion and garlic mixture, along with the chopped parsley, dill, mint, lemon zest, and lemon juice. Season with salt and black pepper. Mix well and let the stuffing mixture cool slightly.

5. Preheat your oven to 375°F (190°C).

6. Carefully stuff each calamari tube with the herbed rice mixture, leaving some space at the top to secure the filling. Use toothpicks or kitchen twine to close the openings and prevent the stuffing from falling out.

7. In the same large pot or Dutch oven, add the remaining olive oil and heat it over medium-high heat. Sear the stuffed calamari tubes for about 2 minutes on each side until they develop a golden-brown color.

8. If using white wine, deglaze the pot by pouring it over the calamari and stirring gently.

9. Transfer the seared calamari to a greased baking dish.

10. Cover the baking dish with aluminum foil and bake the stuffed calamari in the preheated oven for 30-35 minutes or until the calamari becomes tender and fully cooked.

11. Once the stuffed calamari is cooked, remove the foil and bake for an additional 5 minutes to allow the tops to brown slightly.

12. Carefully remove the toothpicks or kitchen twine from the stuffed calamari before serving.

13. Garnish the Stuffed Calamari with Herbs and Rice with fresh herbs and lemon wedges.

14. Serve the delicious and flavorful stuffed calamari hot as a delightful seafood entrée.

Enjoy this Mediterranean-inspired Stuffed Calamari with Herbs and Rice for a memorable meal with family and friends!

Optional Serving Suggestion:
Serve the stuffed calamari with a side of Greek salad or roasted vegetables and crusty bread to create a satisfying and well-rounded meal.

Nutritional Information (per serving - serves 4):
- Calories: 350 kcal
- Protein: 20g
- Carbohydrates: 40g
- Fat: 10g
- Saturated Fat: 1.5g
- Cholesterol: 170mg
- Sodium: 500mg
- Fiber: 2g
- Sugar: 2g

Recipe Notes:
- When buying calamari tubes, look for large ones that are about 4-6 inches long and already cleaned.
- You can use any fresh herbs of your choice, but the combination of parsley, dill, and mint provides a wonderful Mediterranean flavor.
- If you prefer a non-alcoholic version, you can replace the white wine with additional broth.

Italian Seafood Risotto

Preparation Time: 20 minutes **Cooking Time:** 30 minutes **Total Time:** 50 minutes

Ingredients:
- 1 lb (450g) mixed seafood (such as shrimp, scallops, calamari, and mussels), cleaned and deveined
- 1 1/2 cups Arborio rice
- 4 cups fish or seafood broth (warmed)
- 1/4 cup dry white wine (optional)
- 2 tablespoons olive oil
- 1/2 cup finely chopped onion
- 3 cloves garlic, minced
- 1/4 cup dry white wine (optional)
- 1/4 cup grated Parmesan cheese
- 2 tablespoons unsalted butter
- 2 tablespoons fresh parsley, chopped
- Salt and black pepper to taste
- Lemon wedges for serving (optional)

Utensils Needed:
1. Large saucepan or Dutch oven
2. Medium saucepan
3. Wooden spoon or spatula
4. Cutting board
5. Chef's knife
6. Whisk or fork

Instructions:
1. In a medium saucepan, bring the fish or seafood broth to a simmer. Keep it warm over low heat while preparing the risotto.

2. In a large saucepan or Dutch oven, heat the olive oil over medium heat. Add the finely chopped onion and sauté for 3-4 minutes until it becomes translucent.

3. Add the minced garlic to the onions and cook for an additional minute until fragrant.

4. Add the Arborio rice to the saucepan and stir it with the onions and garlic, coating the rice with the oil. Toast the rice for about 2 minutes until it starts to become lightly golden.

5. If using, pour in the white wine and stir constantly until it's mostly absorbed by the rice.

6. Begin adding the warmed seafood broth to the rice, one ladleful at a time, stirring constantly until the liquid is mostly absorbed before adding the next ladleful. Continue this process for about 20 minutes or until the rice is cooked "al

dente" and has a creamy consistency.

7. While the risotto is cooking, prepare the seafood. Heat a separate pan over medium-high heat and add a drizzle of olive oil. Sauté the mixed seafood until they are cooked through. Season with salt and black pepper to taste.

8. Once the rice is cooked to your desired consistency, stir in the grated Parmesan cheese and unsalted butter, allowing the risotto to become rich and creamy.

9. Gently fold in the sautéed seafood and chopped parsley, reserving some parsley for garnish.

10. Taste the Italian Seafood Risotto and adjust the seasoning with salt and black pepper if needed.

11. Serve the delicious and creamy Italian Seafood Risotto hot in individual bowls.

12. Garnish each serving with a sprinkle of fresh parsley and serve with lemon wedges on the side, if desired, for an extra burst of citrus flavor.

Enjoy this hearty and flavorful Italian Seafood Risotto as a delightful main course for a special occasion or a comforting family meal!

Optional Serving Suggestion: Serve the Italian Seafood Risotto with a side of steamed vegetables or a crisp green salad to add more freshness to the dish. A glass of chilled white wine complements this seafood risotto perfectly.

Recipe Notes:

- *Use fresh or frozen seafood for this recipe. If using frozen seafood, ensure it is fully thawed before cooking.*

- *The seafood broth can be store-bought or homemade. If you cannot find seafood broth, you can substitute it with fish or vegetable broth.*

- *Arborio rice is the best choice for risotto as it releases starch while cooking, giving the dish its creamy texture.*

- *To make this dish alcohol-free, omit the white wine and replace it with additional broth.*

Baked Red Snapper with Mediterranean Salsa

Preparation Time: 20 minutes   **Marinating Time:** 30 minutes (optional)   **Cooking Time:** 15-20 minutes
Total Time: 1 hour and 10 minutes (including marinating time, if applicable)

Ingredients:
For the Baked Red Snapper:
- 4 red snapper fillets (about 6 ounces each), skin-on or skinless
- 2 tablespoons olive oil
- 2 tablespoons lemon juice
- 2 cloves garlic, minced
- 1 teaspoon dried oregano
- 1/2 teaspoon paprika
- 1/2 teaspoon ground cumin
- Salt and black pepper to taste

For the Mediterranean Salsa:
- 1 cup cherry tomatoes, quartered
- 1/2 cup cucumber, diced
- 1/4 cup red onion, finely chopped
- 1/4 cup Kalamata olives, pitted and chopped
- 2 tablespoons fresh parsley, chopped
- 2 tablespoons fresh mint, chopped
- 1 tablespoon lemon juice
- 2 tablespoons extra-virgin olive oil
- Salt and black pepper to taste

Utensils Needed:
1. Baking dish (9x13 inches)
2. Aluminum foil (optional, for easy cleanup)
3. Mixing bowl
4. Whisk or fork
5. Cutting board
6. Chef's knife
7. Tongs or spatula

Instructions:
1. Preheat your oven to 400°F (200°C). Grease the baking dish with a little olive oil or line it with aluminum foil for easy cleanup.

2. In a mixing bowl, whisk together the olive oil, lemon juice, minced garlic, dried oregano, paprika, ground cumin, salt, and black pepper to make the marinade.

3. Place the red snapper fillets in the prepared baking dish.

4. Pour the marinade over the red snapper fillets, making sure they are evenly coated. If marinating, cover the dish with plastic wrap and refrigerate for 30 minutes.

5. While the red snapper is marinating (if applicable), prepare the Mediterranean salsa. In a separate bowl, combine the quartered cherry tomatoes, diced cucumber, finely chopped red onion, chopped Kalamata olives, chopped parsley, chopped mint, lemon juice, and extra-virgin olive oil. Season the salsa with salt and black pepper to taste. Mix well and set aside.

6. Once the red snapper is marinated (if applicable), remove the plastic wrap and place the baking dish in the preheated oven.

7. Bake the red snapper for 15-20 minutes or until the fish is cooked through and flakes easily with a fork. The baking time may vary depending on the thickness of the fillets.

8. While the red snapper is baking, you can prepare any side dishes or set the table.

9. Once the red snapper is cooked, remove the baking dish from the oven.

10. Carefully transfer the baked red snapper fillets to individual serving plates using tongs or a spatula.

11. Spoon the Mediterranean salsa over the baked red snapper fillets, distributing it evenly.

12. Serve the delicious and flavorful Baked Red Snapper with Mediterranean Salsa hot, garnished with additional fresh herbs if desired.

Enjoy the delightful Mediterranean flavors of this Baked Red Snapper with Mediterranean Salsa for a memorable seafood meal!

Optional Serving Suggestion:
Serve the Baked Red Snapper with Mediterranean Salsa with a side of lemon-infused couscous or quinoa for a complete and satisfying meal. The couscous or quinoa will soak up the delicious juices from the salsa, adding extra flavor to the dish.

Nutritional Information (per serving - serves 4):
- Calories: 300 kcal
- Protein: 30g
- Carbohydrates: 7g
- Fat: 17g
- Saturated Fat: 2.5g
- Cholesterol: 70mg
- Sodium: 450mg
- Fiber: 2g
- Sugar: 3g

Recipe Notes:
- Red snapper is the preferred fish for this recipe, but you can use other white fish fillets such as sea bass or grouper.
- If you prefer a spicier flavor, you can add a pinch of red pepper flakes to the marinade or salsa.
- Marinating the red snapper is optional, but it helps enhance the flavors. If marinating, cover the baking dish with plastic wrap and refrigerate for 30 minutes.

Greek Lemon Chicken with Potatoes

Preparation Time: 20 minutes **Cooking Time:** 1 hour 30 minutes **Total Time:** 1 hour 50 minutes **Servings:** 4-6

Ingredients:
- 1 whole chicken (about 3.5-4 lbs), cut into pieces
- 4 large russet potatoes, peeled and cut into wedges
- 1/3 cup extra-virgin olive oil
- 1/4 cup fresh lemon juice
- 4 garlic cloves, minced
- 1 tablespoon dried oregano
- 1 teaspoon dried thyme
- 1 teaspoon dried rosemary
- 1 teaspoon paprika
- 1/2 teaspoon ground cumin
- 1/4 teaspoon cayenne pepper (adjust to your spice preference)
- Salt and black pepper, to taste
- 1 large lemon, sliced
- 1/2 cup chicken broth or water
- Fresh parsley, chopped (for garnish)

Utensils Needed:
- Large mixing bowl
- Large roasting pan or baking dish
- Aluminum foil
- Tongs
- Basting brush

Instructions:
1. Preheat your oven to 400°F (200°C).

2. In a large mixing bowl, combine the olive oil, lemon juice, minced garlic, dried oregano, thyme, rosemary, paprika, cumin, cayenne pepper, salt, and black pepper. Mix well to create the marinade.

3. Pat the chicken pieces dry with paper towels, then add them to the marinade. Toss the chicken in the marinade until each piece is well coated. Allow it to marinate for at least 20 minutes. For best results, marinate the chicken in the refrigerator for a few hours or overnight.

4. While the chicken is marinating, peel and cut the potatoes into wedges. Place them in a large roasting pan or baking dish, and drizzle with a little olive oil and season with salt and pepper.

5. Arrange the marinated chicken pieces on top of the potatoes in the roasting pan. Pour any remaining marinade over the chicken and potatoes. Add the lemon slices on top of the chicken.

6. Pour the chicken broth or water into the bottom of the roasting pan to create some steam while cooking, which helps keep the chicken moist.

7. Cover the roasting pan tightly with aluminum foil to seal in the flavors and moisture.

8. Place the roasting pan in the preheated oven and bake for about 1 hour, covered.

9. After 1 hour, remove the foil and continue baking for another 20-30 minutes or until the chicken and potatoes are golden brown and cooked through. The internal temperature of the chicken should reach 165°F (74°C) when measured with a meat thermometer.

10. Once cooked, remove the roasting pan from the oven. Let the chicken rest for a few minutes before serving.

11. Garnish with chopped fresh parsley and serve hot with some of the pan juices drizzled over the chicken and potatoes.

Nutritional Information (per serving, based on 4 servings):
- Calories: 625 kcal
- Protein: 34g
- Carbohydrates: 34g
- Fat: 38g
- Saturated Fat: 7g
- Cholesterol: 132mg
- Sodium: 273mg
- Fiber: 4g
- Sugar: 2g

Recipe Notes:
- You can use chicken thighs, drumsticks, or a mix of both instead of a whole chicken.
- For a healthier version, you can use chicken breast pieces and remove the skin.
- The nutritional information provided is approximate and may vary based on the specific ingredients and portion sizes used.

Enjoy your delicious Greek Lemon Chicken with Potatoes! This dish pairs well with a side salad or some crusty bread. It's a flavorful and satisfying meal perfect for gatherings or family dinners.

Moroccan Chicken Tagine with Olives and Preserved Lemons

Preparation Time: 30 minutes **Cooking Time:** 1 hour 30 minutes **Total Time:** 2 hours **Servings:** 4-6

Ingredients:
- 2.5 lbs (1.1 kg) chicken pieces (thighs and drumsticks recommended), skin-on and bone-in
- 1 large onion, finely chopped
- 3 garlic cloves, minced
- 2 tablespoons olive oil
- 1 teaspoon ground ginger
- 1 teaspoon ground cumin
- 1 teaspoon ground coriander
- 1 teaspoon paprika
- 1/2 teaspoon ground cinnamon
- 1/4 teaspoon ground turmeric
- 1/4 teaspoon saffron threads (optional but highly recommended)
- 1/4 cup chopped fresh cilantro
- 1/4 cup chopped fresh parsley
- 1 cup green olives, pitted
- 2 preserved lemons, pulp discarded, rind rinsed and thinly sliced (available in specialty stores or you can make your own)
- 1 cup chicken broth
- Salt and black pepper, to taste
- Water, as needed

Utensils Needed:
- Tagine (traditional Moroccan cooking pot) or a large, heavy-bottomed pot with a lid
- Cutting board and knife
- Wooden spoon
- Small bowl for soaking saffron (if using)

Instructions:

1. If using saffron, place the saffron threads in a small bowl with 1 tablespoon of warm water. Let it steep for 10-15 minutes.

2. In the tagine or pot, heat the olive oil over medium heat. Add the chopped onions and sauté until they become translucent, about 5 minutes.

3. Stir in the minced garlic and sauté for another 1-2 minutes until fragrant.

4. Add the chicken pieces to the tagine, and season with ground ginger, ground cumin, ground coriander, paprika, ground cinnamon, ground turmeric, salt, and black pepper. Brown the chicken on

all sides for about 5 minutes.

5. Pour in the chicken broth and add the soaked saffron (if using). Bring the mixture to a simmer.

6. Reduce the heat to low, cover the tagine with its lid, and let it simmer gently for about 1 hour, or until the chicken is tender and fully cooked. Check and stir occasionally, adding water if needed to maintain some liquid in the tagine.

7. After an hour, add the chopped fresh cilantro, chopped fresh parsley, olives, and preserved lemon slices. Stir gently to combine all the flavors.

8. Continue to cook, uncovered, for an additional 10-15 minutes, allowing the sauce to thicken slightly and the flavors to meld together.

9. Taste and adjust seasoning if necessary, adding more salt or spices to your preference.

10. Serve the Moroccan Chicken Tagine with Olives and Preserved Lemons hot, with couscous or warm crusty bread on the side.

Nutritional Information (per serving, based on 4 servings):
- Calories: 460 kcal
- Protein: 37g
- Carbohydrates: 10g
- Fat: 30g
- Saturated Fat: 7g
- Cholesterol: 150mg
- Sodium: 890mg
- Fiber: 4g
- Sugar: 2g

Recipe Notes:

- *If you don't have a tagine, you can use a Dutch oven or any large, heavy-bottomed pot with a tight-fitting lid.*
- *Preserved lemons have a unique tangy flavor. If you can't find them, you can make your own by quartering lemons, packing them with salt, and letting them ferment for a few weeks.*

Enjoy this aromatic and flavorful Moroccan dish that balances the richness of the chicken with the bright, tangy notes of preserved lemons and olives. It's a delightful and hearty meal perfect for sharing with family and friends.

Italian Herb-Roasted Chicken

Preparation Time: 15 minutes **Marinating Time:** 2 hours (optional but recommended) **Cooking Time:** 1 hour 15 minutes **Total Time:** 3 hours 30 minutes (including marinating time) **Servings:** 4-6

Ingredients:
- 1 whole chicken (about 4 lbs), giblets removed and patted dry
- 1/4 cup extra-virgin olive oil
- 3 tablespoons balsamic vinegar
- 4 garlic cloves, minced
- 2 tablespoons fresh lemon juice
- 1 tablespoon dried oregano
- 1 tablespoon dried thyme
- 1 tablespoon dried rosemary
- 1 tablespoon dried basil
- 1 teaspoon dried parsley
- 1 teaspoon salt
- 1/2 teaspoon black pepper
- 1 lemon, sliced
- Fresh herbs (such as thyme, rosemary, or parsley) for garnish (optional)

Utensils Needed:
- Large mixing bowl
- Roasting pan or baking dish
- Basting brush
- Kitchen twine (optional)
- Meat thermometer

Instructions:
1. In a large mixing bowl, combine the extra-virgin olive oil, balsamic vinegar, minced garlic, fresh lemon juice, dried oregano, dried thyme, dried rosemary, dried basil, dried parsley, salt, and black pepper. Mix well to create the marinade.

2. Place the chicken in the bowl with the marinade, making sure to coat the chicken thoroughly. If time allows, cover the bowl with plastic wrap and refrigerate for 2-4 hours to marinate (optional but recommended).

3. Preheat your oven to 400°F (200°C).

4. Remove the chicken from the marinade, allowing any excess marinade to drip off, and transfer it to a roasting pan or baking dish.

5. Stuff the cavity of the chicken with lemon slices and any leftover herb sprigs for added flavor. You can also truss the chicken with kitchen twine if desired.

6. Brush the chicken with any remaining marinade or a little extra olive oil for a beautiful golden finish.

7. Place the roasting pan in the preheated

oven, and roast the chicken for about 1 hour and 15 minutes, or until the internal temperature of the thickest part of the chicken reaches 165°F (74°C) when measured with a meat thermometer.

8. While the chicken is roasting, baste it with the pan juices every 20-30 minutes to keep it moist and flavorful.

9. Once cooked, remove the roasting pan from the oven, and let the chicken rest for about 10 minutes before carving.

10. Garnish with fresh herbs if desired, and serve the Italian Herb-Roasted Chicken with your favorite sides, such as roasted vegetables, garlic mashed potatoes, or a fresh salad.

Nutritional Information (per serving, based on 4 servings):
- Calories: 465 kcal
- Protein: 37g
- Carbohydrates: 4g
- Fat: 33g
- Saturated Fat: 7g
- Cholesterol: 142mg
- Sodium: 663mg
- Fiber: 1g
- Sugar: 1g

Recipe Notes:
- For a more intense flavor, you can marinate the chicken in the refrigerator for 2-4 hours before roasting. If marinating, be sure to bring the chicken to room temperature for about 30 minutes before roasting.
- Kitchen twine can be used to truss the chicken to help it cook more evenly and retain its shape.
- The nutritional information provided is approximate and may vary based on the specific ingredients and portion sizes used.

Enjoy the succulent and aromatic Italian Herb-Roasted Chicken, infused with the flavors of Mediterranean herbs and tangy balsamic vinegar. It's a comforting and satisfying dish that's perfect for special occasions or family dinners.

Grilled Balsamic Chicken with Vegetables

Preparation Time: 20 minutes **Marinating Time:** 2 hours (or overnight) **Grilling Time:** 20 minutes
Total Time: 2 hours 40 minutes (including marinating time) **Servings:** 4

Ingredients:
- 4 boneless, skinless chicken breasts (about 1.5 lbs or 680g)
- 1/4 cup balsamic vinegar
- 1/4 cup extra-virgin olive oil
- 2 tablespoons honey or maple syrup
- 3 garlic cloves, minced
- 1 teaspoon dried thyme
- 1 teaspoon dried rosemary
- 1 teaspoon dried oregano
- 1/2 teaspoon red pepper flakes (optional, for some heat)
- Salt and black pepper, to taste
- 2 cups cherry tomatoes
- 2 bell peppers (any color), cut into chunks
- 1 red onion, cut into chunks
- 1 zucchini, sliced
- 1 tablespoon olive oil (for vegetables)
- Fresh basil leaves, for garnish (optional)

Utensils Needed:
- Large mixing bowl
- Ziplock bag or airtight container for marinating
- Grill or grill pan
- Tongs
- Skewers (if using wooden skewers, soak them in water for 30 minutes before grilling)
- Basting brush

Instructions:
1. In a large mixing bowl, whisk together the balsamic vinegar, extra-virgin olive oil, honey (or maple syrup), minced garlic, dried thyme, dried rosemary, dried oregano, red pepper flakes (if using), salt, and black pepper.

2. Place the chicken breasts in the marinade, making sure they are fully coated. If time allows, cover the bowl with plastic wrap or transfer the chicken and marinade to a ziplock bag or airtight container. Marinate in the refrigerator for at least 2 hours or preferably overnight for the best flavor.

3. Preheat your grill or grill pan to medium-high heat.

4. While the grill is heating up, prepare the vegetables. In a separate bowl, toss the cherry tomatoes, bell peppers, red onion, and zucchini with a tablespoon of olive oil, salt, and black pepper.

5. Thread the vegetables onto skewers, alternating the different vegetables for even cooking.

6. Remove the chicken from the marinade and let any excess drip off. Discard the marinade.

7. Grill the chicken breasts and vegetable skewers over medium-high heat. The grilling

time for the chicken will be about 4-5 minutes per side, depending on the thickness of the chicken breasts. Cook until the internal temperature of the chicken reaches 165°F (74°C) when measured with a meat thermometer.

8. Grill the vegetable skewers for about 8-10 minutes, turning occasionally until they are lightly charred and tender.

9. While grilling, baste the chicken with any remaining marinade or a little extra olive oil using a basting brush to keep it moist and enhance the flavors.

10. Once the chicken and vegetables are grilled to perfection, remove them from the grill.

11. Let the chicken rest for a few minutes before slicing.

12. Serve the Grilled Balsamic Chicken with the vegetable skewers on the side. Garnish with fresh basil leaves if desired.

Nutritional Information (per serving):
- *Calories: 390 kcal*
- *Protein: 31g*
- *Carbohydrates: 25g*
- *Fat: 18g*
- *Saturated Fat: 3g*
- *Cholesterol: 85mg*
- *Sodium: 240mg*
- *Fiber: 4g*
- *Sugar: 17g*

Recipe Notes:
- *You can substitute chicken thighs or a mix of chicken pieces for variety.*
- *For a smokier flavor, use a charcoal grill.*
- *Feel free to customize the vegetable selection based on your preferences or what's in season.*
- *The nutritional information provided is approximate and may vary based on the specific ingredients and portion sizes used.*

Enjoy this delightful and healthy Grilled Balsamic Chicken with Vegetables, bursting with Mediterranean flavors. It's a delicious and colorful dish that makes for a satisfying meal, perfect for outdoor gatherings or a flavorful weeknight dinner.

Spanish Chicken and Chorizo Rice

Preparation Time: 15 minutes **Cooking Time:** 40 minutes **Total Time:** 55 minutes **Servings:** 4-6

Ingredients:
- 1.5 lbs (680g) boneless, skinless chicken thighs, cut into bite-sized pieces
- 8 oz (225g) Spanish chorizo sausage, sliced
- 1 cup long-grain white rice
- 2 tablespoons olive oil
- 1 onion, finely chopped
- 3 garlic cloves, minced
- 1 red bell pepper, diced
- 1 green bell pepper, diced
- 1 teaspoon smoked paprika
- 1/2 teaspoon ground cumin
- 1/2 teaspoon dried oregano
- 1/4 teaspoon cayenne pepper (adjust to your spice preference)
- 1 can (14 oz/400g) diced tomatoes
- 2 cups chicken broth
- 1/2 cup frozen peas
- Salt and black pepper, to taste
- Fresh parsley or cilantro, chopped (for garnish)

Utensils Needed:
- Large skillet or paella pan
- Cutting board and knife
- Wooden spoon
- Medium saucepan (if using regular rice instead of instant)
- Aluminum foil (if needed to cover the skillet)

Instructions:
1. In a large skillet or paella pan, heat the olive oil over medium-high heat.

2. Add the chicken pieces to the pan and brown them on all sides. Remove the chicken from the pan and set it aside.

3. In the same pan, add the sliced chorizo and sauté until it releases its oils and becomes slightly crispy. Remove the chorizo and set it aside with the chicken.

4. In the same pan, sauté the chopped onion until it becomes translucent, about 3-4 minutes. Stir in the minced garlic and cook for an additional minute until fragrant.

5. Add the diced red and green bell peppers to the pan and cook for another 3-4 minutes until they start to soften.

6. Stir in the smoked paprika, ground cumin, dried oregano, and cayenne pepper. Cook for a minute to release the flavors.

7. If using regular rice, add it to the pan and toast it for a minute, stirring to coat it with the spices. If using instant rice, skip this step.

8. Pour in the diced tomatoes (with their juice) and chicken broth. Stir well to combine.

9. If using instant rice, add the frozen peas and return the chicken and chorizo to the pan. Cover the skillet

with a lid or aluminum foil and simmer for about 10 minutes or until the rice is cooked and the chicken is tender.

10. If using regular rice, let the mixture come to a simmer, then cover the skillet with a lid or aluminum foil, and cook for about 20-25 minutes or until the rice is tender and has absorbed the liquid.

11. Once the rice is cooked, remove the skillet from the heat and let it rest for a few minutes.

12. Fluff the rice with a fork and adjust the seasoning with salt and black pepper if needed.

13. Garnish with chopped fresh parsley or cilantro before serving.

Nutritional Information (per serving, based on 4 servings):
- Calories: 585 kcal
- Protein: 37g
- Carbohydrates: 42g
- Fat: 30g
- Saturated Fat: 9g
- Cholesterol: 144mg
- Sodium: 1122mg
- Fiber: 3g
- Sugar: 5g

Recipe Notes:

- Spanish chorizo is a dry, cured sausage with a smoky flavor. If you can't find it, you can use Mexican chorizo, but it will have a different taste.
- Instant rice can be used for a quicker version, but traditional long-grain rice adds more texture and absorbs the flavors better.
- Adjust the spice level by increasing or reducing the amount of cayenne pepper.
- The nutritional information provided is approximate and may vary based on the specific ingredients and portion sizes used.

Serve this Spanish Chicken and Chorizo Rice as a flavorful one-pot meal that captures the essence of Spanish cuisine. It's a delicious combination of tender chicken, smoky chorizo, and vibrant vegetables, all infused with aromatic spices. Perfect for a family dinner or when you want to impress your guests with a hearty and satisfying dish!

Lebanese Chicken Shawarma

Preparation Time: 20 minutes **Marinating Time:** 2-4 hours (or overnight) **Cooking Time:** 20 minutes **Total Time:** 3 hours (including marinating time) **Servings:** 4-6

Ingredients:
For the Chicken Shawarma:
- 2 lbs (900g) boneless, skinless chicken thighs
- 1/4 cup lemon juice
- 1/4 cup plain yogurt
- 2 tablespoons olive oil
- 4 garlic cloves, minced
- 1 teaspoon ground cumin
- 1 teaspoon ground coriander
- 1 teaspoon smoked paprika
- 1/2 teaspoon ground turmeric
- 1/2 teaspoon ground cinnamon
- 1/4 teaspoon cayenne pepper (adjust to your spice preference)
- Salt and black pepper, to taste

For Serving:
- Pita bread or flatbread
- Hummus
- Tahini sauce
- Sliced tomatoes
- Sliced cucumbers
- Chopped lettuce
- Pickles
- Chopped fresh parsley or cilantro
- Hot sauce (optional)

Utensils Needed:
- Large mixing bowl
- Ziplock bag or airtight container for marinating
- Grill or grill pan
- Tongs
- Cutting board and knife

Instructions:
1. In a large mixing bowl, combine the lemon juice, plain yogurt, olive oil, minced garlic, ground cumin, ground coriander, smoked paprika, ground turmeric, ground cinnamon, cayenne pepper, salt, and black pepper to make the marinade.

2. Add the chicken thighs to the marinade and toss them until they are fully coated. Cover the bowl with plastic wrap or transfer the chicken and marinade to a ziplock bag or airtight container. Marinate in the refrigerator for at least 2-4 hours, or preferably overnight, to allow the flavors to develop.

3. Preheat your grill or grill pan to medium-high heat.

4. Remove the chicken from the marinade, allowing any excess marinade to drip off.

5. Cook the chicken on the grill or grill pan for about 8-10 minutes per side or until the

internal temperature reaches 165°F (74°C) when measured with a meat thermometer. The cooking time may vary based on the thickness of the chicken thighs.

6. Once cooked, transfer the chicken to a cutting board and let it rest for a few minutes. Slice the chicken into thin strips.

7. Warm the pita bread or flatbread on the grill or in the oven.

8. To assemble the Lebanese Chicken Shawarma, spread some hummus and tahini sauce on the warmed pita bread. Add the sliced chicken on top.

9. Garnish with sliced tomatoes, sliced cucumbers, chopped lettuce, pickles, chopped fresh parsley or cilantro, and hot sauce if desired.

10. Roll up the pita bread tightly to form a shawarma wrap.

Serve the delicious Lebanese Chicken Shawarma wraps as a flavorful and satisfying meal. Enjoy the juicy and spiced chicken with the creamy hummus, tangy tahini sauce, and fresh vegetables—all wrapped in soft and warm pita bread. It's a popular street food in Lebanon and will surely become a favorite at your dining table too!

Nutritional Information (per serving, based on 4 servings):
- *Calories: 520 kcal*
- *Protein: 39g*
- *Carbohydrates: 24g*
- *Fat: 30g*
- *Saturated Fat: 7g*
- *Cholesterol: 185mg*
- *Sodium: 530mg*
- *Fiber: 4g*
- *Sugar: 2g*

Recipe Notes:

- Chicken thighs are used in this recipe for their tenderness and juiciness, but you can also use chicken breast if you prefer.

- For an authentic touch, cook the chicken shawarma on a vertical rotisserie or spit. If you don't have one, a grill or grill pan works well too.

- You can customize the toppings based on your preferences. Traditionally, shawarma is served with garlic sauce, pickles, and other vegetables, but you can get creative with the fillings.

Chicken Souvlaki with Tzatziki Sauce

Preparation Time: 20 minutes **Marinating Time:** 1-2 hours (or overnight) **Cooking Time:** 10 minutes **Total Time:** 2 hours 30 minutes (including marinating time) **Servings:** 4

Ingredients:
For Chicken Souvlaki:
- 1.5 lbs (680g) boneless, skinless chicken breasts or thighs, cut into bite-sized pieces
- 1/4 cup olive oil
- 2 tablespoons fresh lemon juice
- 3 garlic cloves, minced
- 1 tablespoon dried oregano
- 1 teaspoon dried thyme
- 1 teaspoon dried rosemary
- 1/2 teaspoon dried mint
- 1/2 teaspoon paprika
- Salt and black pepper, to taste
- Wooden skewers (if using wooden skewers, soak them in water for 30 minutes before grilling)

For Tzatziki Sauce:
- 1 cup Greek yogurt
- 1/2 cucumber, grated and squeezed to remove excess moisture
- 2 garlic cloves, minced
- 1 tablespoon fresh lemon juice
- 1 tablespoon fresh dill, chopped
- Salt and black pepper, to taste

For Serving:
- Pita bread or flatbread
- Sliced tomatoes
- Sliced red onions
- Sliced cucumbers
- Fresh parsley or dill, chopped
- Lemon wedges

Utensils Needed:
- Large mixing bowl
- Ziplock bag or airtight container for marinating
- Grill or grill pan
- Tongs
- Small mixing bowl for tzatziki sauce

Instructions:
For Chicken Souvlaki:
1. In a large mixing bowl, combine the olive oil, fresh lemon juice, minced garlic, dried oregano, dried thyme, dried rosemary, dried mint, paprika, salt, and black pepper to create the marinade.

2. Add the bite-sized chicken pieces to the marinade, tossing them to ensure they are fully coated. Cover the bowl with plastic wrap or transfer the chicken and marinade to a ziplock bag or airtight container. Marinate in the refrigerator for 1-2 hours, or preferably overnight, to let the flavors infuse into the chicken.

3. Preheat your grill or grill pan to medium-high heat.

4. Thread the marinated chicken pieces onto wooden skewers (if using). Discard the leftover marinade.

5. Grill the chicken souvlaki skewers for about 3-4 minutes per side or until the chicken is fully cooked and has a nice char on the outside.

6. Once cooked, remove the chicken souvlaki from the grill and let them rest for a few minutes.

For Tzatziki Sauce:
1. In a small mixing bowl, combine the Greek yogurt, grated cucumber, minced garlic, fresh lemon juice, chopped dill, salt, and black pepper. Mix well

until all the ingredients are fully incorporated.

2. Taste the tzatziki sauce and adjust the seasoning if needed. You can add more lemon juice, salt, or dill according to your taste preferences.

For Serving:
1. Warm the pita bread or flatbread on the grill or in the oven.

2. Spread a generous amount of tzatziki sauce on each warmed pita bread.

3. Add the grilled chicken souvlaki on top of the tzatziki sauce.

4. Garnish with sliced tomatoes, sliced red onions, sliced cucumbers, and chopped fresh parsley or dill.

5. Serve the Chicken Souvlaki with Tzatziki Sauce along with lemon wedges on the side for an extra burst of flavor.

Enjoy this delicious and authentic Greek dish! The tender and well-seasoned chicken, paired with the creamy and refreshing tzatziki sauce, make for a delightful meal. Serve it with your favorite side salads or roasted vegetables for a complete and satisfying Mediterranean-inspired experience.

Nutritional Information (per serving):
- Calories: 400 kcal
- Protein: 42g
- Carbohydrates: 12g
- Fat: 20g
- Saturated Fat: 3g
- Cholesterol: 110mg
- Sodium: 250mg
- Fiber: 2g
- Sugar: 6g

Recipe Notes:
- *You can use either chicken breasts or thighs for the souvlaki. Both work well and provide juicy and flavorful results.*
- *Feel free to adjust the seasonings in the marinade and tzatziki sauce to suit your taste preferences.*
- *The tzatziki sauce can be made a day ahead and stored in the refrigerator.*

Turkish Chicken Kebabs with Yogurt Sauce

Preparation Time: 30 minutes **Marinating Time:** 1-2 hours (or overnight) **Cooking Time:** 10-12 minutes
Total Time: 2 hours (including marinating time) **Servings:** 4-6

Ingredients:
For Chicken Kebabs:
- 1.5 lbs (680g) boneless, skinless chicken breasts or thighs, cut into bite-sized pieces
- 1/4 cup olive oil
- 2 tablespoons plain yogurt
- 2 tablespoons tomato paste
- 2 tablespoons fresh lemon juice
- 3 garlic cloves, minced
- 1 teaspoon ground cumin
- 1 teaspoon ground coriander
- 1 teaspoon smoked paprika
- 1/2 teaspoon ground turmeric
- 1/4 teaspoon cayenne pepper (adjust to your spice preference)
- Salt and black pepper, to taste
- Wooden skewers (if using wooden skewers, soak them in water for 30 minutes before grilling)

For Yogurt Sauce:
- 1 cup plain yogurt
- 1 tablespoon fresh lemon juice
- 2 tablespoons fresh parsley, chopped
- 1 tablespoon fresh mint, chopped
- Salt and black pepper, to taste

For Serving:
- Pita bread or flatbread
- Sliced tomatoes
- Sliced cucumbers
- Red onion slices
- Fresh parsley or mint, chopped
- Lemon wedges

Utensils Needed:
- Large mixing bowl
- Ziplock bag or airtight container for marinating
- Grill or grill pan
- Tongs
- Small mixing bowl for yogurt sauce

Instructions:
For Chicken Kebabs:
1. In a large mixing bowl, combine the olive oil, plain yogurt, tomato paste, fresh lemon juice, minced garlic, ground cumin, ground coriander, smoked paprika, ground turmeric, cayenne pepper, salt, and black pepper to create the marinade.

2. Add the bite-sized chicken pieces to the marinade, tossing them to ensure they are fully coated. Cover the bowl with plastic wrap or transfer the chicken and marinade to a ziplock bag or airtight container. Marinate in the refrigerator for 1-2 hours, or preferably overnight, to let the flavors infuse into the chicken.

3. Preheat your grill or grill pan to medium-high heat.

4. Thread the marinated chicken pieces onto wooden skewers (if using). Discard the leftover marinade.

5. Grill the chicken kebabs for about 5-6 minutes per side or until the chicken is fully cooked and has a nice char on the outside.

6. Once cooked, remove the chicken kebabs from the grill and let them rest for a few minutes.

For Yogurt Sauce:

1. In a small mixing bowl, combine the plain yogurt, fresh lemon juice, chopped parsley, chopped mint, salt, and black pepper. Mix well until all the ingredients are fully incorporated.

2. Taste the yogurt sauce and adjust the seasoning if needed. You can add more lemon juice, salt, or herbs according to your taste preferences.

For Serving:

1. Warm the pita bread or flatbread on the grill or in the oven.

2. Spread a generous amount of yogurt sauce on each warmed pita bread.

3. Add the grilled chicken kebabs on top of the yogurt sauce.

4. Garnish with sliced tomatoes, sliced cucumbers, red onion slices, and chopped fresh parsley or mint.

5. Serve the Turkish Chicken Kebabs with Yogurt Sauce along with lemon wedges on the side for an extra burst of flavor.

Nutritional Information (per serving, based on 4 servings):
- Calories: 320 kcal
- Protein: 31g
- Carbohydrates: 9g
- Fat: 18g
- Saturated Fat: 3g
- Cholesterol: 90mg
- Sodium: 280mg
- Fiber: 2g
- Sugar: 5g

Recipe Notes:
- You can use either chicken breasts or thighs for the kebabs. Both work well and provide juicy and flavorful results.
- Feel free to adjust the seasonings in the marinade and yogurt sauce to suit your taste preferences.
- The yogurt sauce can be made a day ahead and stored in the refrigerator.

Enjoy this delicious and authentic Turkish dish! The well-spiced and tender chicken, paired with the creamy and refreshing yogurt sauce, make for a delightful meal. Serve it with your favorite side salads or roasted vegetables for a complete and satisfying Mediterranean-inspired experience.

Sicilian Chicken Marsala

Preparation Time: 15 minutes **Cooking Time:** 25 minutes **Total Time:** 40 minutes **Servings:** 4

Ingredients:
- 4 boneless, skinless chicken breasts (about 1.5 lbs or 680g)
- 1/2 cup all-purpose flour
- Salt and black pepper, to taste
- 2 tablespoons olive oil
- 4 tablespoons unsalted butter, divided
- 1 cup sliced mushrooms
- 1/2 cup Marsala wine (sweet or dry, depending on your preference)
- 1/2 cup chicken broth
- 1/2 cup heavy cream
- 2 tablespoons chopped fresh parsley (for garnish)

Utensils Needed:
- Large shallow dish for flouring the chicken
- Large skillet or frying pan
- Tongs
- Cutting board and knife

Instructions:
1. Pat the chicken breasts dry with paper towels. Place the all-purpose flour in a large shallow dish and season it with salt and black pepper.

2. Dredge each chicken breast in the seasoned flour, shaking off any excess flour.

3. In a large skillet or frying pan, heat the olive oil and 2 tablespoons of butter over medium-high heat.

4. Once the butter is melted and the oil is hot, add the floured chicken breasts to the pan. Cook the chicken for about 4-5 minutes per side, or until they are browned and fully cooked through. Use a meat thermometer to check the internal temperature, which should reach 165°F (74°C).

5. Once the chicken is cooked, remove it from the pan and set it aside on a plate.

6. In the same pan, add the sliced mushrooms and sauté them for about 2-3 minutes until they are tender and slightly browned.

7. Pour the Marsala wine into the pan, stirring to deglaze and scrape up any browned bits from the bottom of the pan.

8. Add the chicken broth to the pan and bring the mixture to a simmer. Let it cook for about 2-3 minutes to allow the alcohol to cook off and the flavors to meld.

9. Reduce the heat to low and stir in the heavy cream. Let the

sauce simmer for an additional 2 minutes to thicken slightly.

10. Stir in the remaining 2 tablespoons of butter to add richness and a velvety texture to the sauce.

11. Return the cooked chicken breasts to the pan, coating them with the Marsala sauce. Let them warm through for a minute or two.

12. Garnish the Sicilian Chicken Marsala with chopped fresh parsley.

Serve this delectable Sicilian Chicken Marsala over pasta, rice, or mashed potatoes, and enjoy the rich and savory flavors of this classic Italian dish. It's a restaurant-quality meal that you can easily prepare at home, perfect for special occasions or a delightful weeknight dinner with loved ones.

Nutritional Information (per serving):
- Calories: 450 kcal
- Protein: 33g
- Carbohydrates: 12g
- Fat: 29g
- Saturated Fat: 14g
- Cholesterol: 155mg
- Sodium: 420mg
- Fiber: 1g
- Sugar: 3g

Recipe Notes:
- *Marsala wine is a key ingredient in this recipe. You can use either sweet or dry Marsala wine, depending on your preference. Sweet Marsala wine will give the dish a richer, sweeter flavor, while dry Marsala wine will provide a more savory taste.*
- *If you don't have Marsala wine, you can substitute with dry sherry or Madeira wine, but the flavor will be slightly different.*
- *Chicken thighs can be used instead of chicken breasts if you prefer dark meat.*
- *For a gluten-free version, you can use a gluten-free all-purpose flour.*

Stuffed Chicken Breasts with Spinach and Feta

Preparation Time: 20 minutes **Cooking Time:** 25 minutes **Total Time:** 45 minutes **Servings:** 4

Ingredients:
- 4 boneless, skinless chicken breasts (about 1.5 lbs or 680g)
- 2 cups fresh baby spinach, chopped
- 1 cup crumbled feta cheese
- 1/4 cup sun-dried tomatoes, chopped (optional, for added flavor)
- 2 garlic cloves, minced
- 1 tablespoon olive oil
- 1 teaspoon dried oregano
- 1/2 teaspoon dried thyme
- 1/2 teaspoon dried basil
- Salt and black pepper, to taste
- 1 tablespoon butter, melted
- 1 tablespoon lemon juice
- Toothpicks or kitchen twine (to secure the stuffed chicken)

Utensils Needed:
- Cutting board and knife
- Meat mallet or rolling pin
- Small mixing bowl
- Baking dish
- Toothpicks or kitchen twine for securing the stuffed chicken
- Meat thermometer (optional but helpful)

Instructions:
1. Preheat your oven to 400°F (200°C).

2. Using a sharp knife, create a pocket in each chicken breast by making a horizontal cut along one side. Be careful not to cut all the way through to the other side.

3. In a small mixing bowl, combine the chopped baby spinach, crumbled feta cheese, sun-dried tomatoes (if using), minced garlic, olive oil, dried oregano, dried thyme, dried basil, salt, and black pepper. Mix well to create the stuffing.

4. Stuff each chicken breast with an equal amount of the spinach and feta mixture. Press the edges of the chicken together to seal the pocket. Use toothpicks or kitchen twine to secure the stuffed chicken and prevent the filling from spilling out during cooking.

5. Place the stuffed chicken breasts in a baking dish.

6. In a separate small bowl, mix together the melted butter and lemon juice.

7. Brush the melted butter and lemon mixture over the stuffed chicken breasts.

8. Bake the stuffed chicken in the preheated oven for about 20-25 minutes or until the internal temperature of the chicken reaches 165°F (74°C) when measured with a meat thermometer.

9. Once cooked, remove the stuffed chicken from the oven and let it rest for a few minutes.

10. Carefully remove the toothpicks or kitchen twine before serving.

Serve these delicious Stuffed Chicken Breasts with Spinach and Feta alongside your favorite side dishes, such as roasted vegetables, garlic mashed potatoes, or a fresh salad. The tender and flavorful chicken, combined with the savory spinach and tangy feta filling, creates a delightful meal that's sure to impress your family or guests. Enjoy!

Nutritional Information (per serving):
- *Calories: 310 kcal*
- *Protein: 39g*
- *Carbohydrates: 4g*
- *Fat: 15g*
- *Saturated Fat: 7g*
- *Cholesterol: 125mg*
- *Sodium: 560mg*
- *Fiber: 1g*
- *Sugar: 1g*

Recipe Notes:
- You can customize the filling by adding ingredients like chopped olives or roasted red peppers for additional flavor and texture.
- If you prefer a crispier crust on the chicken, you can brush the stuffed breasts with olive oil before baking.
- For a gluten-free version, ensure that your feta cheese and sun-dried tomatoes are gluten-free.

Mediterranean Main Courses: Vegetarian Recipes

Eggplant Parmesan

Preparation Time: 30 minutes **Cooking Time:** 1 hour **Total Time:** 1 hour 30 minutes **Servings:** 6

Ingredients:
- 2 large eggplants
- 2 cups all-purpose flour
- 4 large eggs
- 2 cups breadcrumbs (preferably Italian-style)
- 1 cup grated Parmesan cheese
- 2 cups marinara sauce (homemade or store-bought)
- 2 cups shredded mozzarella cheese
- 1/4 cup chopped fresh basil leaves
- Salt and pepper to taste
- Olive oil for frying

Utensils Needed:
- Cutting board
- Knife
- 3 shallow dishes (for dredging)
- Whisk
- Large skillet or frying pan
- Baking sheet
- Paper towels
- 9x13 inch baking dish
- Aluminum foil

Instructions:

1. Preheat your oven to 375°F (190°C).

2. Wash the eggplants, then trim off the ends. Cut the eggplants into 1/2-inch thick slices, either crosswise or lengthwise, depending on your preference.

3. Sprinkle salt on both sides of the eggplant slices and place them in a colander or on a wire rack. Let them sit for about 20 minutes to draw out excess moisture and bitterness. This process helps improve the texture and flavor of the eggplant.

4. While the eggplants are resting, set up your dredging stations. In one shallow dish, place the all-purpose flour. In another dish, beat the eggs with a pinch of salt and pepper. In the third dish, combine the breadcrumbs and grated Parmesan cheese.

5. After 20 minutes, pat the eggplant slices dry with paper towels to remove the excess salt and moisture.

6. Dip each eggplant slice into the flour, shaking off any excess. Then dip it into the beaten eggs, allowing any excess egg to drip off. Finally, coat the eggplant in the breadcrumb-Parmesan mixture, pressing the breadcrumbs gently onto the surface to adhere.

7. In a large skillet or frying pan, pour enough olive oil to cover the bottom (about 1/4 inch deep) and heat it over medium-high heat. Fry

the breaded eggplant slices in batches for 2-3 minutes per side, or until they turn golden brown. Place the fried eggplant slices on a paper towel-lined baking sheet to absorb any excess oil.

8. In a 9x13 inch baking dish, spread a thin layer of marinara sauce on the bottom. Arrange half of the fried eggplant slices in a single layer over the sauce.

9. Sprinkle half of the shredded mozzarella cheese over the eggplant slices and add half of the chopped basil leaves.

10. Pour another layer of marinara sauce over the cheese, then repeat the layers with the remaining eggplant, mozzarella, and basil.

11. For the final layer, spread a generous amount of marinara sauce over the top and sprinkle with any remaining mozzarella and basil.

12. Cover the baking dish with aluminum foil and bake in the preheated oven for 25 minutes.

13. After 25 minutes, remove the foil and bake for an additional 10-15 minutes, or until the cheese is bubbly and lightly browned.

14. Let the Eggplant Parmesan rest for a few minutes before serving. It goes well with a side of pasta or a fresh green salad.

Enjoy your delicious and comforting Eggplant Parmesan!

Nutritional Information (per serving):
- Calories: 350
- Total Fat: 15g
- Saturated Fat: 7g
- Cholesterol: 95mg
- Sodium: 850mg
- Total Carbohydrates: 35g
- Dietary Fiber: 5g
- Sugars: 7g
- Protein: 18g

Recipe Notes:
- You can reduce the calorie and fat content by baking the eggplant instead of frying it. Simply coat the eggplant slices in olive oil and bake in a preheated oven at 400°F (200°C) for 20-25 minutes or until golden brown.
- For a spicier version, add red pepper flakes to the marinara sauce or sprinkle them on top before baking.
- This dish is best served fresh, but any leftovers can be refrigerated for up to 3 days or frozen for up to 1 month.

Ratatouille

Preparation Time: 30 minutes **Cooking Time:** 45 minutes **Total Time:** 1 hour 15 minutes **Servings:** 6

Ingredients:
- 1 large eggplant, diced
- 2 zucchinis, diced
- 1 large yellow bell pepper, diced
- 1 large red bell pepper, diced
- 1 large onion, finely chopped
- 4 cloves garlic, minced
- 4 large tomatoes, diced
- 1/4 cup tomato paste
- 1/4 cup olive oil
- 1 teaspoon dried thyme
- 1 teaspoon dried oregano
- 1/2 teaspoon dried rosemary
- Salt and pepper to taste
- Fresh basil leaves, chopped, for garnish

Utensils Needed:
- Cutting board
- Knife
- Large pot or Dutch oven
- Wooden spoon or spatula
- Measuring cups and spoons

Instructions:

1. Heat the olive oil in a large pot or Dutch oven over medium heat.

2. Add the chopped onions and sauté until they become translucent, about 3-4 minutes.

3. Stir in the minced garlic and cook for an additional 1-2 minutes until the garlic becomes fragrant.

4. Add the diced eggplant, zucchinis, yellow and red bell peppers to the pot. Season with salt, pepper, dried thyme, dried oregano, and dried rosemary.

5. Cook the vegetables, stirring occasionally, for about 10 minutes or until they begin to soften.

6. Add the diced tomatoes and tomato paste to the pot. Stir well to combine all the ingredients.

7. Reduce the heat to low, cover the pot, and let the ratatouille simmer for 30 minutes. Stir occasionally to prevent sticking.

8. After 30 minutes, check the seasoning and adjust with more salt and pepper if needed.

9. Once the vegetables are tender and the flavors have melded together, remove the pot from the heat.

10. Garnish the ratatouille with

chopped fresh basil leaves just before serving.

Serve the Ratatouille hot as a delightful and flavorful vegetable dish that's perfect for any season.

Optional: Ratatouille can be served as a side dish or as a main course. If you want to make it a heartier meal, consider adding cooked chickpeas or serving it with a side of crusty bread for dipping.

Nutritional Information (per serving):
- Calories: 160
- Total Fat: 8g
- Saturated Fat: 1g
- Cholesterol: 0mg
- Sodium: 200mg
- Total Carbohydrates: 22g
- Dietary Fiber: 7g
- Sugars: 12g
- Protein: 4g

Recipe Notes:
- Ratatouille is a versatile dish, and you can adjust the vegetables and herbs to your taste. Feel free to add other vegetables like mushrooms or carrots.
- This dish tastes even better the next day, so consider making it ahead of time and reheating it for serving.
- Ratatouille can be served as a side dish, but it's also delicious on its own or over rice, pasta, or couscous.

Spinach and Feta Stuffed Peppers

Preparation Time: 20 minutes **Cooking Time**: 40 minute **Total Time**: 1 hour **Servings**: 4

Ingredients:
- 4 large bell peppers (red, yellow, or orange)
- 2 cups fresh spinach, chopped
- 1 cup crumbled feta cheese
- 1 cup cooked quinoa or rice
- 1 small onion, finely chopped
- 2 cloves garlic, minced
- 1 tablespoon olive oil
- 1 teaspoon dried oregano
- 1 teaspoon dried basil
- 1/2 teaspoon red pepper flakes (optional, for heat)
- Salt and pepper to taste
- 1/4 cup grated Parmesan cheese (for topping)

Utensils Needed:
- Cutting board
- Knife
- Large pot
- Large skillet or frying pan
- Mixing bowl
- Spoon
- Baking dish
.

Instructions:
1. Preheat your oven to 375°F (190°C).

2. Cut the tops off the bell peppers and remove the seeds and membranes. Rinse the peppers under cold water and set them aside.

3. In a large pot of boiling water, blanch the whole bell peppers for 2-3 minutes to soften them slightly. Drain and set aside.

4. In a large skillet or frying pan, heat the olive oil over medium heat.

5. Add the chopped onions and sauté until they become translucent, about 3-4 minutes.

6. Stir in the minced garlic and cook for an additional 1-2 minutes until the garlic becomes fragrant.

7. Add the chopped spinach to the skillet and cook until it wilts, about 2-3 minutes. Season with dried oregano, dried basil, red pepper flakes (if using), salt, and pepper.

8. Remove the skillet from the heat and stir in the cooked quinoa or rice and crumbled feta cheese. Mix everything well until the filling is evenly combined.

9. Stuff each blanched bell pepper with the spinach and feta filling, pressing it down gently to pack it inside.

10. Place the stuffed peppers in a baking dish. If there is any remaining filling, you can scatter it around the peppers.

11. Sprinkle grated Parmesan cheese over the top of each stuffed pepper.

12. Cover the baking dish with foil and bake in the preheated oven for 20 minutes.

13. After 20 minutes, remove the foil and continue baking for an additional 15-20 minutes or until the peppers are tender and the cheese is golden and bubbly.

14. Once cooked, remove the stuffed peppers from the oven and let them cool for a few minutes before serving.

Serve the Spinach and Feta Stuffed Peppers as a delightful and wholesome meal, either on their own or accompanied by a side salad or crusty bread. Enjoy this nutritious and flavorful dish!

Nutritional Information (per serving):
- Calories: 280
- Total Fat: 14g
- Saturated Fat: 6g
- Cholesterol: 30mg
- Sodium: 600mg
- Total Carbohydrates: 28g
- Dietary Fiber: 6g
- Sugars: 9g
- Protein: 12g

Recipe Notes:
- You can customize this recipe by adding other vegetables or herbs, such as diced tomatoes, black olives, or fresh parsley.
- If you prefer a spicier version, you can increase the amount of red pepper flakes or add some diced jalapenos to the filling.
- This dish is vegetarian-friendly and can be made gluten-free by using gluten-free quinoa or rice.

Lentil and Chickpea Stew

Preparation Time: 15 minutes **Cooking Time:** 45 minutes **Total Time:** 1 hour **Servings:** 6

Ingredients:
- 1 cup dried green or brown lentils, rinsed and picked over
- 1 can (15 ounces) chickpeas, drained and rinsed
- 1 large onion, finely chopped
- 3 cloves garlic, minced
- 2 large carrots, peeled and diced
- 2 stalks celery, diced
- 1 red bell pepper, diced
- 1 can (28 ounces) crushed tomatoes
- 4 cups vegetable broth
- 2 tablespoons tomato paste
- 1 teaspoon ground cumin
- 1 teaspoon ground coriander
- 1/2 teaspoon smoked paprika
- 1/4 teaspoon cayenne pepper (optional, for heat)
- 2 tablespoons olive oil
- Salt and pepper to taste
- Fresh parsley or cilantro, chopped, for garnish

Utensils Needed:
- Cutting board
- Knife
- Large pot or Dutch oven
- Wooden spoon or spatula
- Measuring cups and spoons

Instructions:
1. In a large pot or Dutch oven, heat the olive oil over medium heat.

2. Add the chopped onions and sauté until they become translucent, about 3-4 minutes.

3. Stir in the minced garlic and cook for an additional 1-2 minutes until the garlic becomes fragrant.

4. Add the diced carrots, celery, and red bell pepper to the pot. Season with ground cumin, ground coriander, smoked paprika, cayenne pepper (if using), salt, and pepper.

5. Cook the vegetables, stirring occasionally, for about 5 minutes or until they start to soften.

6. Pour in the crushed tomatoes, vegetable broth, and tomato paste. Stir well to combine all the ingredients.

7. Add the rinsed lentils to the pot and stir to incorporate them into the mixture.

8. Bring the stew to a boil, then reduce the

heat to low, cover the pot, and let it simmer for 30 minutes. Stir occasionally to prevent sticking.

9. After 30 minutes, add the drained and rinsed chickpeas to the stew and stir them in gently.

10. Continue simmering the stew for an additional 10-15 minutes, or until the lentils are tender and fully cooked.

11. Taste the stew and adjust the seasoning with more salt and pepper if needed.

12. Once the lentils are tender and the flavors have melded together, remove the pot from the heat.

13. Garnish the Lentil and Chickpea Stew with chopped fresh parsley or cilantro just before serving.

Serve the flavorful and hearty Lentil and Chickpea Stew in bowls, and enjoy it as a satisfying and nutritious meal, perfect for chilly days or anytime you crave a comforting dish. It pairs well with crusty bread or a side salad for a complete and wholesome meal.

Nutritional Information (per serving):
- Calories: 270
- Total Fat: 7g
- Saturated Fat: 1g
- Cholesterol: 0mg
- Sodium: 750mg
- Total Carbohydrates: 41g
- Dietary Fiber: 13g
- Sugars: 9g
- Protein: 14g

Recipe Notes:
- You can customize this stew by adding other vegetables like spinach, kale, or bell peppers.
- If you prefer a thicker stew, you can add an extra tablespoon of tomato paste or simmer the stew without the lid for the last 10 minutes of cooking.
- This stew can be made ahead of time and stored in the refrigerator for up to 3 days. It also freezes well for up to 2 months.

Vegetable Moussaka

Preparation Time: 30 minutes **Cooking Time:** 1 hour 30 minutes **Total Time:** 2 hours **Servings:** 6

Ingredients:
- 2 large eggplants, sliced lengthwise into 1/4-inch thick slices
- 4 medium potatoes, peeled and sliced into 1/4-inch thick rounds
- 2 zucchinis, sliced into 1/4-inch thick rounds
- 1 large onion, finely chopped
- 4 cloves garlic, minced
- 1 can (15 ounces) chickpeas, drained and rinsed
- 1 can (28 ounces) crushed tomatoes
- 1/4 cup tomato paste
- 1/4 cup red wine (optional)
- 2 teaspoons dried oregano
- 2 teaspoons dried basil
- 1/2 teaspoon ground cinnamon
- 1/4 teaspoon ground nutmeg
- 1/4 teaspoon cayenne pepper (optional, for heat)
- 2 cups shredded mozzarella cheese
- 1/2 cup grated Parmesan cheese
- 2 tablespoons olive oil
- Salt and pepper to taste
- Fresh parsley, chopped, for garnish

Utensils Needed:
- Cutting board
- Knife
- Mandoline or sharp vegetable slicer (optional)
- Large skillet or frying pan
- Baking sheet
- 9x13 inch baking dish
- Wooden spoon or spatula
- Measuring cups and spoons

Instructions:
1. Preheat your oven to 375°F (190°C).

2. Lay the eggplant slices on a baking sheet, brush them with olive oil, and season with salt and pepper. Bake in the preheated oven for 15-20 minutes or until the slices are tender and slightly browned. Remove from the oven and set aside.

3. In a large skillet or frying pan, heat 1 tablespoon of olive oil over medium heat.

4. Add the chopped onions and sauté until they become translucent, about 3-4 minutes.

5. Stir in the minced garlic and cook for an additional 1-2 minutes until the garlic becomes fragrant.

6. Add the sliced zucchinis to the skillet and cook for 3-4 minutes until they begin to soften. Season with dried oregano, dried basil, ground cinnamon, ground nutmeg, cayenne pepper (if using), salt, and pepper.

7. Stir in the crushed tomatoes and tomato paste. If using red wine, add it to the sauce as well. Simmer the sauce for 10 minutes, allowing the flavors to meld together.

8. In a separate skillet, heat the remaining tablespoon of olive oil over medium heat.

9. Add the sliced potatoes and cook for about 5 minutes on each side until they are lightly browned and slightly tender.

10. In a 9x13 inch baking dish, layer half of the cooked eggplant slices on the bottom.

11. Next, spread half of the tomato sauce mixture over the eggplant layer.

12. Layer half of the cooked potatoes on top of the tomato sauce.

13. Add half of the drained and rinsed chickpeas over the potato layer.

14. Sprinkle half of the shredded mozzarella cheese and grated Parmesan cheese over the chickpeas.

15. Repeat the layers with the remaining ingredients, ending with a layer of cheese on top.

16. Cover the baking dish with aluminum foil and bake in the preheated oven for 40 minutes.

17. After 40 minutes, remove the foil and bake for an additional 10-15 minutes or until the cheese is bubbly and lightly browned.

18. Once cooked, remove the Vegetable Moussaka from the oven and let it rest for a few minutes before serving.

19. Garnish the moussaka with chopped fresh parsley and serve it hot.

Enjoy the delicious and hearty Vegetable Moussaka, a flavorful and comforting dish that will delight your taste buds! Serve it with a side salad or some crusty bread for a complete meal.

Nutritional Information (per serving):
- *Calories: 380*
- *Total Fat: 15g*
- *Saturated Fat: 7g*
- *Cholesterol: 30mg*
- *Sodium: 600mg*
- *Total Carbohydrates: 45g*
- *Dietary Fiber: 10g*
- *Sugars: 9g*
- *Protein: 20g*

Recipe Notes:
- *Feel free to add other vegetables such as red bell peppers or mushrooms to the moussaka for extra flavor and texture.*
- *If you prefer a meaty version, you can add cooked ground beef or lamb to the tomato sauce layer.*
- *Moussaka tastes even better the next day, so consider making it ahead of time and reheating it for serving.*

Italian Eggplant Rollatini

Preparation Time: 30 minutes **Cooking Time:** 45 minutes **Total Time:** 1 hour 15 minutes **Servings:** 4-6

Ingredients:
- 2 large eggplants, sliced lengthwise into 1/4-inch thick slices
- 2 cups ricotta cheese
- 1 cup shredded mozzarella cheese
- 1/2 cup grated Parmesan cheese
- 2 large eggs, lightly beaten
- 1/4 cup chopped fresh parsley
- 2 cups marinara sauce (homemade or store-bought)
- 2 tablespoons olive oil
- Salt and pepper to taste

Utensils Needed:
- Cutting board
- Knife
- Mandoline or sharp vegetable slicer (optional)
- Paper towels
- Baking sheet
- Mixing bowl
- Whisk
- 9x13 inch baking dish
- Aluminum foil

Instructions:
1. Preheat your oven to 375°F (190°C).

2. Lay the eggplant slices on a baking sheet, sprinkle salt on both sides, and let them sit for about 20 minutes. This process helps draw out excess moisture and bitterness from the eggplants. After 20 minutes, pat the slices dry with paper towels.

3. Brush both sides of the eggplant slices with olive oil and season with salt and pepper.

4. Arrange the eggplant slices on a baking sheet and bake in the preheated oven for 15-20 minutes or until they become tender and slightly browned. Remove from the oven and set aside.

5. In a mixing bowl, combine the ricotta cheese, shredded mozzarella cheese, grated Parmesan cheese, chopped fresh parsley, and beaten eggs. Mix well until all ingredients are thoroughly combined.

6. Spoon a generous amount of the ricotta mixture onto each eggplant slice, spreading it evenly.

7. Carefully roll up the eggplant slices, starting from the narrower end, to form a roll. Place each roll seam-side down in a 9x13 inch baking dish.

8. Pour the marinara sauce over the eggplant rolls, making sure they are well coated.

9. Cover the baking dish with aluminum foil and bake in the preheated oven for 25 minutes.

10. After 25 minutes, remove the foil and bake for an additional 15 minutes, or until the sauce is bubbly and the cheese on top is lightly browned.

11. Once cooked, remove the Italian Eggplant Rollatini from the oven and let it rest for a few minutes before serving.

Serve the delectable Italian Eggplant Rollatini as a delightful and comforting dish that's perfect for a special dinner or any occasion. It pairs well with a side of pasta or a fresh green salad. Enjoy the flavors of Italy in this delicious dish!

Nutritional Information (per serving, based on 6 servings):
- Calories: 380
- Total Fat: 24g
- Saturated Fat: 12g
- Cholesterol: 135mg
- Sodium: 800mg
- Total Carbohydrates: 18g
- Dietary Fiber: 5g
- Sugars: 10g
- Protein: 24g

Recipe Notes:

- *You can use part-skim ricotta cheese and low-fat mozzarella cheese to reduce the fat content.*
- *Feel free to add some fresh basil leaves or other herbs to the ricotta mixture for extra flavor.*
- *This dish is best served fresh, but any leftovers can be refrigerated for up to 3 days.*

Stuffed Zucchini with Quinoa and Feta

Preparation Time: 30 minutes **Cooking Time:** 40 minutes **Total Time:** 1 hour 10 minutes **Servings:** 4

Ingredients:
- 4 medium-sized zucchini
- 1 cup cooked quinoa (about 1/2 cup uncooked)
- 1/2 cup crumbled feta cheese
- 1/4 cup chopped fresh parsley
- 1/4 cup chopped fresh dill
- 1/4 cup chopped red onion
- 2 cloves garlic, minced
- 1 tablespoon lemon juice
- 2 tablespoons olive oil
- Salt and pepper to taste

Utensils Needed:
- Cutting board
- Knife
- Spoon or melon baller (for scooping out zucchini)
- Mixing bowl
- Baking dish
- Aluminum foil

Instructions:
1. Preheat your oven to 375°F (190°C).

2. Cut the zucchini in half lengthwise and scoop out the flesh, leaving about 1/4-inch thick shell. Chop the scooped-out zucchini flesh and set it aside.

3. In a mixing bowl, combine the cooked quinoa, crumbled feta cheese, chopped parsley, chopped dill, chopped red onion, minced garlic, lemon juice, olive oil, and the chopped zucchini flesh. Season with salt and pepper to taste.

4. Mix all the ingredients well until the filling is evenly combined.

5. Stuff each zucchini half with the quinoa and feta mixture, pressing it down gently to pack it inside.

6. Place the stuffed zucchini halves in a baking dish.

7. Cover the baking dish with aluminum foil and bake in the preheated oven for 20 minutes.

8. After 20 minutes, remove the foil and bake for an additional 15-20 minutes, or until the zucchini is tender and the filling is lightly browned on top.

9. Once cooked, remove the Stuffed Zucchini with Quinoa and Feta from the oven and let them cool for a few minutes before serving.

Serve the delicious and nutritious Stuffed Zucchini with Quinoa and Feta as a flavorful and satisfying meal. It can be enjoyed on its own or accompanied by a side salad for a complete and wholesome dish. Enjoy the delightful flavors and textures in this healthy recipe!

Nutritional Information (per serving):
- Calories: 190
- Total Fat: 9g
- Saturated Fat: 3g
- Cholesterol: 15mg
- Sodium: 240mg
- Total Carbohydrates: 22g
- Dietary Fiber: 4g
- Sugars: 5g
- Protein: 7g

Recipe Notes:
- *You can customize this recipe by adding other vegetables like cherry tomatoes, bell peppers, or cooked spinach.*
- *If you want to make it a heartier meal, consider adding cooked ground turkey, chicken, or chickpeas to the quinoa filling.*
- *This dish is vegetarian-friendly and can easily be made vegan by omitting the feta cheese or using a dairy-free alternative.*

Lebanese Mujadara

Preparation Time: 15 minutes **Cooking Time:** 1 hour **Total Time:** 1 hour 15 minutes **Servings:** 4-6

Ingredients:
- 1 cup brown or green lentils, rinsed and drained
- 1 cup long-grain white rice
- 2 large onions, thinly sliced
- 4 tablespoons olive oil, divided
- 1 teaspoon ground cumin
- 1/2 teaspoon ground cinnamon
- 1/4 teaspoon ground allspice
- 4 cups vegetable broth or water
- Salt and pepper to taste
- Fresh parsley, chopped, for garnish (optional)

Utensils Needed:
- Cutting board
- Knife
- Large pot or Dutch oven
- Wooden spoon or spatula
- Measuring cups and spoons

Instructions:
1. In a large pot or Dutch oven, heat 2 tablespoons of olive oil over medium heat.

2. Add the thinly sliced onions and sauté until they become caramelized and golden brown, about 15-20 minutes. Stir occasionally to prevent burning. Once caramelized, remove half of the onions from the pot and set them aside for later use.

3. To the remaining onions in the pot, add the ground cumin, ground cinnamon, and ground allspice. Stir and cook for 1-2 minutes to toast the spices and enhance their flavors.

4. Add the rinsed lentils to the spiced onions in the pot and stir to coat the lentils with the spices.

5. Pour in the vegetable broth or water, season with salt and pepper, and bring the mixture to a boil.

6. Reduce the heat to low, cover the pot with a lid, and let the lentils simmer for about 30 minutes or until they are tender and most of the liquid is absorbed.

7. While the lentils are cooking, rinse the white rice under cold water until the water runs clear. This step helps remove excess starch from the rice and prevents it from becoming sticky.

8. In a separate pot, cook the rice according to the package instructions, using 2 cups of water or vegetable broth.

Once the rice is cooked, fluff it with a fork.

9. In a small skillet, heat the remaining 2 tablespoons of olive oil over medium heat.

10. Add the reserved caramelized onions to the skillet and cook for a few minutes to warm them up.

11. Combine the cooked rice and half of the caramelized onions in a large serving bowl, mixing them gently.

12. To serve, spread the rice and onion mixture on a large platter or individual plates, and then top it with the spiced lentils.

13. Garnish the Lebanese Mujadara with the remaining caramelized onions and chopped fresh parsley, if desired.

Enjoy the flavorful and hearty Lebanese Mujadara as a satisfying and comforting dish that's perfect for sharing with family and friends. It can be served as a main course or as a side dish alongside other Middle Eastern delicacies.

Nutritional Information (per serving, based on 6 servings):
- *Calories: 350*
- *Total Fat: 12g*
- *Saturated Fat: 1.5g*
- *Cholesterol: 0mg*
- *Sodium: 700mg*
- *Total Carbohydrates: 49g*
- *Dietary Fiber: 9g*
- *Sugars: 4g*
- *Protein: 11g*

Recipe Notes:
- *Traditionally, mujadara is served with yogurt or a side salad, which adds a refreshing contrast to the warm and spiced lentils and rice.*
- *You can adjust the spices to your taste. Some variations of mujadara include adding ground coriander, ground cardamom, or ground cloves for extra flavor.*
- *Leftovers of this dish can be refrigerated and enjoyed the next day or frozen for up to 3 months.*

Spanish Vegetable Paella

Preparation Time: 20 minutes **Cooking Time:** 40 minutes **Total Time:** 1 hour **Servings:** 4-6

Ingredients:
- 1 1/2 cups paella rice (short-grain rice)
- 4 cups vegetable broth
- 1/4 cup olive oil
- 1 large onion, finely chopped
- 3 cloves garlic, minced
- 1 red bell pepper, thinly sliced
- 1 yellow bell pepper, thinly sliced
- 1 cup green beans, trimmed and cut into 1-inch pieces
- 1 cup frozen peas
- 1 teaspoon saffron threads (or 1/2 teaspoon ground turmeric)
- 1 teaspoon smoked paprika
- 1/2 teaspoon ground cumin
- 1/4 teaspoon cayenne pepper (optional, for heat)
- Salt and pepper to taste
- Lemon wedges, for serving
- Fresh parsley, chopped, for garnish

Utensils Needed:
- Paella pan or a large skillet with a wide, flat base
- Cutting board
- Knife
- Wooden spoon or spatula
- Measuring cups and spoons

Instructions:
1. In a small bowl, crush the saffron threads with your fingers and steep them in 1/4 cup of hot vegetable broth. Set it aside for later use.

2. In a paella pan or a large skillet, heat the olive oil over medium heat.

3. Add the chopped onion and sauté until it becomes translucent, about 3-4 minutes.

4. Stir in the minced garlic and cook for an additional 1-2 minutes until the garlic becomes fragrant.

5. Add the sliced red and yellow bell peppers to the pan and sauté for 2-3 minutes until they start to soften.

6. Stir in the green beans and frozen peas, and cook for another 2-3 minutes.

7. Sprinkle the smoked paprika, ground cumin, and cayenne pepper (if using) over the vegetables. Season with salt and pepper to taste.

8. Add the paella rice to the pan, stirring it to coat it with the oil and spices.

9. Pour the saffron-infused vegetable broth over the rice, followed by the remaining vegetable broth. Stir everything gently to distribute the ingredients evenly.

10. Bring the mixture to a simmer, and then reduce the heat to low. Cook the paella uncovered for about 20-25 minutes or until the rice is tender and has absorbed most of the liquid. Avoid stirring the rice during this time to allow the formation of the coveted socarrat, the slightly crispy layer at the bottom of the pan.

11. Once the rice is cooked and the liquid is mostly absorbed, remove the paella from the heat.

12. Let the paella rest for a few minutes before serving.

13. To serve, garnish the Spanish Vegetable Paella with chopped fresh parsley and serve with lemon wedges on the side.

Enjoy the delicious and vibrant Spanish Vegetable Paella as a flavorful and satisfying dish that brings the taste of Spain to your table. It's perfect for sharing with friends and family, and it pairs wonderfully with a crisp Spanish white wine. Buen provecho!

Nutritional Information (per serving, based on 6 servings):
- *Calories: 350*
- *Total Fat: 10g*
- *Saturated Fat: 1.5g*
- *Cholesterol: 0mg*
- *Sodium: 750mg*
- *Total Carbohydrates: 60g*
- *Dietary Fiber: 6g*
- *Sugars: 8g*
- *Protein: 7g*

Recipe Notes:
- *Traditional paella rice, such as Bomba rice or Calasparra rice, is preferred for its ability to absorb flavors and remain firm. However, you can use short-grain rice as a substitute.*
- *Feel free to add other vegetables, such as artichoke hearts or asparagus, to the paella for additional variety and flavor.*
- *For a non-vegetarian version, you can add cooked chicken, shrimp, or mussels to the paella.*

Greek Spinach and Feta Pie (Spanakopita)

Preparation Time: 30 minutes **Cooking Time:** 45 minutes **Total Time:** 1 hour 15 minutes **Servings:** 8-10

Ingredients:
- 1 package (16 ounces) frozen spinach, thawed and drained
- 1 cup crumbled feta cheese
- 1 cup ricotta cheese
- 1/2 cup grated Parmesan cheese
- 4 green onions, finely chopped
- 3 cloves garlic, minced
- 2 tablespoons chopped fresh dill
- 2 tablespoons chopped fresh parsley
- 1/4 teaspoon ground nutmeg
- 1/4 teaspoon black pepper
- 1/4 cup olive oil
- 1 package (16 sheets) phyllo dough, thawed
- 1/2 cup unsalted butter, melted

Utensils Needed:
- Cutting board
- Knife
- Large mixing bowl
- Baking dish (9x13 inches)
- Pastry brush

Instructions:
1. Preheat your oven to 375°F (190°C).

2. In a large mixing bowl, combine the thawed and drained spinach, crumbled feta cheese, ricotta cheese, grated Parmesan cheese, chopped green onions, minced garlic, chopped dill, chopped parsley, ground nutmeg, black pepper, and olive oil. Mix everything well until the filling is evenly combined.

3. Prepare the phyllo dough by laying one sheet in the bottom of the baking dish. Brush it lightly with melted butter. Repeat this process, layering and buttering each sheet, until you have used half of the phyllo sheets.

4. Spread the spinach and feta filling evenly over the layered phyllo sheets in the baking dish.

5. Continue layering the remaining phyllo sheets on top of the filling, brushing each sheet with melted butter.

6. Once all the phyllo sheets are used and the filling is covered, brush the top layer with melted butter as well.

7. Using a sharp knife, score the top layer of the pie into serving-sized pieces.

8. Bake the Greek Spinach and Feta Pie in the preheated oven for about 40-45

minutes or until the phyllo is golden brown and crispy.

9. Once cooked, remove the pie from the oven and let it cool for a few minutes before serving.

Serve the delightful Greek Spinach and Feta Pie warm or at room temperature as a flavorful and savory dish that's perfect for any occasion. It can be served as an appetizer, side dish, or even a main course with a side of Greek salad. Enjoy the wonderful taste of Greece in this delicious spanakopita!

Nutritional Information (per serving, based on 8 servings):
- *Calories: 360*
- *Total Fat: 26g*
- *Saturated Fat: 12g*
- *Cholesterol: 60mg*
- *Sodium: 700mg*
- *Total Carbohydrates: 20g*
- *Dietary Fiber: 2g*
- *Sugars: 1g*
- *Protein: 12g*

Recipe Notes:
- You can use fresh spinach instead of frozen, but be sure to blanch and drain it well before using in the recipe.
- Traditional spanakopita uses dill and parsley for flavor, but you can also add other herbs like mint or basil if desired.
- Phyllo dough can dry out quickly, so keep it covered with a damp cloth while you work with it to prevent it from becoming brittle.

Moroccan Lamb Tagine with Apricots and Almonds

Preparation Time 30 minutes **Cooking Time** 2 hours **Total Time** 2 hours 30 minutes **Servings** 4

Ingredients
- 1.5 lbs (700g) boneless lamb shoulder, cut into 1.5-inch cubes
- 2 tablespoons olive oil
- 1 large onion, finely chopped
- 3 garlic cloves, minced
- 1 teaspoon ground cumin
- 1 teaspoon ground coriander
- 12 teaspoon ground cinnamon
- 14 teaspoon ground ginger
- 14 teaspoon ground turmeric
- 14 teaspoon ground paprika
- 14 teaspoon saffron threads (optional)
- 1 cup dried apricots, halved
- 12 cup whole blanched almonds
- 2 cups chicken or lamb broth
- 2 tablespoons honey
- 1 tablespoon preserved lemon peel (optional but recommended)
- Salt and pepper to taste
- Fresh cilantro or parsley, chopped, for garnish

Utensils Needed
- Tagine pot (traditional Moroccan cooking pot) or a heavy-bottomed Dutch oven with a lid
- Cutting board and knife
- Large skillet or frying pan
- Wooden spoon or spatula
- Measuring cups and spoons
- Mixing bowl

Instructions

1. Heat the olive oil in a skillet or frying pan over medium-high heat. Season the lamb cubes with salt and pepper, then brown them in batches until they are nicely seared on all sides. Transfer the browned lamb to a plate and set aside.

2. In the same skillet, add the chopped onion and cook over medium heat until softened and translucent, about 5 minutes. Stir in the minced garlic and cook for another minute.

3. Add the ground cumin, coriander, cinnamon, ginger, turmeric, and paprika to the onions and garlic. Cook for a couple of minutes, stirring constantly, until the spices release their aromas.

4. If using saffron, crush it into a powder between your fingers and add it to the spice mixture. This will enhance the color and flavor of the tagine.

5. Return the browned lamb cubes to the skillet, along with any juices that have accumulated on the plate. Stir everything together, ensuring the lamb is coated in the spice mixture.

6. Now, add the halved dried apricots and blanched almonds to the skillet, distributing them evenly among the lamb.

7. Pour in the chicken or lamb broth and drizzle the honey over the ingredients. Stir gently to combine all the flavors.

8. If you have preserved lemon peel, chop it finely and add it to the tagine. The preserved lemon will add a tangy and slightly salty taste to the dish.

9. Bring the mixture to a simmer, then reduce the heat to low. Cover the tagine pot or Dutch oven with a lid.

10. Let the tagine simmer gently for about 1.5 to 2 hours or until the lamb is tender and the flavors have melded together beautifully. Stir occasionally to prevent sticking, and adjust the seasoning with salt and pepper to taste.

11. Once the lamb is tender and the sauce has thickened slightly, the tagine is ready. Remove it from the heat.

12. Garnish the Moroccan Lamb Tagine with chopped fresh cilantro or parsley.

13. Serve the tagine hot over cooked couscous or with crusty bread to soak up the flavorful sauce.

Enjoy your delicious Moroccan Lamb Tagine with Apricots and Almonds, a dish that captures the rich and aromatic flavors of Moroccan cuisine!

Nutritional Information (per serving)
- *Calories 450*
- *Total Fat 25g*
- *Saturated Fat 6g*
- *Cholesterol 95mg*
- *Sodium 520mg*
- *Total Carbohydrates 30g*
- *Dietary Fiber 5g*
- *Sugars 21g*
- *Protein 30g*

Recipe Notes
- You can prepare the preserved lemon peel at home, but it requires a few weeks to ferment. If you can't find preserved lemon, you can substitute with fresh lemon zest.
- If you don't have a tagine pot, a heavy-bottomed Dutch oven with a lid will work just fine.
- Saffron adds a unique flavor and aroma, but it can be expensive. If you prefer, you can omit it from the recipe.
- If using a tagine pot, it's essential to season it before first use according to the manufacturer's instructions.

Greek Moussaka

Preparation Time 45 minutes **Cooking Time** 1 hour **Total Time** 1 hour 45 minutes **Servings** 6-8

Ingredients

For the Eggplant Layers
- 2 large eggplants, sliced lengthwise into 14-inch thick slices
- Olive oil for brushing
- Salt and pepper to taste

For the Meat Sauce
- 1.5 lbs (700g) ground lamb or beef
- 1 large onion, finely chopped
- 3 garlic cloves, minced
- 1 can (14 oz) crushed tomatoes
- 2 tablespoons tomato paste
- 1 teaspoon dried oregano
- 12 teaspoon ground cinnamon
- Salt and pepper to taste
- Olive oil for cooking

For the Béchamel Sauce
- 12 cup (1 stick) unsalted butter
- 12 cup all-purpose flour
- 4 cups whole milk
- Pinch of ground nutmeg
- 1 cup grated Parmesan or Kefalotyri cheese
- 2 large eggs, lightly beaten
- Salt and pepper to taste

Utensils Needed
- Large baking sheet
- Brush for oiling eggplant
- Large skillet or frying pan
- Wooden spoon or spatula
- 9x13-inch baking dish
- Whisk
- Saucepan

Instructions

1. Preheat your oven to 400°F (200°C). Line a baking sheet with parchment paper or lightly grease it.

2. Slice the eggplants lengthwise into approximately 14-inch thick slices. Brush both sides of the slices with olive oil and season with salt and pepper. Place the slices on the prepared baking sheet.

3. Bake the eggplant slices in the preheated oven for about 15-20 minutes or until they are tender and slightly browned. Remove from the oven and set aside.

4. In a large skillet or frying pan, heat some olive oil over medium heat. Add the chopped onion and cook until it becomes translucent, about 5 minutes. Stir in the minced garlic and cook for another minute.

5. Add the ground lamb or beef to the skillet, breaking it up with a wooden spoon. Cook until the meat is browned and cooked through.

6. Stir in the crushed tomatoes, tomato paste, dried oregano, ground cinnamon, salt, and pepper. Simmer the sauce for about 15 minutes, allowing the flavors to meld together. Adjust the seasoning to your taste.

7. While the meat sauce simmers, prepare the béchamel sauce. In a saucepan, melt the butter over medium heat. Whisk in the flour and cook for 1-2 minutes, stirring constantly.

8. Gradually pour in the milk while whisking continuously to avoid lumps. Add a pinch of

ground nutmeg, salt, and pepper. Keep whisking until the sauce thickens and comes to a gentle boil.

9. Remove the saucepan from the heat and whisk in the grated Parmesan or Kefalotyri cheese. Allow the sauce to cool slightly, then whisk in the lightly beaten eggs until the sauce is smooth.

10. Preheat your oven to 375°F (190°C).

11. To assemble the moussaka, layer half of the baked eggplant slices in the bottom of a 9x13-inch baking dish.

12. Spread the meat sauce evenly over the eggplant layer.

13. Add the remaining eggplant slices on top of the meat sauce.

14. Pour the béchamel sauce over the eggplant layer, spreading it evenly to cover the entire dish.

15. Bake the moussaka in the preheated oven for about 40-45 minutes or until the top is golden brown and bubbling.

16. Remove the moussaka from the oven and allow it to cool for a few minutes before serving.

17. Serve the Greek Moussaka warm with a side salad and crusty bread.

Enjoy the delicious layers of flavors in this classic Greek Moussaka! It's a comforting and hearty dish that will satisfy your taste buds.

Nutritional Information (per serving)
- *Calories 460*
- *Total Fat 28g*
- *Saturated Fat 15g*
- *Cholesterol 153mg*
- *Sodium 460mg*
- *Total Carbohydrates 20g*
- *Dietary Fiber 4g*
- *Sugars 11g*
- *Protein 32g*

Recipe Notes
- *You can prepare the moussaka ahead of time and reheat it when serving. It often tastes even better the next day as the flavors have more time to meld together.*
- *Traditionally, moussaka is made with lamb, but you can substitute with beef if preferred.*
- *Kefalotyri cheese is a Greek hard cheese commonly used in moussaka, but Parmesan works well as a substitute.*
- *Moussaka is often served with a side salad and crusty bread.*

Italian Bolognese Sauce with Whole Wheat Pasta

Preparation Time 20 minutes **Cooking Time** 2 hours **Total Time** 2 hours 20 minutes **Servings** 6

Ingredients

For the Bolognese Sauce
- 2 tablespoons olive oil
- 1 large onion, finely chopped
- 2 carrots, peeled and finely chopped
- 2 celery stalks, finely chopped
- 3 garlic cloves, minced
- 1 lb (450g) ground beef
- 1 lb (450g) ground pork
- 1 cup whole milk
- 1 cup dry white wine
- 1 can (28 oz) crushed tomatoes
- 2 tablespoons tomato paste
- 1 teaspoon dried oregano
- 12 teaspoon dried thyme
- 1 bay leaf
- Salt and pepper to taste

For the Whole Wheat Pasta
- 1 lb (450g) whole wheat pasta (such as spaghetti, fettuccine, or penne)
- Salt for boiling water

For Serving
- Grated Parmesan cheese
- Fresh basil leaves, chopped

Utensils Needed
- Large pot for boiling pasta
- Large skillet or frying pan
- Wooden spoon or spatula
- Saucepan
- Colander

Instructions

1. Bring a large pot of water to a boil. Add a generous amount of salt to the boiling water, and cook the whole wheat pasta according to the package instructions until al dente. Drain the pasta in a colander and set it aside.

2. In a large skillet or frying pan, heat the olive oil over medium heat. Add the chopped onion, carrots, and celery. Cook for about 5 minutes or until the vegetables become soft and translucent.

3. Stir in the minced garlic and cook for another minute until fragrant.

4. Add the ground beef and pork to the skillet, breaking it up with a wooden spoon. Cook until the meat is browned and cooked through.

5. Pour in the whole milk and let it simmer for a few minutes, allowing the meat to absorb the flavors.

6. Stir in the white wine and cook until the liquid has mostly evaporated.

7. Add the crushed tomatoes, tomato paste, dried oregano, dried thyme, bay leaf, salt, and pepper. Mix everything well.

8. Reduce the heat to low, cover the skillet with a lid, and let the Bolognese sauce simmer gently for about 1.5 to 2 hours. Stir occasionally to prevent sticking and adjust the seasoning as needed.

9. While the sauce simmers, prepare the whole wheat pasta as per the instructions mentioned earlier.

10. Once the Bolognese sauce has thickened and the flavors have melded together beautifully, remove the bay leaf, and the sauce is ready.

11. To serve, ladle the Bolognese sauce over the cooked whole wheat pasta. Garnish with grated Parmesan cheese and chopped fresh basil leaves.

12. Enjoy your delicious and comforting Italian Bolognese Sauce with Whole Wheat Pasta!

The rich and flavorful Bolognese sauce pairs perfectly with whole wheat pasta, making this dish not only delicious but also a healthier option. It's a classic Italian favorite that's sure to satisfy your taste buds!

Nutritional Information (per serving with whole wheat pasta)
- *Calories 560*
- *Total Fat 20g*
- *Saturated Fat 7g*
- *Cholesterol 85mg*
- *Sodium 360mg*
- *Total Carbohydrates 57g*
- *Dietary Fiber 10g*
- *Sugars 10g*
- *Protein 35g*

Recipe Notes
- For a healthier option, you can use lean ground beef and pork or substitute with ground turkey or chicken.
- Whole wheat pasta adds extra fiber and nutrients, but you can use regular pasta if desired.
- The Bolognese sauce tastes even better the next day, so consider making it ahead of time and reheating when serving.
- You can freeze any leftover Bolognese sauce for future use.

Lebanese Kofta Kebabs with Tzatziki Sauce

Preparation Time 30 minutes **Marinating Time** 1 hour (optional) **Cooking Time** 15 minutes **Total Time** 1 hour 45 minutes (including marinating time) **Servings** 4

Ingredients
For the Kofta Kebabs
- 1 lb (450g) ground lamb or beef (or a combination of both)
- 1 small onion, finely grated
- 3 garlic cloves, minced
- 14 cup fresh parsley, finely chopped
- 14 cup fresh mint, finely chopped
- 1 teaspoon ground cumin
- 1 teaspoon ground coriander
- 12 teaspoon ground cinnamon
- 14 teaspoon ground allspice
- 14 teaspoon cayenne pepper (optional, for heat)
- Salt and pepper to taste
- Skewers (wooden or metal)

For the Tzatziki Sauce
- 1 cup Greek yogurt
- 12 cucumber, grated and drained
- 2 garlic cloves, minced
- 1 tablespoon fresh dill, chopped
- 1 tablespoon fresh mint, chopped
- 1 tablespoon lemon juice
- 1 tablespoon extra-virgin olive oil
- Salt and pepper to taste

For Serving
- Pita bread or Lebanese flatbread
- Sliced tomatoes
- Sliced red onions
- Fresh parsley or mint for garnish

Utensils Needed
- Mixing bowl
- Grater
- Skewers (if using wooden, soak them in water for at least 30 minutes before using to prevent burning during cooking)
- Grill or stovetop griddle pan
- Serving platter

Instructions
1. In a mixing bowl, combine the ground lamb or beef with the grated onion, minced garlic, chopped parsley, chopped mint, ground cumin, ground coriander, ground cinnamon, ground allspice, cayenne pepper (if using), salt, and pepper.

2. Mix the ingredients together thoroughly using your hands until well combined. Cover the bowl with plastic wrap and refrigerate for an hour to allow the flavors to meld (marinating is optional).

3. While the kofta mixture is marinating, prepare the Tzatziki sauce. In a separate bowl, combine the Greek yogurt, grated and drained cucumber, minced garlic, chopped dill, chopped mint, lemon juice, olive oil, salt, and pepper. Stir well to

combine, then cover and refrigerate until serving.

4. After the kofta mixture has marinated (if you chose to marinate), take it out of the refrigerator. Preheat your grill or stovetop griddle pan to medium-high heat.

5. Divide the kofta mixture into equal portions and shape each portion into elongated cylinders, about 3-4 inches long, around the skewers.

6. Place the kofta kebabs on the preheated grill or griddle pan. Cook for about 4-6 minutes on each side or until they are cooked through and slightly charred on the outside.

7. While the kofta kebabs are cooking, warm the pita bread or Lebanese flatbread on the grill or in a separate pan.

8. Once the kofta kebabs are done, remove them from the heat and assemble the kebabs on a serving platter.

9. Serve the Lebanese Kofta Kebabs with warm pita bread, Tzatziki sauce, sliced tomatoes, sliced red onions, and fresh parsley or mint for garnish.

10. Enjoy the delicious flavors of these Lebanese Kofta Kebabs with Tzatziki Sauce!

This dish offers a wonderful combination of aromatic spices and fresh herbs, making it a delightful and satisfying meal to enjoy with family and friends.

Nutritional Information (per serving)
- *Calories 420*
- *Total Fat 28g*
- *Saturated Fat 11g*
- *Cholesterol 95mg*
- *Sodium 230mg*
- *Total Carbohydrates 11g*
- *Dietary Fiber 1g*
- *Sugars 5g*
- *Protein 30g*

Recipe Notes
- *For a leaner option, you can use ground turkey instead of lamb or beef.*
- *If you prefer a milder flavor, you can reduce or omit the cayenne pepper in the kofta mixture.*
- *Marinating the kofta for an hour or more in the refrigerator can enhance the flavors, but it's optional if you're short on time.*
- *You can use store-bought Tzatziki sauce, but making it from scratch gives it a fresher taste.*

Spanish Beef and Chorizo Paella

Preparation Time 20 minutes **Cooking Time** 40 minutes **Total Time** 1 hour **Servings** 4-6

Ingredients
- 1 lb (450g) beef sirloin, cut into 1-inch cubes
- 6 oz (170g) Spanish chorizo sausage, sliced
- 1 large onion, finely chopped
- 3 garlic cloves, minced
- 1 red bell pepper, diced
- 1 yellow bell pepper, diced
- 1 cup Arborio rice (or other short-grain rice suitable for paella)
- 4 cups beef or chicken broth
- 12 cup dry white wine
- 1 teaspoon smoked paprika
- 12 teaspoon saffron threads
- 12 cup frozen peas
- 14 cup chopped fresh parsley
- 1 lemon, cut into wedges
- Olive oil for cooking
- Salt and pepper to taste

Utensils Needed
- Large paella pan or wide, shallow skillet
- Cutting board and knife
- Wooden spoon or spatula
- Small bowl for soaking saffron
- Measuring cups and spoons

Instructions
1. In a small bowl, soak the saffron threads in a couple of tablespoons of warm water, and set it aside to infuse.

2. Heat some olive oil in a large paella pan or skillet over medium-high heat. Add the beef cubes and season with salt and pepper. Cook the beef until browned on all sides, then remove it from the pan and set it aside.

3. In the same pan, add the sliced chorizo and cook until it releases its flavorful oil. Remove the chorizo from the pan and set it aside with the beef.

4. Lower the heat to medium, and in the same pan, add the chopped onion and diced bell peppers. Cook until they become soft and slightly caramelized, about 5 minutes.

5. Stir in the minced garlic and smoked paprika, and cook for another minute until the aroma is released.

6. Add the Arborio rice to the pan and stir it to coat it with the oil and spices. Toast the rice for a couple of minutes until it starts to turn translucent.

7. Pour in the white wine and let it simmer for a minute to deglaze the pan,

scraping any bits from the bottom.

8. Now, add the soaked saffron along with its water to the pan, distributing the saffron evenly.

9. Pour in the beef or chicken broth and bring it to a gentle boil. Lower the heat to a simmer and let the rice cook uncovered for about 15-20 minutes or until most of the liquid has been absorbed and the rice is al dente.

10. While the rice is cooking, preheat your oven to 400°F (200°C).

11. Once the rice is cooked, add the browned beef, chorizo, and frozen peas to the pan. Mix everything gently, distributing the ingredients evenly.

12. Transfer the paella pan to the preheated oven and cook for an additional 5-7 minutes. This step, known as socarrat, crisps the bottom layer of rice, adding texture and flavor.

13. Remove the paella from the oven, and let it rest for a couple of minutes before serving.

14. Garnish the Spanish Beef and Chorizo Paella with chopped fresh parsley and serve it with lemon wedges on the side for squeezing over the dish.

Enjoy the delightful flavors of this classic Spanish Beef and Chorizo Paella! It's a hearty and satisfying one-pan meal that's perfect for sharing with family and friends.

Nutritional Information (per serving)
- Calories 470
- Total Fat 20g
- Saturated Fat 7g
- Cholesterol 75mg
- Sodium 930mg
- Total Carbohydrates 38g
- Dietary Fiber 3g
- Sugars 4g
- Protein 29g

Recipe Notes
- *Spanish chorizo is a cured, smoked sausage. If you can't find it, you can use Mexican chorizo, but the flavor will be different.*
- *For a traditional paella, use short-grain rice like Arborio or Bomba rice, which absorbs the flavors and creates a creamy texture.*
- *Saffron is a key ingredient in paella, providing the signature golden color and unique flavor. If you can't find saffron, you can use a pinch of ground turmeric as a substitute, though the flavor won't be the same.*
- *You can customize the paella by adding seafood like shrimp or mussels or using chicken instead of beef.*
- *Paella is typically cooked outdoors over an open flame in Spain, but a large stovetop paella pan or a wide skillet works well for this recipe.*

Moroccan Kefta Meatballs with Tomato Sauce

Preparation Time 30 minutes **Cooking Time** 30 minutes **Total Time** 1 hour **Servings** 4-6

Ingredients

For the Kefta Meatballs

- 1 lb (450g) ground beef or lamb (or a combination of both)
- 1 small onion, grated
- 2 garlic cloves, minced
- 14 cup fresh parsley, finely chopped
- 14 cup fresh cilantro, finely chopped
- 1 teaspoon ground cumin
- 1 teaspoon ground paprika
- 12 teaspoon ground cinnamon
- 14 teaspoon ground coriander
- 14 teaspoon cayenne pepper (optional, for heat)
- Salt and pepper to taste

For the Tomato Sauce

- 1 tablespoon olive oil
- 1 large onion, finely chopped
- 3 garlic cloves, minced
- 1 can (14 oz) crushed tomatoes
- 1 tablespoon tomato paste
- 1 teaspoon ground cumin
- 1 teaspoon ground paprika
- 12 teaspoon ground cinnamon
- 14 teaspoon cayenne pepper (optional, for heat)
- 1 cup beef or vegetable broth
- Salt and pepper to taste

For Serving

- Cooked couscous or rice
- Fresh parsley or cilantro for garnish
- Lemon wedges

Utensils Needed

- Mixing bowl
- Large skillet or frying pan
- Wooden spoon or spatula
- Measuring cups and spoons

Instructions

1. In a mixing bowl, combine the ground beef or lamb with the grated onion, minced garlic, chopped parsley, chopped cilantro, ground cumin, ground paprika, ground cinnamon, ground coriander, cayenne pepper (if using), salt, and pepper.

2. Mix the ingredients together thoroughly using your hands until well combined.

3. Shape the mixture into small meatballs, about 1 to 1.5 inches in diameter. Set the meatballs aside.

4. In a large skillet or frying pan, heat the olive oil over medium heat. Add the chopped onion and cook until it becomes soft and translucent, about 5 minutes.

5. Stir in the minced garlic and cook for another minute until fragrant.

6. Add the crushed tomatoes, tomato paste, ground cumin, ground paprika, ground cinnamon, cayenne pepper (if using), salt, and pepper to the skillet. Mix everything well.

7. Pour in the beef or vegetable broth and bring the sauce to a simmer.

8. Carefully add the meatballs to the simmering tomato sauce, ensuring they are partially submerged. You may need to cook the meatballs in batches if your pan is not large enough.

9. Cover the skillet with a lid and let the meatballs cook in the sauce for about 15-20 minutes, or until they are cooked through and tender.

10. While the meatballs are cooking, prepare couscous or rice according to the package instructions.

11. Once the meatballs are cooked, remove the skillet from the heat.

12. To serve, place the cooked couscous or rice on a serving platter. Arrange the Kefta Meatballs on top of the couscous or rice.

13. Pour the Tomato Sauce over the meatballs and couscous.

14. Garnish with fresh parsley or cilantro, and serve the Moroccan Kefta Meatballs with Tomato Sauce with lemon wedges on the side for squeezing over the dish.

Enjoy the rich and flavorful Moroccan Kefta Meatballs with Tomato Sauce served over couscous or rice! This dish is sure to impress with its aromatic spices and comforting flavors.

Nutritional Information (per serving)
- *Calories 300*
- *Total Fat 15g*
- *Saturated Fat 5g*
- *Cholesterol 75mg*
- *Sodium 420mg*
- *Total Carbohydrates 10g*
- *Dietary Fiber 2g*
- *Sugars 4g*
- *Protein 30g*

Recipe Notes
- *You can use any combination of ground beef and lamb according to your preference.*
- *Adjust the amount of cayenne pepper according to your desired level of spiciness.*
- *For a complete meal, serve the Kefta Meatballs and Tomato Sauce over cooked couscous or rice.*

Greek Lamb Souvlaki with Pita and Toppings

Preparation Time 20 minutes **Marinating Time** 1-2 hours (optional) **Cooking Time** 10 minutes **Total Time** 1 hour 30 minutes (including marinating time) **Servings** 4

Ingredients
For the Lamb Souvlaki
- 1.5 lbs (700g) boneless lamb leg or shoulder, cut into 1-inch cubes
- 14 cup olive oil
- 2 tablespoons fresh lemon juice
- 2 garlic cloves, minced
- 1 tablespoon dried oregano
- 1 teaspoon dried thyme
- 1 teaspoon dried rosemary
- 12 teaspoon ground cumin
- Salt and pepper to taste
- Skewers (wooden or metal)

For Serving
- Pita bread or Greek flatbread
- Sliced tomatoes
- Sliced red onions
- Sliced cucumbers
- Crumbled feta cheese
- Kalamata olives
- Tzatziki sauce (store-bought or homemade)
- Lemon wedges

Utensils Needed
- Mixing bowl
- Skewers (if using wooden, soak them in water for at least 30 minutes before using to prevent burning during cooking)
- Grill or stovetop griddle pan
- Cutting board and knife
- Serving platter

Instructions
1. In a mixing bowl, combine the olive oil, fresh lemon juice, minced garlic, dried oregano, dried thyme, dried rosemary, ground cumin, salt, and pepper.

2. Add the cubed lamb to the marinade and toss to coat the meat evenly. Cover the bowl with plastic wrap and refrigerate for 1 to 2 hours to allow the flavors to meld (marinating is optional but recommended).

3. While the lamb is marinating, prepare the toppings and the tzatziki sauce if making it from scratch. Slice the tomatoes, red onions, and cucumbers, and crumble the feta cheese. Set aside.

4. If you're making homemade tzatziki sauce, combine Greek yogurt, grated cucumber, minced garlic, chopped dill, lemon juice, salt, and a drizzle of olive oil in a bowl. Stir well and refrigerate until serving.

5. Preheat your grill or stovetop griddle pan to medium-high heat.

6. Thread the marinated lamb cubes onto skewers, dividing the meat evenly among them.

7. Place the lamb skewers on the preheated grill or griddle pan and cook for about 2-3 minutes on each side or until the meat is cooked through and slightly charred.

8. While the lamb is cooking, warm the pita bread on the grill or in a separate pan.

9. Once the lamb is cooked, remove the skewers from the heat and let them rest for a minute.

10. To serve, place the warm pita bread on a serving platter. Remove the lamb from the skewers and arrange it on top of the pita.

11. Add the sliced tomatoes, red onions, cucumbers, crumbled feta cheese, and Kalamata olives on top of the lamb.

12. Drizzle tzatziki sauce over the toppings.

13. Garnish with fresh parsley and serve the Greek Lamb Souvlaki with Pita and Toppings with lemon wedges on the side for squeezing over the dish.

Enjoy the delicious flavors of this Greek Lamb Souvlaki with Pita and Toppings! It's a mouthwatering and satisfying meal that captures the essence of Greek cuisine.

Nutritional Information (per serving)
- *Calories 480*
- *Total Fat 27g*
- *Saturated Fat 8g*
- *Cholesterol 120mg*
- *Sodium 590mg*
- *Total Carbohydrates 25g*
- *Dietary Fiber 2g*
- *Sugars 3g*
- *Protein 35g*

Recipe Notes
- *You can also use chicken, pork, or beef instead of lamb for the souvlaki.*
- *Marinating the lamb in the olive oil, lemon juice, and herbs enhances the flavor, but it's optional if you're short on time.*
- *If using wooden skewers, make sure to soak them in water before threading the lamb to prevent them from burning during cooking.*
- *Tzatziki sauce is a classic condiment for souvlaki, and you can easily make it by combining Greek yogurt, grated cucumber, minced garlic, chopped dill, lemon juice, and a drizzle of olive oil.*

Recipe Italian Osso Buco

Preparation Time 20 minutes **Cooking Time** 2 hours 30 minutes **Total Time** 2 hours 50 minutes
Servings 4

Ingredients
- 4 pieces of veal shanks, about 1.5 inches thick (about 2 lbs or 900g)
- All-purpose flour for dredging
- 14 cup olive oil
- 1 large onion, finely chopped
- 2 medium carrots, peeled and finely chopped
- 2 celery stalks, finely chopped
- 4 garlic cloves, minced
- 1 cup dry white wine
- 1 can (14 oz) diced tomatoes
- 1 cup beef or veal broth
- 1 tablespoon tomato paste
- 2 bay leaves
- 1 teaspoon dried thyme
- 1 teaspoon dried oregano
- Salt and pepper to taste
- Gremolata (optional, for garnish)
- 2 tablespoons fresh parsley, finely chopped
- Zest of 1 lemon
- 2 garlic cloves, minced

Utensils Needed
- Large Dutch oven or heavy-bottomed pot with a lid
- Plate for dredging
- Wooden spoon or spatula
- Measuring cups and spoons

Instructions
1. Preheat your oven to 325°F (160°C).

2. Season the veal shanks with salt and pepper. Dredge each piece in flour, shaking off any excess.

3. In a large Dutch oven or heavy-bottomed pot, heat the olive oil over medium-high heat.

4. Brown the veal shanks on all sides until they are nicely seared. This should take about 5-6 minutes per side. Once browned, remove the shanks from the pot and set them aside on a plate.

5. In the same pot, add the chopped onion, carrots, celery, and minced garlic. Cook the vegetables over medium heat until they become soft and translucent, about 5 minutes.

6. Pour in the dry white wine and deglaze the pot, scraping up any browned bits from the bottom.

7. Stir in the diced tomatoes, beef or veal broth, and tomato paste. Add the bay leaves, dried thyme, dried oregano, salt, and pepper. Mix everything well.

8. Return the browned veal shanks to the pot, nestling them into the sauce.

9. Bring the mixture to a gentle simmer, then cover the pot with the lid.

10. Transfer the covered pot to the preheated oven and let it braise for about 2 to 2.5 hours or until the meat is tender and falls off the bone.

11. While the Osso Buco is cooking, prepare the gremolata (if using) by combining the chopped fresh parsley, lemon zest, and minced garlic in a small bowl. Set it aside for garnishing.

12. Once the Osso Buco is done cooking, remove the pot from the oven. If the sauce is too thin, you can simmer it on the stovetop for a few minutes to reduce it to your desired consistency.

13. To serve, place one or two veal shanks on each plate, spooning the sauce and vegetables over the top.

14. Garnish with a sprinkle of gremolata, if using.

15. Serve the Italian Osso Buco with your choice of side dish, such as creamy polenta, mashed potatoes, or risotto.

Enjoy the delectable flavors of this classic Italian Osso Buco! Its tender, braised veal shanks in rich tomato-based sauce are sure to impress and delight your taste buds.

Nutritional Information (per serving)
- *Calories 540*
- *Total Fat 28g*
- *Saturated Fat 7g*
- *Cholesterol 150mg*
- *Sodium 720mg*
- *Total Carbohydrates 19g*
- *Dietary Fiber 4g*
- *Sugars 7g*
- *Protein 47g*

Recipe Notes
- *Osso Buco traditionally uses veal shanks, but you can use beef shanks if veal is not available.*
- *If you don't have dry white wine, you can substitute with chicken or beef broth.*
- *Gremolata is a classic garnish for Osso Buco, but it's optional. The bright flavors of the lemon and garlic complement the rich dish.*

Lebanese Lamb Shawarma

Preparation Time 20 minutes Marinating Time 2 hours to overnight Cooking Time 15 minutes Total Time 2 hours 35 minutes to 8 hours 35 minutes (including marinating time) Servings 4

Ingredients
For the Lamb Shawarma
- 1.5 lbs (700g) boneless lamb leg or shoulder, thinly sliced or cut into small, thin strips
- 1 large onion, finely grated
- 4 garlic cloves, minced
- 14 cup olive oil
- 2 tablespoons lemon juice
- 1 tablespoon ground cumin
- 1 tablespoon ground coriander
- 1 teaspoon ground paprika
- 1 teaspoon ground turmeric
- 12 teaspoon ground cinnamon
- 14 teaspoon cayenne pepper (optional, for heat)
- Salt and pepper to taste

For Serving
- Pita bread or Lebanese flatbread
- Sliced tomatoes
- Sliced cucumbers
- Pickles (such as pickled turnips or cucumbers)
- Fresh parsley or mint leaves
- Tahini sauce or garlic yogurt sauce (optional)
- Hummus (optional)

Utensils Needed
- Large bowl for marinating
- Skewers (if using wooden, soak them in water for at least 30 minutes before using to prevent burning during cooking)
- Grill or stovetop griddle pan
- Cutting board and knife
- Serving platter.

Instructions
1. In a large bowl, combine the grated onion, minced garlic, olive oil, lemon juice, ground cumin, ground coriander, ground paprika, ground turmeric, ground cinnamon, cayenne pepper (if using), salt, and pepper.

2. Add the thinly sliced or cut lamb to the marinade and toss to coat the meat evenly. Cover the bowl with plastic wrap and refrigerate for at least 2 hours, or preferably overnight, to allow the flavors to meld and the meat to tenderize.

3. If using wooden skewers, soak them in water for at least 30 minutes to prevent them from burning during cooking.

4. Preheat your grill or stovetop griddle pan to medium-high heat.

5. Thread the marinated lamb slices onto skewers, dividing the meat evenly among them.

6. Place the lamb skewers on the preheated grill or

griddle pan and cook for about 6-8 minutes on each side or until the meat is cooked through and slightly charred.

7. While the lamb is cooking, warm the pita bread on the grill or in a separate pan.

8. Once the lamb is cooked, remove the skewers from the heat and let them rest for a minute.

9. To serve, place the warm pita bread on a serving platter. Remove the lamb from the skewers and arrange it on top of the pita.

10. Add sliced tomatoes, sliced cucumbers, pickles, and fresh parsley or mint leaves on top of the lamb.

11. Optionally, drizzle tahini sauce or garlic yogurt sauce over the toppings and serve with hummus on the side.

12. Fold the pita bread to create a wrap, and enjoy the Lebanese Lamb Shawarma!

This flavorful and aromatic Lebanese Lamb Shawarma is a delightful dish that brings the taste of the Middle East to your table. It's perfect for a satisfying and tasty meal with family and friends.

Nutritional Information (per serving)
- *Calories 520*
- *Total Fat 29g*
- *Saturated Fat 10g*
- *Cholesterol 120mg*
- *Sodium 140mg*
- *Total Carbohydrates 12g*
- *Dietary Fiber 3g*
- *Sugars 3g*
- *Protein 49g*

Recipe Notes
- For a more traditional touch, you can use a vertical rotisserie for cooking the lamb shawarma.
- Marinating the lamb for at least 2 hours (or even overnight) enhances the flavors and tenderizes the meat.
- You can customize the toppings and sauces according to your preference and availability

Spanish Beef and Potato Stew

Preparation Time 20 minutes **Cooking Time** 2 hours 30 minutes **Total Time** 2 hours 50 minutes
Servings 6

Ingredients
- 2 lbs (900g) beef stew meat, cut into bite-sized pieces
- 2 tablespoons olive oil
- 1 large onion, chopped
- 3 garlic cloves, minced
- 2 large potatoes, peeled and diced
- 2 large carrots, peeled and diced
- 1 red bell pepper, diced
- 1 can (14 oz) diced tomatoes
- 4 cups beef broth
- 1 cup dry red wine (optional, you can replace with additional beef broth)
- 2 bay leaves
- 1 teaspoon dried thyme
- 1 teaspoon paprika
- 12 teaspoon ground cumin
- Salt and pepper to taste
- Fresh parsley for garnish

Utensils Needed
- Large Dutch oven or heavy-bottomed pot with a lid
- Cutting board and knife
- Wooden spoon or spatula
- Measuring cups and spoons

Instructions
1. In a large Dutch oven or heavy-bottomed pot, heat the olive oil over medium-high heat.

2. Add the beef stew meat to the pot, season with salt and pepper, and cook until it's browned on all sides. This should take about 5-7 minutes. Once browned, remove the beef from the pot and set it aside.

3. In the same pot, add the chopped onion and cook until it becomes soft and translucent, about 5 minutes.

4. Stir in the minced garlic and cook for another minute until fragrant.

5. Add the diced potatoes, carrots, and red bell pepper to the pot. Cook for about 5 minutes, stirring occasionally.

6. Pour in the diced tomatoes and their juices, beef broth, and dry red wine (if using). Add the bay leaves, dried thyme, paprika, ground cumin, salt, and pepper. Mix everything well.

7. Return the browned beef to the pot,

nestling it into the vegetables and broth.

8. Bring the mixture to a boil, then reduce the heat to low. Cover the pot with the lid and let the stew simmer gently for about 2 hours, or until the beef is tender and the flavors have melded together beautifully.

9. Stir the stew occasionally during the cooking process to prevent sticking and ensure even cooking.

10. Once the beef and vegetables are tender and the stew has thickened to your desired consistency, remove the pot from the heat.

11. To serve, ladle the Spanish Beef and Potato Stew into bowls. Garnish with fresh parsley.

12. Enjoy the heartwarming and comforting flavors of this delicious Spanish Beef and Potato Stew!

This stew is a hearty and satisfying dish that showcases the rich and comforting flavors of Spanish cuisine. It's perfect for a comforting family meal on a chilly day.

Nutritional Information (per serving)
- *Calories 420*
- *Total Fat 18g*
- *Saturated Fat 6g*
- *Cholesterol 105mg*
- *Sodium 660mg*
- *Total Carbohydrates 25g*
- *Dietary Fiber 4g*
- *Sugars 6g*
- *Protein 38g*

Recipe Notes
- *You can use any preferred cut of beef for stew, such as chuck roast or beef stew cubes.*
- *The addition of dry red wine enhances the flavors of the stew, but it's optional. You can replace it with more beef broth if desired.*
- *For a thicker stew, you can mix a couple of tablespoons of flour with water and stir it into the stew during the cooking process.*

Mediterranean Stews And Soups

Mediterranean Fish Soup

Time to Prepare: 20 minutes **Cooking Time:** 30 minutes **Total Time:** 50 minutes **Servings:** 4

Ingredients:
- 1 lb (450g) firm white fish fillets (such as cod, haddock, or snapper), cut into bite-sized pieces
- 1 large onion, finely chopped
- 2 cloves garlic, minced
- 1 large fennel bulb, thinly sliced
- 1 large carrot, thinly sliced
- 1 red bell pepper, diced
- 1 can (14 oz/400g) diced tomatoes, with juices
- 4 cups (1 liter) fish or vegetable broth
- 1 cup (250ml) dry white wine
- 1/4 cup (60ml) extra-virgin olive oil
- 2 tablespoons tomato paste
- 1 bay leaf
- 1 teaspoon dried oregano
- 1 teaspoon dried thyme
- 1/2 teaspoon red pepper flakes (adjust to taste)
- Salt and black pepper to taste
- Fresh parsley, chopped, for garnish
- Crusty bread, for serving

Utensils Needed:
- Large pot or Dutch oven
- Wooden spoon or spatula
- Knife and cutting board
- Ladle

Instructions:
1. Heat the olive oil in a large pot or Dutch oven over medium heat. Add the chopped onion and sauté for 2-3 minutes until it becomes translucent.

2. Stir in the minced garlic and cook for another 1 minute until the garlic releases its aroma.

3. Add the sliced fennel, carrot, and diced red bell pepper to the pot. Cook for 5 minutes, stirring occasionally, until the vegetables start to soften.

4. Pour in the white wine and let it simmer for a couple of minutes to allow some of the alcohol to evaporate.

5. Add the diced tomatoes (with their juices), fish or vegetable broth, tomato paste, bay leaf, dried oregano, dried thyme, and red pepper flakes to the pot. Stir well to combine all the ingredients.

6. Season the soup with salt and black pepper to taste. Remember that the fish broth might already contain some salt, so adjust accordingly.

7. Bring the soup to a gentle boil, then reduce the heat to low. Cover the pot and let it simmer for about 15 minutes to allow the flavors to meld together.

8. After 15 minutes, gently add the bite-sized fish pieces to the soup. Be careful not to

stir too vigorously to avoid breaking up the fish.

9. Simmer the soup for another 5-7 minutes or until the fish is cooked through and flakes easily with a fork.

10. Taste the soup and adjust the seasoning if needed.

11. Remove the bay leaf from the soup and discard it.

12. Ladle the Mediterranean Fish Soup into bowls, and garnish with chopped fresh parsley.

13. Serve the soup hot with crusty bread on the side.

Enjoy your delicious and comforting Mediterranean Fish Soup! It's a nutritious and flavorful dish that will transport your taste buds to the shores of the Mediterranean.

Nutritional Information (per serving):
- *Calories: approximately 320 kcal*
- *Total Fat: 12g*
- *Saturated Fat: 2g*
- *Cholesterol: 60mg*
- *Sodium: 800mg*
- *Total Carbohydrates: 18g*
- *Dietary Fiber: 4g*
- *Sugars: 8g*
- *Protein: 24g*
- *Vitamin D: 20% DV*
- *Calcium: 10% DV*
- *Iron: 15% DV*
- *Potassium: 25% DV*
- *Vitamin C: 70% DV*

Recipe Notes:
- *You can use any firm white fish for this soup. Make sure to choose sustainable options.*
- *Adjust the amount of red pepper flakes according to your spice preference.*
- *If you prefer a thicker soup, you can add a small amount of cornstarch mixed with water to the soup while it's simmering.*
- *This soup tastes even better the next day, so consider making it ahead of time and reheating it before serving.*
- *Serve the Mediterranean Fish Soup with crusty bread or croutons to soak up the flavorful broth.*

Tuscan White Bean Soup

Time to Prepare: 15 minutes **Cooking Time:** 1 hour 15 minutes **Total Time:** 1 hour 30 minutes
Servings: 6

Ingredients:
- 2 cups dried cannellini beans (or 3 cans of canned cannellini beans, drained and rinsed)
- 2 tablespoons olive oil
- 1 large onion, chopped
- 2 carrots, diced
- 2 celery stalks, diced
- 4 garlic cloves, minced
- 1 can (14 oz/400g) diced tomatoes, with juices
- 6 cups (1.5 liters) vegetable or chicken broth
- 2 sprigs fresh rosemary
- 2 bay leaves
- 1 teaspoon dried thyme
- 1 teaspoon dried oregano
- 1/2 teaspoon red pepper flakes (optional, adjust to taste)
- Salt and black pepper to taste
- Grated Parmesan cheese, for serving (optional)
- Fresh parsley, chopped, for garnish
- Crusty bread, for serving

Utensils Needed:
- Large pot or Dutch oven
- Colander (if using dried beans)
- Wooden spoon or spatula
- Knife and cutting board
- Ladle

Instructions:
1. If using dried beans, rinse them under cold water and pick out any debris. Soak the beans overnight in plenty of water. Drain and rinse them before using in the recipe.

2. Heat the olive oil in a large pot or Dutch oven over medium heat. Add the chopped onion, diced carrots, and diced celery. Sauté for about 5 minutes, stirring occasionally, until the vegetables soften.

3. Add the minced garlic to the pot and cook for another 1 minute until the garlic becomes fragrant.

4. Pour in the diced tomatoes (with their juices) and stir well to combine with the vegetables.

5. Add the soaked or canned cannellini beans to the pot and mix them with the vegetables.

6. Pour in the vegetable or chicken broth, and add the fresh rosemary sprigs, bay leaves, dried thyme, dried oregano, and red pepper flakes (if using). Stir everything together.

7. Bring the soup to a boil, then reduce the heat to low. Cover the pot and let the soup

simmer for about 1 hour or until the beans are tender and the flavors have melded together. If using canned beans, simmer for 30 minutes to allow the flavors to develop.

8. Once the beans are tender, remove the rosemary sprigs and bay leaves from the soup and discard them.

9. Season the soup with salt and black pepper to taste.

10. Ladle the Tuscan White Bean Soup into bowls, and if desired, top each serving with grated Parmesan cheese and chopped fresh parsley.

11. Serve the soup hot with crusty bread on the side.

Enjoy the comforting and hearty Tuscan White Bean Soup! It's a classic Italian dish that is perfect for chilly days and will leave you feeling satisfied and nourished.

Nutritional Information (per serving):
- *Calories: approximately 300 kcal*
- *Total Fat: 7g*
- *Saturated Fat: 1g*
- *Cholesterol: 0mg*
- *Sodium: 800mg*
- *Total Carbohydrates: 47g*
- *Dietary Fiber: 12g*
- *Sugars: 6g*
- *Protein: 14g*
- *Vitamin D: 0% DV*
- *Calcium: 15% DV*
- *Iron: 25% DV*
- *Potassium: 20% DV*
- *Vitamin C: 20% DV*

Recipe Notes:
- *If using dried beans, remember to soak them overnight or use the quick soak method (boil beans for 2 minutes, then let them soak for 1 hour) before starting the recipe.*
- *The red pepper flakes add a bit of heat to the soup. Adjust the amount according to your preference.*
- *You can use vegetable broth for a vegetarian version or chicken broth for a heartier flavor.*
- *This soup tends to thicken as it sits, so you can add more broth or water when reheating leftovers, if desired.*

Greek Lemon Chicken Soup (Avgolemono)

Time to Prepare: 15 minutes **Cooking Time:** 30 minutes **Total Time:** 45 minutes **Servings:** 4

Ingredients:
- 1 lb (450g) boneless, skinless chicken breast, cooked and shredded (you can use rotisserie chicken for convenience)
- 6 cups (1.5 liters) chicken broth
- 1/2 cup (100g) long-grain white rice
- 3 large eggs, separated
- Juice of 2 lemons (about 1/4 cup or 60ml)
- Zest of 1 lemon
- Salt and black pepper to taste
- Fresh dill, chopped, for garnish

Utensils Needed:
- Large pot or Dutch oven
- Small mixing bowl
- Whisk
- Fork
- Knife and cutting board
- Ladle

Instructions:
1. In a large pot or Dutch oven, bring the chicken broth to a boil over medium-high heat.

2. Add the white rice to the boiling broth and reduce the heat to medium. Cook the rice for about 15 minutes or until tender, stirring occasionally.

3. While the rice is cooking, shred the cooked chicken into bite-sized pieces using a fork.

4. In a small mixing bowl, whisk the egg yolks until smooth. Slowly add the lemon juice while whisking continuously until well combined. Set the lemon and egg mixture aside.

5. Once the rice is tender, add the shredded chicken and lemon zest to the pot. Stir to combine and let it simmer for a few more minutes to heat the chicken.

6. Season the soup with salt and black pepper to taste.

7. Remove the pot from the heat. While continuously whisking the soup, slowly pour the lemon and egg mixture into the hot broth. The eggs will thicken the soup and give it a creamy consistency.

8. Return the pot to low heat and continue to whisk the soup for a minute or two until it thickens slightly. Be careful not to boil the soup at this stage to avoid curdling the eggs.

9. Taste the soup and adjust the seasoning if needed.

10. Ladle the Greek Lemon Chicken Soup into bowls, and garnish with chopped fresh dill.

11. Serve the soup hot, and you can accompany it with some crusty bread if desired.

Enjoy the tangy and comforting Greek Lemon Chicken Soup! It's a classic Greek dish that is both delicious and nourishing. The lemony flavor adds a refreshing twist to the traditional chicken soup, making it a favorite for many.

Nutritional Information (per serving):
- *Calories: approximately 250 kcal*
- *Total Fat: 6g*
- *Saturated Fat: 2g*
- *Cholesterol: 180mg*
- *Sodium: 950mg*
- *Total Carbohydrates: 17g*
- *Dietary Fiber: 1g*
- *Sugars: 1g*
- *Protein: 30g*
- *Vitamin D: 6% DV*
- *Calcium: 4% DV*
- *Iron: 10% DV*
- *Potassium: 10% DV*
- *Vitamin C: 20% DV*

Recipe Notes:
- *You can use leftover cooked chicken or rotisserie chicken to save time. If using uncooked chicken breast, poach it in the chicken broth for about 15-20 minutes until fully cooked, then shred it.*
- *Traditional Avgolemono is made with orzo pasta, but you can use white rice as a substitute for a gluten-free version.*
- *Be sure to temper the eggs properly to prevent curdling in the soup. It's essential to add the lemon juice and egg mixture slowly to the hot broth while whisking continuously.*
- *The soup can thicken upon cooling, so you can add more chicken broth or water when reheating leftovers if needed.*

Moroccan Vegetable Tagine

Time to Prepare: 20 minutes **Cooking Time:** 1 hour 15 minutes **Total Time:** 1 hour 35 minutes **Servings:** 4

Ingredients:
- 2 tablespoons olive oil
- 1 large onion, finely chopped
- 3 garlic cloves, minced
- 2 large carrots, peeled and cut into thick slices
- 2 medium zucchinis, cut into thick slices
- 1 large sweet potato, peeled and cut into chunks
- 1 red bell pepper, seeded and cut into strips
- 1 yellow bell pepper, seeded and cut into strips
- 1 can (14 oz/400g) chickpeas, drained and rinsed
- 1 can (14 oz/400g) diced tomatoes, with juices
- 1 cup (250ml) vegetable broth
- 1/2 cup (125ml) water
- 1 tablespoon honey or maple syrup
- 1 tablespoon ground cumin
- 1 tablespoon ground coriander
- 1 teaspoon ground turmeric
- 1 teaspoon ground cinnamon
- 1/2 teaspoon ground ginger
- 1/2 teaspoon ground paprika
- Pinch of saffron threads (optional)
- Salt and black pepper to taste
- Fresh cilantro or parsley, chopped, for garnish
- Cooked couscous or quinoa, for serving

Utensils Needed:
- Tagine (traditional Moroccan cooking vessel) or a large pot with a tight-fitting lid
- Wooden spoon or spatula
- Knife and cutting board
- Small bowl (if using saffron threads)
- Serving platter

Instructions:
1. If using saffron, place the saffron threads in a small bowl and add a tablespoon of warm water. Let it steep for a few minutes.

2. In a tagine or a large pot, heat the olive oil over medium heat. Add the finely chopped onion and sauté for 3-4 minutes until it becomes translucent.

3. Add the minced garlic to the tagine and cook for another minute until the garlic releases its aroma.

4. Stir in the ground cumin, ground coriander, ground turmeric, ground cinnamon, ground ginger, and ground paprika. Mix well to coat the onions and garlic with the spices.

5. Add the sweet potato, carrots, zucchinis, red bell pepper, and yellow bell pepper to the tagine. Mix the vegetables with the spices to coat them evenly.

6. Pour in the vegetable broth, water, and the steeped saffron (if using). Stir everything together.

7. Add the diced tomatoes with their juices and the drained and rinsed chickpeas to the tagine. Mix well to combine all the ingredients.

8. Drizzle the honey or maple syrup over the vegetables and season with salt and black pepper to taste.

9. Bring the tagine to a boil, then reduce the heat to low. Cover the tagine with its lid and let it simmer for about 1 hour or until the vegetables are tender, stirring occasionally.

10. Taste the tagine and adjust the seasoning if needed.

11. Once the vegetables are tender and the flavors have melded together, remove the tagine from the heat.

12. Sprinkle the chopped fresh cilantro or parsley over the tagine as a garnish.

13. Serve the Moroccan Vegetable Tagine over cooked couscous or quinoa on a serving platter.

Enjoy the flavorful and aromatic Moroccan Vegetable Tagine! It's a hearty and wholesome dish that showcases the vibrant and diverse flavors of Moroccan cuisine.

Nutritional Information (per serving):
- *Calories: approximately 350 kcal*
- *Total Fat: 8g*
- *Saturated Fat: 1g*
- *Cholesterol: 0mg*
- *Sodium: 850mg*
- *Total Carbohydrates: 63g*
- *Dietary Fiber: 14g*
- *Sugars: 15g*
- *Protein: 11g*
- *Vitamin D: 0% DV*
- *Calcium: 10% DV*
- *Iron: 20% DV*
- *Potassium: 25% DV*
- *Vitamin C: 150% DV*

Recipe Notes:
- *You can customize this tagine with other vegetables like eggplant, butternut squash, or green beans.*
- *If you don't have a tagine, you can use a large pot with a tight-fitting lid for cooking. The tagine provides a beautiful presentation, but the flavors will still be fantastic without it.*
- *Adjust the sweetness by varying the amount of honey or maple syrup according to your taste.*
- *Saffron adds a distinct flavor and color to the tagine, but it's optional if you don't have it on hand.*
- *Serve the Moroccan Vegetable Tagine over cooked couscous or quinoa for a complete meal.*

Spanish Gazpacho

Time to Prepare: 20 minutes **Chilling Time:** 2 hours or overnight **Total Time:** 2 hours 20 minutes (including chilling time) **Servings:** 4-6

Ingredients:
- 2 lbs (900g) ripe tomatoes, cored and roughly chopped
- 1 cucumber, peeled and roughly chopped
- 1 red bell pepper, seeded and roughly chopped
- 1 small red onion, peeled and roughly chopped
- 2 cloves garlic, peeled
- 3 cups (750ml) tomato juice or vegetable broth
- 1/4 cup (60ml) extra-virgin olive oil
- 2 tablespoons red wine vinegar
- 1 teaspoon salt (adjust to taste)
- 1/2 teaspoon black pepper
- 1/2 teaspoon ground cumin
- 1/2 teaspoon smoked paprika (optional, for added smokiness)
- 1/2 cup (50g) stale bread, torn into pieces
- Garnish options: chopped cucumber, bell pepper, red onion, fresh basil, croutons, or a drizzle of olive oil

Utensils Needed:
- Blender or food processor
- Large bowl
- Wooden spoon or spatula
- Knife and cutting board

Instructions:
1. In a blender or food processor, combine the chopped tomatoes, cucumber, red bell pepper, red onion, garlic, and stale bread pieces.

2. Blend the mixture on high until it becomes smooth and well combined.

3. While the blender is running, gradually pour in the tomato juice or vegetable broth to thin out the mixture.

4. Add the extra-virgin olive oil, red wine vinegar, salt, black pepper, ground cumin, and smoked paprika (if using). Blend again until all the ingredients are fully incorporated and the gazpacho is smooth and creamy.

5. Taste the gazpacho and adjust the seasoning if needed. You can add more salt, vinegar, or spices according to your taste preference.

6. Pour the gazpacho into a large bowl and give it a good stir with a wooden spoon or spatula.

7. Cover the bowl with plastic wrap or a lid, and refrigerate the gazpacho for at least 2 hours or overnight to

allow the flavors to develop.

8. Before serving, give the gazpacho another stir to ensure it is well-mixed.

9. Ladle the chilled Spanish Gazpacho into individual bowls or glasses.

10. Garnish each serving with chopped cucumber, bell pepper, red onion, fresh basil, croutons, or a drizzle of olive oil, as desired.

11. Serve the gazpacho cold and enjoy the refreshing and flavorful taste of this classic Spanish soup.

Spanish Gazpacho is a perfect dish for hot summer days, as it provides a refreshing and cooling experience. It's not only delicious but also packed with nutrients from fresh vegetables and olive oil, making it a healthy addition to your diet.

Nutritional Information (per serving, based on 4 servings):
- *Calories: approximately 230 kcal*
- *Total Fat: 15g*
- *Saturated Fat: 2g*
- *Cholesterol: 0mg*
- *Sodium: 630mg*
- *Total Carbohydrates: 21g*
- *Dietary Fiber: 4g*
- *Sugars: 12g*
- *Protein: 4g*
- *Vitamin D: 0% DV*
- *Calcium: 6% DV*
- *Iron: 15% DV*
- *Potassium: 25% DV*
- *Vitamin C: 100% DV*

Recipe Notes:
- *Use ripe tomatoes for the best flavor. If they are not fully ripe, you can add a tablespoon of tomato paste to enhance the taste.*
- *For a smoother texture, you can peel the tomatoes before chopping them, but it's not necessary.*
- *The bread in this recipe helps to thicken the gazpacho and give it a velvety consistency. Traditionally, stale bread is used, but you can use fresh bread if you don't have stale bread on hand.*
- *If you prefer a spicier gazpacho, you can add a small amount of chopped jalapeno or red chili pepper to the ingredients.*
- *Gazpacho tastes even better when it's chilled for a few hours or overnight. This allows the flavors to meld together.*

Italian Minestrone Soup

Time to Prepare: 20 minutes **Cooking Time:** 40 minutes **Total Time:** 1 hour **Servings:** 6

Ingredients:
- 2 tablespoons olive oil
- 1 medium onion, chopped
- 2 cloves garlic, minced
- 2 medium carrots, diced
- 2 celery stalks, diced
- 1 medium zucchini, diced
- 1 cup green beans, cut into 1-inch pieces
- 1 can (14 oz/400g) diced tomatoes, with juices
- 1 can (14 oz/400g) kidney beans, drained and rinsed
- 1 can (14 oz/400g) cannellini beans, drained and rinsed
- 6 cups (1.5 liters) vegetable broth
- 2 cups (500ml) water
- 1 teaspoon dried oregano
- 1 teaspoon dried basil
- 1/2 teaspoon dried thyme
- 1 bay leaf
- 1 cup small pasta (such as macaroni or small shells)
- Salt and black pepper to taste
- Grated Parmesan cheese, for serving (optional)
- Fresh parsley, chopped, for garnish

Utensils Needed:
- Large pot or Dutch oven
- Wooden spoon or spatula
- Knife and cutting board
- Ladle

Instructions:
1. Heat the olive oil in a large pot or Dutch oven over medium heat. Add the chopped onion and sauté for 2-3 minutes until it becomes translucent.

2. Stir in the minced garlic and cook for another 1 minute until the garlic releases its aroma.

3. Add the diced carrots, diced celery, diced zucchini, and cut green beans to the pot. Cook for 5 minutes, stirring occasionally, until the vegetables start to soften.

4. Pour in the diced tomatoes (with their juices), drained kidney beans, and drained cannellini beans. Mix well to combine all the ingredients.

5. Add the vegetable broth, water, dried oregano, dried basil, dried thyme, and bay leaf to the pot. Stir everything together.

6. Bring the soup to a boil, then reduce the heat to low. Cover the pot and let it simmer for about 15 minutes

to allow the flavors to meld together.

7. After 15 minutes, add the small pasta to the soup. Continue to simmer the soup for the time specified on the pasta's package instructions, usually around 10-12 minutes or until the pasta is cooked al dente.

8. Taste the soup and season with salt and black pepper to your liking.

9. Remove the bay leaf from the soup and discard it.

10. Ladle the Italian Minestrone Soup into bowls, and if desired, sprinkle some grated Parmesan cheese and chopped fresh parsley on top.

11. Serve the soup hot with some crusty bread on the side.

Enjoy the hearty and flavorful Italian Minestrone Soup! It's a comforting dish that is perfect for chilly days and will leave you feeling nourished and satisfied.

Nutritional Information (per serving):
- *Calories: approximately 300 kcal*
- *Total Fat: 7g*
- *Saturated Fat: 1g*
- *Cholesterol: 0mg*
- *Sodium: 800mg*
- *Total Carbohydrates: 50g*
- *Dietary Fiber: 13g*
- *Sugars: 6g*
- *Protein: 12g*
- *Vitamin D: 0% DV*
- *Calcium: 10% DV*
- *Iron: 25% DV*
- *Potassium: 25% DV*
- *Vitamin C: 25% DV*

Recipe Notes:
- *You can customize this Minestrone Soup with other vegetables you prefer, such as cabbage, spinach, or bell peppers.*
- *Feel free to use any type of small pasta you like. Adjust the cooking time according to the pasta's package instructions.*
- *To make this soup gluten-free, use gluten-free pasta or rice.*
- *Minestrone Soup is often made with a combination of vegetable broth and water. However, you can use chicken broth or beef broth if preferred.*
- *The Parmesan cheese adds a delicious savory touch, but you can omit it for a vegan version.*

Lentil Soup with Spinach and Lemon

Time to Prepare: 15 minutes **Cooking Time:** 35 minutes **Total Time:** 50 minutes **Servings:** 4-6

Ingredients:
- 1 cup dried green or brown lentils, rinsed and picked over
- 1 tablespoon olive oil
- 1 large onion, finely chopped
- 2 carrots, diced
- 2 celery stalks, diced
- 3 cloves garlic, minced
- 6 cups (1.5 liters) vegetable broth or water
- 1 can (14 oz/400g) diced tomatoes, with juices
- 2 cups packed fresh spinach leaves, chopped
- Juice of 1 lemon (about 2-3 tablespoons)
- 1 teaspoon ground cumin
- 1 teaspoon ground coriander
- 1/2 teaspoon ground turmeric
- 1 bay leaf
- Salt and black pepper to taste
- Lemon wedges, for serving
- Fresh parsley, chopped, for garnish

Utensils Needed:
- Large pot or Dutch oven
- Wooden spoon or spatula
- Knife and cutting board
- Lemon juicer (if using fresh lemon)
- Ladle

Instructions:
1. In a large pot or Dutch oven, heat the olive oil over medium heat. Add the chopped onion, diced carrots, and diced celery. Sauté for about 5 minutes until the vegetables soften.

2. Stir in the minced garlic and cook for another minute until the garlic becomes fragrant.

3. Add the rinsed lentils to the pot and mix them with the sautéed vegetables.

4. Pour in the vegetable broth or water, and add the diced tomatoes (with their juices), ground cumin, ground coriander, ground turmeric, and bay leaf. Stir everything together.

5. Bring the soup to a boil, then reduce the heat to low. Cover the pot and let the soup simmer for about 20-25 minutes or until the lentils are tender.

6. Once the lentils are cooked, add the chopped fresh spinach to the pot. Stir the spinach into the soup and let it wilt for a few minutes.

7. Squeeze the lemon juice into the soup and stir to incorporate the citrus flavor.

8. Season the soup with salt and black pepper to taste.

9. Remove the bay leaf from the soup and discard it.

10. Ladle the Lentil Soup with Spinach and Lemon into bowls, and if desired, garnish with chopped fresh parsley.

11. Serve the soup hot, and you can offer lemon wedges on the side for an extra zesty touch.

Enjoy the wholesome and flavorful Lentil Soup with Spinach and Lemon! It's a nutritious and comforting dish that is perfect for any time of the year. The combination of lentils, vegetables, spinach, and lemon creates a delightful harmony of flavors.

Nutritional Information (per serving, based on 4 servings):
- *Calories: approximately 240 kcal*
- *Total Fat: 4g*
- *Saturated Fat: 1g*
- *Cholesterol: 0mg*
- *Sodium: 800mg*
- *Total Carbohydrates: 40g*
- *Dietary Fiber: 15g*
- *Sugars: 7g*
- *Protein: 14g*
- *Vitamin D: 0% DV*
- *Calcium: 10% DV*
- *Iron: 25% DV*
- *Potassium: 20% DV*
- *Vitamin C: 30% DV*

Recipe Notes:
- *You can use other types of lentils if green or brown lentils are not available, but cooking times may vary.*
- *Fresh spinach works best in this recipe, but you can use frozen spinach if fresh is unavailable.*
- *Adjust the amount of lemon juice according to your taste preference. The lemon adds a bright and tangy flavor to the soup.*
- *For extra richness, you can stir in a tablespoon of unsalted butter or olive oil just before serving.*

Turkish Red Lentil Soup (Mercimek Çorbasi)

Time to Prepare: 10 minutes **Cooking Time:** 25 minutes **Total Time:** 35 minutes **Servings:** 4-6

Ingredients:
- 1 cup red lentils, rinsed and picked over
- 1 large onion, finely chopped
- 2 cloves garlic, minced
- 2 tablespoons olive oil
- 2 large carrots, peeled and diced
- 2 medium potatoes, peeled and diced
- 1 tablespoon tomato paste
- 6 cups (1.5 liters) vegetable broth or water
- 1 teaspoon ground cumin
- 1 teaspoon ground paprika
- Salt and black pepper to taste
- Juice of 1 lemon (about 2-3 tablespoons), plus lemon wedges for serving
- Fresh parsley, chopped, for garnish
- Red pepper flakes or ground red pepper (optional, for added spice)

Utensils Needed:
- Large pot or Dutch oven
- Wooden spoon or spatula
- Knife and cutting board
- Lemon juicer (if using fresh lemon)
- Immersion blender or regular blender (optional, for a smoother consistency)
- Ladle

Instructions:
1. In a large pot or Dutch oven, heat the olive oil over medium heat. Add the chopped onion and sauté for 2-3 minutes until it becomes translucent.

2. Stir in the minced garlic and cook for another minute until the garlic releases its aroma.

3. Add the diced carrots and diced potatoes to the pot. Sauté for 3-4 minutes to soften the vegetables.

4. Stir in the tomato paste and cook for another minute, coating the vegetables with the paste.

5. Add the rinsed red lentils to the pot and mix them with the sautéed vegetables.

6. Pour in the vegetable broth or water, and add the ground cumin and ground paprika. Stir everything together.

7. Bring the soup to a boil, then reduce the heat to low. Cover the pot and let the soup simmer for about 15-20 minutes or until the lentils and vegetables are tender.

8. Once the lentils and vegetables are cooked, season the soup with

salt and black pepper to taste.

9. Using an immersion blender or regular blender, if desired, blend part of the soup to achieve a smoother consistency. This step is optional, and you can leave the soup chunky if you prefer.

10. Squeeze the lemon juice into the soup and stir to incorporate the citrus flavor.

11. Taste the soup and adjust the seasoning or add more lemon juice if desired. For added spice, sprinkle some red pepper flakes or ground red pepper on top.

12. Ladle the Turkish Red Lentil Soup into bowls, and garnish with chopped fresh parsley.

13. Serve the soup hot, and offer lemon wedges on the side for individual drizzling.

Enjoy the delicious and comforting Turkish Red Lentil Soup! It's a classic Turkish dish that is not only flavorful but also quick and easy to make. The combination of red lentils, vegetables, and spices creates a hearty and nutritious soup that is perfect for any time of the year.

Nutritional Information (per serving, based on 4 servings):
- *Calories: approximately 240 kcal*
- *Total Fat: 6g*
- *Saturated Fat: 1g*
- *Cholesterol: 0mg*
- *Sodium: 800mg*
- *Total Carbohydrates: 35g*
- *Dietary Fiber: 12g*
- *Sugars: 6g*
- *Protein: 11g*
- *Vitamin D: 0% DV*
- *Calcium: 6% DV*
- *Iron: 25% DV*
- *Potassium: 25% DV*
- *Vitamin C: 20% DV*

Recipe Notes:
- *Red lentils cook faster than other lentil varieties and give a smooth texture to the soup. However, you can use green or brown lentils if red lentils are not available, but the cooking time may vary.*
- *You can customize the soup by adding other vegetables like celery or bell peppers.*
- *For a creamier consistency, you can use an immersion blender to blend part of the soup before serving. Alternatively, transfer a portion of the soup to a blender and puree it before returning it to the pot.*
- *Turkish Red Lentil Soup is traditionally served with a drizzle of lemon juice and some red pepper flakes for added spice.*

Sicilian Fish Stew

Time to Prepare: 20 minutes **Cooking Time:** 30 minutes **Total Time:** 50 minutes **Servings:** 4-6

Ingredients:
- 1 lb (450g) firm white fish fillets (such as cod, halibut, or snapper), cut into chunks
- 1 lb (450g) large shrimp, peeled and deveined
- 2 tablespoons olive oil
- 1 large onion, finely chopped
- 2 cloves garlic, minced
- 1 fennel bulb, thinly sliced
- 1 red bell pepper, thinly sliced
- 1 yellow bell pepper, thinly sliced
- 1 can (14 oz/400g) diced tomatoes, with juices
- 2 cups (500ml) fish or seafood broth
- 1 cup (250ml) dry white wine
- 1/2 cup (125ml) water
- 1 teaspoon dried oregano
- 1 teaspoon dried basil
- 1/2 teaspoon red pepper flakes (adjust to taste)
- Salt and black pepper to taste
- Fresh parsley, chopped, for garnish
- Crusty bread or cooked couscous, for serving

Utensils Needed:
- Large pot or Dutch oven
- Wooden spoon or spatula
- Knife and cutting board
- Lemon juicer (if using fresh lemon)
- Ladle

Instructions:
1. In a large pot or Dutch oven, heat the olive oil over medium heat. Add the finely chopped onion and sauté for 2-3 minutes until it becomes translucent.

2. Stir in the minced garlic and cook for another minute until the garlic releases its aroma.

3. Add the thinly sliced fennel bulb, red bell pepper, and yellow bell pepper to the pot. Sauté for 5 minutes until the vegetables start to soften.

4. Pour in the dry white wine and let it simmer for a couple of minutes to cook off the alcohol.

5. Add the diced tomatoes (with their juices), fish or seafood broth, and water to the pot. Stir everything together.

6. Sprinkle the dried oregano, dried basil, and red pepper flakes into the stew. Mix well to incorporate the herbs and spices.

7. Bring the stew to a gentle simmer and let it cook for about 15 minutes to allow the flavors to meld together.

8. Season the stew with salt and black pepper to taste.

9. Add the chunks of white fish fillets and the peeled and deveined shrimp to the pot. Stir gently to submerge the fish and shrimp in the broth.

10. Cover the pot and let the stew simmer for another 5-7 minutes or until the fish is cooked through and the shrimp are pink and opaque.

11. Taste the stew and adjust the seasoning if needed.

12. Remove the pot from the heat and ladle the Sicilian Fish Stew into bowls.

13. Garnish each serving with chopped fresh parsley.

14. Serve the stew hot, along with crusty bread or cooked couscous on the side.

Enjoy the rich and flavorful Sicilian Fish Stew! It's a delightful dish that showcases the abundance of fresh seafood and aromatic Mediterranean flavors. The combination of fish, shrimp, and vegetables in a savory broth makes it a hearty and satisfying meal.

Nutritional Information (per serving, based on 4 servings):
- *Calories: approximately 350 kcal*
- *Total Fat: 10g*
- *Saturated Fat: 2g*
- *Cholesterol: 150mg*
- *Sodium: 800mg*
- *Total Carbohydrates: 20g*
- *Dietary Fiber: 4g*
- *Sugars: 7g*
- *Protein: 35g*
- *Vitamin D: 20% DV*
- *Calcium: 10% DV*
- *Iron: 20% DV*
- *Potassium: 30% DV*
- *Vitamin C: 150% DV*

Recipe Notes:
- *You can use a variety of fish and seafood in this stew, depending on what's available and fresh. Along with white fish and shrimp, you can consider adding mussels, clams, or squid.*
- *The fennel bulb gives a distinctive flavor to the stew. If you're not a fan of fennel, you can omit it or replace it with thinly sliced celery for a similar texture.*
- *The red pepper flakes add some heat to the stew. Adjust the amount according to your preference for spiciness.*
- *Serve the Sicilian Fish Stew with crusty bread to soak up the flavorful broth or with cooked couscous for a heartier meal.*

Chicken and Chickpea Stew

Time to Prepare: 15 minutes **Cooking Time:** 40 minutes **Total Time:** 55 minutes **Servings:** 4-6

Ingredients:
- 1.5 lbs (680g) boneless, skinless chicken thighs, cut into bite-sized pieces
- 1 can (14 oz/400g) chickpeas, drained and rinsed
- 2 tablespoons olive oil
- 1 large onion, finely chopped
- 3 cloves garlic, minced
- 2 large carrots, peeled and diced
- 2 celery stalks, diced
- 1 red bell pepper, diced
- 1 can (14 oz/400g) diced tomatoes, with juices
- 4 cups (1 liter) chicken broth
- 1 teaspoon ground cumin
- 1 teaspoon ground coriander
- 1/2 teaspoon smoked paprika
- 1 bay leaf
- Salt and black pepper to taste
- Fresh parsley or cilantro, chopped, for garnish
- Cooked rice or couscous, for serving

Utensils Needed:
- Large pot or Dutch oven
- Wooden spoon or spatula
- Knife and cutting board
- Ladle

Instructions:
1. In a large pot or Dutch oven, heat the olive oil over medium heat. Add the finely chopped onion, diced carrots, diced celery, and diced red bell pepper. Sauté for about 5 minutes until the vegetables start to soften.

2. Stir in the minced garlic and cook for another minute until the garlic becomes fragrant.

3. Add the bite-sized chicken pieces to the pot. Cook the chicken until it's browned on all sides, about 5 minutes.

4. Sprinkle the ground cumin, ground coriander, and smoked paprika over the chicken and vegetables. Mix well to coat everything with the spices.

5. Pour in the diced tomatoes (with their juices) and the drained and rinsed chickpeas. Stir to combine all the ingredients.

6. Add the chicken broth and the bay leaf to the pot. Season

with salt and black pepper to taste.

7. Bring the stew to a boil, then reduce the heat to low. Cover the pot and let the stew simmer for about 30 minutes to allow the flavors to meld together and the chicken to cook thoroughly.

8. Taste the stew and adjust the seasoning if needed.

9. Remove the bay leaf from the stew and discard it.

10. Ladle the Chicken and Chickpea Stew into bowls, and garnish with chopped fresh parsley or cilantro.

11. Serve the stew hot, and you can accompany it with cooked rice or couscous on the side.

Enjoy the comforting and nutritious Chicken and Chickpea Stew! It's a wholesome and flavorful dish that is sure to please everyone at the table. The combination of tender chicken, hearty chickpeas, and a medley of vegetables in a savory broth makes it a satisfying and balanced meal.

Nutritional Information (per serving, based on 4 servings):
- *Calories: approximately 400 kcal*
- *Total Fat: 18g*
- *Saturated Fat: 4g*
- *Cholesterol: 120mg*
- *Sodium: 900mg*
- *Total Carbohydrates: 28g*
- *Dietary Fiber: 8g*
- *Sugars: 7g*
- *Protein: 32g*
- *Vitamin D: 10% DV*
- *Calcium: 10% DV*
- *Iron: 20% DV*
- *Potassium: 25% DV*
- *Vitamin C: 80% DV*

Recipe Notes:
- You can use chicken breasts instead of chicken thighs if you prefer white meat.
- Feel free to add other vegetables like diced potatoes, green beans, or spinach to enhance the stew's flavor and nutrition.
- The smoked paprika adds a rich smoky flavor, but you can use regular paprika if you don't have smoked paprika on hand.
- Serve the Chicken and Chickpea Stew with cooked rice or couscous for a complete and hearty meal.

Mediterranean Desserts Recipes

Greek Yogurt with Honey and Fresh Fruits

Time to Prepare: 10 minutes **Cooking Time:** None (This is a no-cook recipe) **Servings:** 2

Ingredients:
- 1 cup Greek yogurt (plain, unsweetened)
- 2 tablespoons honey (adjust to taste)
- 1 cup mixed fresh fruits (e.g., berries, sliced peaches, chopped mango, or any fruits of your choice)
- 1 tablespoon chopped nuts (e.g., almonds, walnuts, or pistachios) optional, for added crunch and flavor
- Fresh mint leaves for garnish optional, for presentation

Utensils Needed:
1. Mixing bowl
2. Spoon or whisk for stirring
3. Serving bowls or glasses
4. Knife and cutting board (for preparing fresh fruits)

Recipe:
1. Prepare the Fresh Fruits:
- Wash the fresh fruits thoroughly under running water.
- If needed, peel and chop the fruits into bite-sized pieces. If using berries, you can leave them whole or slice larger ones.

2. Mixing the Greek Yogurt:
- In a mixing bowl, add the Greek yogurt and stir it gently to smoothen its texture.

3. Sweeten with Honey:
- Drizzle the honey over the yogurt.
- Using the spoon or whisk, gently fold the honey into the yogurt until it is well incorporated.
- Taste the yogurt, and if you prefer it sweeter, add more honey to adjust to your liking.

4. Assembling the Dish:
- Take your serving bowls or glasses.
- Spoon a generous amount of the honey-sweetened Greek yogurt into each bowl or glass.

5. Adding the Fresh Fruits:
- Now, it's time to add the fresh fruits. Arrange the chopped or whole fruits on top of the yogurt in an appealing manner.
- Feel free to be creative with the fruit arrangement to make the dish visually appealing.

6. Optional: Add Chopped Nuts:
- If you want some extra crunch and flavor, sprinkle the chopped nuts over the fresh fruits.

7. Garnish and Serve:
- Optionally, garnish the Greek yogurt with

a few fresh mint leaves for a burst of color and presentation.

- Serve immediately and enjoy your delicious and healthy Greek Yogurt with Honey and Fresh Fruits!

Nutritional Information (per serving):
- *Calories: Approximately 200 kcal*
- *Protein: 10g*
- *Fat: 4g*
- *Carbohydrates: 35g*
- *Fiber: 3g*
- *Sugar: 30g*

Recipe Notes:
- *The nutritional information provided is approximate and may vary based on the specific brands of ingredients used.*
- *Greek yogurt is an excellent source of protein and calcium, and it contains probiotics that are beneficial for gut health.*
- *Honey adds natural sweetness and complements the tanginess of the yogurt. You can use more or less honey based on your taste preferences.*
- *Feel free to customize this recipe with your favorite fresh fruits. It's a great way to use seasonal fruits or those that you have on hand.*
- *If you have dietary restrictions or preferences, you can use alternatives such as vegan yogurt and agave nectar for a vegan version of this dish.*
- *For added texture and variety, you can also sprinkle some granola or toasted coconut flakes on top.*
- *This Greek yogurt with honey and fresh fruits is perfect for breakfast, a healthy snack, or a light dessert.*

Enjoy this delightful and refreshing Greek yogurt dish any time of the day!

Orange-Almond Cake

Time to Prepare: 15 minutes **Cooking Time**: 40-45 minutes **Servings**: 10-12

Ingredients:
- 1 ½ cups almond flour
- 1 cup all-purpose flour
- 1 ½ teaspoons baking powder
- ½ teaspoon baking soda
- ¼ teaspoon salt
- 3 large eggs, at room temperature
- 1 cup granulated sugar
- ½ cup unsalted butter, melted
- ½ cup Greek yogurt (plain, unsweetened)
- 1 tablespoon orange zest (from about 2 oranges)
- ½ cup fresh orange juice (from about 2 oranges)
- 1 teaspoon pure vanilla extract
- Sliced almonds and powdered sugar for garnish optional

Utensils Needed:
1. 9-inch round cake pan (springform or regular)
2. Parchment paper or baking spray
3. Mixing bowls
4. Electric mixer or hand whisk
5. Zester or grater (for orange zest)
6. Juicer or citrus reamer (for fresh orange juice)
7. Spatula
8. Cooling rack

Recipe:
1. Preheat the Oven:
- Preheat your oven to 350°F (175°C).
- Grease the bottom and sides of the cake pan with butter or baking spray.
- Cut a piece of parchment paper to fit the bottom of the pan, and place it inside.

2. Combine Dry Ingredients:
- In a mixing bowl, whisk together the almond flour, all-purpose flour, baking powder, baking soda, and salt until well combined. Set aside.

3. Beat Eggs and Sugar:
- In a separate large mixing bowl, beat the eggs and granulated sugar with an electric mixer or hand whisk until pale and fluffy.

4. Add Wet Ingredients:
- Slowly pour in the melted butter, Greek yogurt, orange zest, orange juice, and vanilla extract into the egg-sugar mixture. Mix until everything is well incorporated.

5. Incorporate Dry Ingredients:
- Gradually add the dry ingredient mixture into the wet ingredients. Use a spatula to fold the dry ingredients gently until just combined. Avoid overmixing.

6. Bake the Cake:
- Pour the cake batter into the

prepared cake pan, spreading it evenly.

- Optionally, sprinkle some sliced almonds on top for added texture and a nutty flavor.

- Place the cake pan in the preheated oven and bake for 40-45 minutes or until a toothpick inserted into the center comes out clean.

7. Cool and Serve:

- Once the cake is done, remove it from the oven and let it cool in the pan for about 10 minutes.

- Then, carefully transfer the cake to a cooling rack to cool completely before serving.

8. Garnish and Serve:

- Optionally, dust the top of the cake with powdered sugar for a touch of sweetness and a beautiful presentation.

- Slice the Orange-Almond Cake and serve it as a delightful dessert or a sweet treat for any occasion!

Nutritional Information (per serving, based on 12 servings):
- *Calories: Approximately 290 kcal*
- *Protein: 7g*
- *Fat: 17g*
- *Carbohydrates: 29g*
- *Fiber: 2g*
- *Sugar: 18g*

Recipe Notes:
- *Almond flour gives this cake a rich, nutty flavor and a moist texture. If you prefer, you can use all-purpose flour instead, but the almond flour is what makes this cake special.*
- *Make sure the eggs and Greek yogurt are at room temperature to ensure even mixing and better cake texture.*
- *You can adjust the sweetness by increasing or decreasing the amount of sugar according to your taste.*
- *The cake stays moist for a couple of days, making it a great make-ahead dessert option.*
- *Serve this cake with a dollop of whipped cream or a scoop of vanilla ice cream for an extra indulgent treat.*
- *If you want a gluten-free version of this cake, ensure that the baking powder and baking soda used are certified gluten-free.*
- *You can also add a glaze or a simple orange syrup over the cake for an extra burst of orange flavor.*

Enjoy this delicious Orange-Almond Cake with a cup of tea or coffee, or as a delightful dessert after a meal!

Baklava

Time to Prepare: 30 minutes **Cooking Time:** 45 minutes **Resting Time:** 4 hours (or overnight) **Servings:** 24 pieces

Ingredients:
- 1 package (16 oz) phyllo dough, thawed
- 1 ½ cups unsalted butter, melted
- 1 ½ cups mixed nuts (walnuts, pistachios, and almonds), coarsely chopped or crushed
- 1 teaspoon ground cinnamon
- 1 cup granulated sugar
- 1 cup water
- ½ cup honey
- 1 teaspoon vanilla extract
- 1 teaspoon lemon juice
- Optional: Ground cloves or cardamom for extra flavor

Utensils Needed:
1. 9x13-inch baking dish
2. Pastry brush
3. Sharp knife
4. Small saucepan
5. Food processor or rolling pin (for crushing nuts)
6. Saucepan or microwave-safe bowl (for making syrup)
7. Small bowl (for melting butter)
8. Kitchen towel or plastic wrap

Recipe:
1. Prepare the Nuts:

- In a food processor or using a rolling pin, coarsely chop or crush the mixed nuts.
- Add ground cinnamon and any optional spices, such as ground cloves or cardamom, to the chopped nuts. Mix well and set aside.

2. Preheat the Oven:
- Preheat your oven to 350°F (175°C).

3. Prepare the Phyllo Dough:
- Take the thawed phyllo dough and keep it covered with a slightly damp kitchen towel or plastic wrap to prevent it from drying out while you work.

4. Layer the Phyllo Sheets:
- Brush the bottom of the baking dish with melted butter.
- Carefully place one sheet of phyllo dough into the dish and brush it with melted butter.
- Repeat this process, layering and buttering each phyllo sheet until you have used about half of the phyllo dough.

5. Add the Nut Mixture:
- Spread half of the nut mixture evenly over the layered phyllo sheets.

6. Continue Layering Phyllo and Nuts:
- Layer the remaining phyllo sheets over the nut mixture, buttering each sheet as before.
- Spread the remaining nut mixture over the second layer of phyllo sheets.

7. Finish Layering Phyllo Sheets:

- Continue layering the remaining phyllo sheets on top of the nut mixture, buttering each sheet, until all the phyllo dough is used.

8. Cut the Baklava:

- Using a sharp knife, carefully cut the baklava into diamond or square shapes.

9. Bake the Baklava:

- Place the baking dish in the preheated oven and bake for about 45 minutes or until the baklava turns golden brown and crisp.

10. Make the Syrup:

- While the baklava is baking, prepare the syrup. In a saucepan, combine the granulated sugar, water, honey, vanilla extract, and lemon juice.

- Bring the mixture to a boil, then reduce the heat and let it simmer for about 10 minutes until it thickens slightly.

11. Pour the Syrup:

- Once the baklava is done baking, immediately pour the hot syrup over the hot baklava.

- Allow the baklava to cool and soak up the syrup for at least 4 hours or overnight before serving.

Nutritional Information (per piece, based on 24 servings):
- *Calories: Approximately 200 kcal*
- *Protein: 3g*
- *Fat: 12g*
- *Carbohydrates: 22g*
- *Fiber: 1g*
- *Sugar: 12g*

Recipe Notes:
- *Phyllo dough is delicate, so handle it carefully to avoid tearing or drying out.*
- *You can adjust the nut mixture according to your preference. Some people like more walnuts, while others prefer more pistachios or almonds.*
- *For a crispier baklava, make sure to use melted butter between each phyllo layer generously.*
- *While cutting the baklava, you can make diagonal cuts to create diamond shapes or vertical/horizontal cuts for square pieces.*
- *Let the baklava cool completely before serving to allow the flavors to meld and the syrup to soak in fully.*
- *Store any leftover baklava in an airtight container at room temperature for up to a week.*

Enjoy the delicious and sweet indulgence of Baklava, a classic Middle Eastern dessert!

Fresh Fruit Salad with Mint

Time to Prepare: 20 minutes **Cooking Time:** None (This is a no-cook recipe) **Servings:** 4

Ingredients:
- 2 cups mixed fresh fruits (e.g., strawberries, blueberries, grapes, kiwi, mango, pineapple, watermelon, or any fruits of your choice), washed and chopped/sliced
- 2 tablespoons fresh mint leaves, chopped
- 1 tablespoon honey (adjust to taste)
- 1 tablespoon freshly squeezed lime or lemon juice
- 1 teaspoon lime or lemon zest (optional, for extra citrus flavor)

Utensils Needed:
1. Large mixing bowl
2. Cutting board
3. Knife
4. Measuring cups and spoons
5. Small bowl (for dressing)
6. Whisk or fork (for dressing)
7. Serving bowls or plates

Recipe:
1. Prep the Fresh Fruits:
- Wash all the fresh fruits thoroughly under running water.
- Cut and chop the fruits into bite-sized pieces, or slice them as desired. Remove any pits, seeds, or tough cores.
- Place the chopped fruits in a large mixing bowl.

2. Prepare the Mint Leaves:
- Wash the fresh mint leaves and pat them dry with a paper towel.
- Finely chop the mint leaves and add them to the bowl with the fresh fruits.

3. Make the Dressing:
- In a small bowl, whisk together the honey, freshly squeezed lime or lemon juice, and lime or lemon zest (if using) until well combined.

4. Combine Fruits and Dressing:
- Pour the dressing over the chopped fruits and mint in the large mixing bowl.
- Gently toss the fruits and mint with the dressing until everything is evenly coated.

5. Chill and Serve:
- Cover the fruit salad with plastic wrap or transfer it to an airtight container.
- Refrigerate the fruit salad for at least 30 minutes to allow the flavors to meld and the fruits to chill.

6. Serve with Fresh Mint Garnish:
- Before serving, give the fruit salad a final

toss to redistribute the dressing.

- Optionally, garnish the fruit salad with a few fresh mint leaves for presentation.

Nutritional Information (per serving, based on 4 servings):
- *Calories: Approximately 80 kcal*
- *Protein: 1g*
- *Fat: 0.5g*
- *Carbohydrates: 20g*
- *Fiber: 3g*
- *Sugar: 14g*

Recipe Notes:

- *This fruit salad is highly customizable. You can use any combination of fresh fruits that you enjoy or have on hand. It's a great way to use seasonal fruits or clear out your fruit bowl.*
- *The honey-lime (or honey-lemon) dressing adds a sweet-tangy flavor that enhances the natural sweetness of the fruits. Feel free to adjust the sweetness and tartness to your taste.*
- *The mint leaves provide a refreshing and aromatic touch to the fruit salad. If you prefer, you can use basil or omit the herbs altogether.*
- *For a tropical twist, consider adding shredded coconut or coconut flakes to the fruit salad.*
- *This fruit salad is best served fresh, but you can store any leftovers in the refrigerator for a day or two. Just keep in mind that the fruits may release some juices over time, which could make the salad a bit watery.*
- *You can serve this fruit salad on its own as a healthy and refreshing dessert or snack. It also pairs well with yogurt or ice cream for a more indulgent treat.*
- *If you plan to prepare this fruit salad in advance for a gathering or picnic, consider keeping the dressing separate until just before serving to maintain the fruit's freshness and texture.*

Enjoy this vibrant and flavorful Fresh Fruit Salad with Mint as a delightful and healthy addition to your meals or as a light and refreshing dessert!

Italian Tiramisu

Time to Prepare: 30 minutes **Chilling Time:** 4 hours (or overnight) **Servings:** 8-10

Ingredients:
- 1 cup strong brewed coffee or espresso, cooled to room temperature
- 3 tablespoons coffee liqueur (e.g., Kahlua or Tia Maria) optional, for added flavor
- 3 large egg yolks, at room temperature
- ½ cup granulated sugar
- 1 cup mascarpone cheese, at room temperature
- 1 cup heavy cream, chilled
- 1 teaspoon pure vanilla extract
- 24 to 30 ladyfingers (savoiardi)
- Unsweetened cocoa powder or grated dark chocolate for dusting

Utensils Needed:
1. Medium-sized mixing bowl
2. Electric mixer or hand whisk
3. Shallow dish or plate
4. 9x13-inch dish or serving dish
5. Fine-mesh sieve or sifter
6. Spatula or spoon for spreading
7. Plastic wrap or aluminum foil (for covering)
8. Grater (for chocolate garnish)

Recipe:
1. Brew and Cool the Coffee:
- Brew strong coffee or espresso and allow it to cool to room temperature.
- If using coffee liqueur, stir it into the cooled coffee.

2. Prepare the Mascarpone Filling:
- In a medium-sized mixing bowl, whisk the egg yolks and granulated sugar together until pale and creamy.

3. Add Mascarpone Cheese:
- Gently fold the mascarpone cheese into the egg yolk mixture until smooth and well combined.

4. Whip the Heavy Cream:
- In a separate bowl, whip the chilled heavy cream and vanilla extract until stiff peaks form.

5. Combine Mascarpone and Whipped Cream:
- Gently fold the whipped cream into the mascarpone mixture until the filling is light and airy.

6. Dip Ladyfingers in Coffee:
- One at a time, quickly dip the ladyfingers into the coffee (or coffee liqueur mixture) for a couple of seconds. Do not soak them as they can become too soggy.

7. Layer the Tiramisu:
- Arrange a layer of dipped ladyfingers in

the bottom of the 9x13-inch dish.

8. Add the Filling:

- Spread half of the mascarpone filling over the layer of ladyfingers, making sure it's even.

9. Repeat the Layers:

- Add another layer of dipped ladyfingers on top of the filling.
- Spread the remaining mascarpone filling over the second layer of ladyfingers.

10. Cover and Chill:

- Cover the tiramisu with plastic wrap or aluminum foil and refrigerate for at least 4 hours or preferably overnight. Chilling allows the flavors to meld and the dessert to set.

11. Dust with Cocoa Powder or Grated Chocolate:

- Before serving, remove the tiramisu from the refrigerator.

- Using a fine-mesh sieve or sifter, dust the top of the tiramisu with unsweetened cocoa powder or grated dark chocolate.

Nutritional Information (per serving, based on 10 servings):
- *Calories: Approximately 370 kcal*
- *Protein: 5g*
- *Fat: 25g*
- *Carbohydrates: 30g*
- *Fiber: 1g*
- *Sugar: 17g*

Recipe Notes:
- *Ladyfingers are a classic choice for tiramisu, but you can use other sponge cake or ladyfinger alternatives if you prefer.*
- *Ensure that the egg yolks are at room temperature to achieve a smooth and creamy mascarpone filling.*
- *If you prefer a non-alcoholic version, you can omit the coffee liqueur or replace it with coffee only.*
- *To make a kid-friendly version, you can use decaffeinated coffee or simply soak the ladyfingers in milk instead of coffee.*
- *Tiramisu tastes best when chilled for an extended period, allowing the flavors to develop fully. Overnight chilling is recommended for the best results.*
- *The dusting of cocoa powder or grated chocolate on top adds a nice finishing touch and enhances the visual appeal of the tiramisu.*
- *Tiramisu can be stored in the refrigerator for up to 3-4 days, but it's best enjoyed within the first 2 days after preparation.*

Enjoy this classic and decadent Italian Tiramisu as a delightful ending to any meal or a special treat on its own!

Turkish Delight (Lokum)

Time to Prepare: 20 minutes **Cooking Time:** 40 minutes **Chilling Time:** 4 hours (or overnight) **Servings:** About 40 pieces

Ingredients:
- 1 cup water
- 3 ½ cups granulated sugar
- 1 cup cornstarch
- ¼ teaspoon cream of tartar
- 2 ½ cups cold water
- 2 tablespoons rosewater or orange blossom water (or any desired flavor extract)
- Food coloring (optional)
- ½ cup confectioners' sugar (powdered sugar) for dusting

Utensils Needed:
1. Medium-sized saucepan
2. Candy thermometer
3. Wooden spoon or heat-resistant spatula
4. 8x8-inch square baking dish or pan
5. Parchment paper
6. Knife or pizza cutter
7. Sifter or fine-mesh sieve (for dusting)
8. Airtight container (for storage)

Recipe:

1. Prepare the Baking Dish:
- Line the 8x8-inch baking dish with parchment paper, leaving some excess paper hanging over the edges. This will make it easier to remove the Turkish Delight later.

2. Combine Sugar and Water:
- In a medium-sized saucepan, mix 1 cup of water with granulated sugar over medium heat.
- Stir until the sugar dissolves completely.

3. Cook the Sugar Syrup:
- Insert the candy thermometer into the saucepan, making sure it doesn't touch the bottom.
- Allow the sugar syrup to boil without stirring until it reaches 240°F (116°C), which is the soft-ball stage.

4. Mix Cornstarch and Water:
- In a separate bowl, whisk together the cornstarch and cold water until well combined and smooth.

5. Combine Cornstarch Mixture with Sugar Syrup:
- Slowly pour the cornstarch mixture into the boiling sugar syrup while continuously stirring.

6. Cook the Mixture:
- Add the cream of tartar to the mixture and continue stirring over medium heat.
- Cook the mixture for about 30-40 minutes, stirring frequently, until it thickens and turns a pale color.

7. Add Flavor and Food Coloring:

- Once the mixture thickens, add the rosewater or orange blossom water (or any desired flavor extract) and stir until fully incorporated.

- Optionally, add a few drops of food coloring to achieve the desired color for your Turkish Delight.

8. Pour the Mixture into the Baking Dish:

- Pour the hot Turkish Delight mixture into the prepared baking dish and spread it evenly using a spatula.

9. Let It Cool and Set:

- Allow the Turkish Delight to cool at room temperature for about 30 minutes.

- Once it cools down, cover the baking dish with plastic wrap and refrigerate for at least 4 hours or overnight to allow it to set.

10. Cut and Dust with Confectioners' Sugar:

- Once the Turkish Delight is set, remove it from the baking dish using the excess parchment paper.

- Place it on a clean surface and dust the top with confectioners' sugar.

11. Cut into Pieces:

- Cut the Turkish Delight into small squares or rectangles using a knife or pizza cutter.

- Dust all sides of each piece with more confectioners' sugar to prevent sticking.

Nutritional Information (per piece, based on about 40 servings):
- *Calories: Approximately 60 kcal*
- *Protein: 0g*
- *Fat: 0g*
- *Carbohydrates: 15g*
- *Fiber: 0g*
- *Sugar: 11g*

Recipe Notes:
- Turkish Delight can be flavored with various extracts such as rosewater, orange blossom water, lemon, mint, or other flavors of your choice.
- The addition of food coloring is optional and can be adjusted according to your preferences for visual appeal.
- For a firmer Turkish Delight, you can increase the amount of cornstarch slightly.
- Store the Turkish Delight in an airtight container with parchment paper between the layers to prevent sticking. It will stay fresh for several weeks.
- Turkish Delight is a delightful treat on its own, but it also makes for a wonderful gift during holidays or special occasions.

Enjoy this delicious and traditional Turkish Delight as a sweet and fragrant confectionery that delights the taste buds!

Moroccan Orange Blossom Water Pudding

Time to Prepare: 15 minutes **Cooking Time:** 10 minutes **Chilling Time:** 2-4 hours (or overnight)
Servings: 4-6

Ingredients:
- 4 cups whole milk
- 1/2 cup granulated sugar (adjust to taste)
- 1/2 cup cornstarch
- 2 tablespoons orange blossom water
- 1 teaspoon vanilla extract
- Pinch of salt
- Ground cinnamon, for garnish
- Sliced almonds or pistachios, for garnish (optional)

Utensils Needed:
1. Medium-sized saucepan
2. Whisk or wooden spoon
3. Heat-resistant spatula
4. Serving bowls or glasses
5. Plastic wrap or aluminum foil (for covering)

Recipe:
1. Combine Milk and Sugar:
- In a medium-sized saucepan, whisk together the whole milk and granulated sugar.

2. Warm the Milk Mixture:
- Heat the milk mixture over medium heat, stirring occasionally until it starts to steam. Do not boil.

3. Mix Cornstarch and Orange Blossom Water:
- In a separate bowl, mix the cornstarch with the orange blossom water until it forms a smooth paste.

4. Add Cornstarch Mixture to Milk:
- Gradually pour the cornstarch mixture into the warm milk while stirring constantly. This will thicken the pudding.

5. Continue Cooking:
- Keep stirring the mixture over medium heat until it thickens to a custard-like consistency. This should take about 5-7 minutes.

6. Add Vanilla and Salt:
- Once the pudding has thickened, remove the saucepan from the heat.
- Stir in the vanilla extract and a pinch of salt to enhance the flavors.

7. Pour into Serving Bowls:
- Pour the hot pudding into serving bowls or glasses. You can use one large bowl or individual serving dishes.

8. Chill the Pudding:
- Cover each bowl with plastic wrap or aluminum foil to prevent a skin from

forming on the pudding.

- Refrigerate the pudding for 2-4 hours, or preferably overnight, to cool and set completely.

9. Garnish and Serve:

- Before serving, remove the plastic wrap or aluminum foil from the bowls.

- Optionally, sprinkle ground cinnamon over the top of the pudding for a warm and aromatic touch.

- For added texture and flavor, you can garnish the pudding with sliced almonds or pistachios.

Nutritional Information (per serving, based on 6 servings):
- *Calories: Approximately 260 kcal*
- *Protein: 8g*
- *Fat: 8g*
- *Carbohydrates: 38g*
- *Fiber: 0g*
- *Sugar: 26g*

Recipe Notes:
- Orange blossom water is a key ingredient in this pudding, providing its distinct Moroccan flavor. You can find it in Middle Eastern or specialty stores.
- Adjust the amount of sugar according to your taste preference. Moroccan desserts tend to be moderately sweet, but you can increase or decrease the sugar to suit your liking.
- Make sure to stir the cornstarch mixture thoroughly before adding it to the warm milk to avoid lumps in the pudding.
- While stirring the milk mixture during cooking, pay attention to avoid scorching the bottom of the saucepan.
- The pudding will thicken further as it cools in the refrigerator.
- Moroccan Orange Blossom Water Pudding is traditionally served chilled and makes for a refreshing and delightful dessert, especially during warm weather or after a flavorful Moroccan meal.

Enjoy the delicate flavors and creamy texture of this Moroccan Orange Blossom Water Pudding as a lovely and aromatic treat!

Greek Loukoumades

Time to Prepare: 20 minutes **Cooking Time:** 20 minutes **Rising Time:** 1 hour **Servings:** About 30-40 loukoumades

Ingredients:
- 1 ½ cups all-purpose flour
- 1 cup lukewarm water
- 1 packet (2 ¼ teaspoons) active dry yeast
- ½ teaspoon salt
- 1 tablespoon granulated sugar
- Vegetable oil, for frying
- Honey, for drizzling
- Chopped nuts (e.g., walnuts or pistachios), for garnish optional
- Ground cinnamon, for garnish optional

Utensils Needed:
1. Large mixing bowl
2. Whisk or fork
3. Plastic wrap or clean kitchen towel
4. Deep frying pan or pot
5. Slotted spoon or spider strainer
6. Paper towels (for draining)
7. Serving plate or dish
8. Honey drizzler or spoon (for serving)

Recipe:

1. Prepare the Yeast Mixture:
- In a small bowl, dissolve the granulated sugar in lukewarm water.
- Sprinkle the active dry yeast over the water-sugar mixture.
- Let it sit for about 5-10 minutes until the yeast becomes frothy and activated.

2. Mix the Dough:
- In a large mixing bowl, combine the all-purpose flour and salt.
- Pour the activated yeast mixture into the flour mixture.
- Use a whisk or fork to mix everything together until a smooth batter is formed.

3. Let the Dough Rise:
- Cover the bowl with plastic wrap or a clean kitchen towel.
- Let the dough rise in a warm, draft-free place for about 1 hour or until it doubles in size.

4. Heat the Oil:
- In a deep frying pan or pot, heat vegetable oil to 350°F (175°C) over medium heat.
- You want enough oil to submerge the loukoumades while frying.

5. Fry the Loukoumades:
- Using two spoons or a small ice cream scoop, carefully drop spoonfuls of the risen dough into the hot oil.
- Fry the loukoumades in batches, being careful not to overcrowd the pan, for about 2-3 minutes per side or until they turn golden brown and puffed up.
- Use a slotted spoon or spider

strainer to remove the fried loukoumades from the oil and place them on paper towels to drain any excess oil.

6. Serve the Loukoumades:

- Transfer the loukoumades to a serving plate or dish.

- Drizzle honey generously over the loukoumades while they are still warm.

- Optionally, garnish with chopped nuts (e.g., walnuts or pistachios) and a sprinkle of ground cinnamon for added flavor and presentation.

Nutritional Information (per serving, based on 40 loukoumades):
- *Calories: Approximately 60 kcal*
- *Protein: 1g*
- *Fat: 1g*
- *Carbohydrates: 11g*
- *Fiber: 0g*
- *Sugar: 1g*

Recipe Notes:
- Loukoumades are best served fresh and warm, so try to enjoy them as soon as possible after frying.
- The rising time for the dough may vary depending on the room temperature and yeast activity. The goal is for the dough to double in size and become light and airy.
- Be cautious while frying the loukoumades, as they can puff up and expand quickly in the hot oil.
- You can customize the toppings to your liking. Apart from honey, you can drizzle them with chocolate sauce, caramel, or a flavored syrup like rose or orange blossom.
- Loukoumades are a popular dessert during Greek festivals and celebrations, and they are enjoyed by people of all ages.

Savor the deliciousness of these Greek Loukoumades, delightfully fluffy and coated in sweet honey for an irresistible treat!

Italian Cannoli

Time to Prepare: 1 hour   **Cooking Time**: 30 minutes   **Chilling Time**: 1 hour (for the filling)
Servings: About 16 cannoli

Ingredients:

For the Cannoli Shells:
- 2 cups all-purpose flour
- 2 tablespoons granulated sugar
- 1/4 teaspoon salt
- 2 tablespoons unsalted butter, softened
- 1/2 cup dry white wine or marsala wine
- 1 large egg white (for sealing)

For the Cannoli Filling:
- 2 cups ricotta cheese, drained (preferably whole milk ricotta)
- 1 cup powdered sugar
- 1 teaspoon vanilla extract
- 1/3 cup mini chocolate chips or chopped candied fruit (optional)

For Frying:
- Vegetable oil, for frying

Utensils Needed:
1. Stand mixer or hand mixer
2. Mixing bowls
3. Rolling pin
4. Cannoli tubes or metal cannoli molds
5. Deep-frying pan or pot
6. Slotted spoon
7. Paper towels (for draining)
8. Pastry bag or ziplock bag (for filling)

Recipe:

1. Prepare the Cannoli Dough:
- In a mixing bowl, combine the all-purpose flour, granulated sugar, and salt.
- Add the softened butter and mix until the mixture resembles coarse crumbs.
- Pour in the white wine or marsala wine and mix until a smooth dough forms.

2. Knead and Rest the Dough:
- Transfer the dough to a lightly floured surface and knead it for about 5 minutes until smooth and elastic.
- Wrap the dough in plastic wrap and let it rest at room temperature for 30 minutes.

3. Roll and Cut the Cannoli Shells:
- Divide the rested dough into two portions for easier handling.
- Roll out each portion of the dough thinly on a floured surface, about 1/8 inch thick.
- Using a round cutter or a glass, cut the dough into circles about 4-5 inches in diameter.

4. Wrap the Dough around the Cannoli Tubes:
- Wrap each circle of dough around a cannoli tube or metal cannoli mold, overlapping the edges slightly.
- Seal the edges with a small amount of beaten egg white to ensure they stay closed during frying.

5. Fry the Cannoli Shells:
- In a deep-frying pan or pot, heat vegetable oil to 350°F (175°C).
- Carefully fry the cannoli shells in batches until golden brown, about 2-3 minutes per batch.

- Use a slotted spoon to remove the shells from the hot oil and place them on paper towels to drain any excess oil.

6. Prepare the Cannoli Filling:

- In a mixing bowl, combine the drained ricotta cheese, powdered sugar, and vanilla extract.
- Optionally, add mini chocolate chips or chopped candied fruit for extra flavor and texture.

7. Chill the Cannoli Filling:

- Cover the cannoli filling with plastic wrap and refrigerate for at least 1 hour to allow the flavors to meld and the filling to set.

8. Fill the Cannoli Shells:

- Just before serving, transfer the chilled cannoli filling to a pastry bag or ziplock bag fitted with a large star tip.
- Carefully pipe the filling into each cannoli shell from both ends, filling them completely.

Nutritional Information (per cannoli shell with filling, based on 16 cannoli):
- *Calories: Approximately 180 kcal*
- *Protein: 4g*
- *Fat: 9g*
- *Carbohydrates: 20g*
- *Fiber: 1g*
- *Sugar: 8g*

Recipe Notes:
- For a traditional Italian cannoli experience, use marsala wine in the dough. However, you can substitute it with dry white wine or omit it altogether.
- Make sure to drain the ricotta cheese thoroughly to avoid a watery filling. You can place it in a fine-mesh sieve or cheesecloth-lined colander and refrigerate for a few hours before using.
- Optionally, dip the ends of the filled cannoli into chopped pistachios, chopped chocolate, or powdered sugar for added presentation and taste.
- Cannoli shells are best filled just before serving to maintain their crispy texture. Fill only the cannoli shells that will be consumed immediately and store any unfilled shells in an airtight container to retain their freshness.
- Italian cannoli are a delightful treat and a popular dessert during special occasions and celebrations.

Indulge in the delicious and authentic taste of Italian Cannoli, a beloved pastry filled with creamy ricotta cheese and adorned with delightful flavors!

Almond and Orange Blossom Flourless Cake

Time to Prepare: 20 minutes **Cooking Time:** 40-45 minutes **Servings:** 8-10

Ingredients:
For the Cake:
- 1 1/2 cups almond flour
- 1 cup granulated sugar
- 4 large eggs, separated (at room temperature)
- 1/2 cup unsalted butter, melted and cooled
- 1 tablespoon orange blossom water
- Zest of 1 orange
- Pinch of salt

For the Orange Syrup (optional):
- Juice of 1 orange
- 2 tablespoons granulated sugar
- 1 tablespoon orange blossom water

Utensils Needed:
1. 9-inch round cake pan
2. Parchment paper
3. Mixing bowl
4. Electric mixer or hand whisk
5. Fine-mesh sieve or sifter
6. Spatula or wooden spoon
7. Zester or grater (for orange zest)
8. Small saucepan (for syrup, if using)
9. Serving plate

Recipe:
1. Preheat the Oven:
- Preheat your oven to 350°F (175°C).
- Grease a 9-inch round cake pan and line the bottom with parchment paper.

2. Mix the Dry Ingredients:
- In a mixing bowl, whisk together the almond flour, granulated sugar, and a pinch of salt until well combined.

3. Add Egg Yolks and Butter:
- Add the egg yolks, melted butter, orange blossom water, and orange zest to the dry ingredients.
- Stir everything together until you have a smooth batter.

4. Whip the Egg Whites:
- In a separate bowl, using an electric mixer or hand whisk, whip the egg whites until stiff peaks form.

5. Fold Egg Whites into Batter:
- Gently fold the whipped egg whites into the almond batter using a spatula or wooden spoon.
- Be careful not to deflate the egg whites; you want to keep the batter light and airy.

6. Bake the Cake:
- Pour the batter into the prepared cake pan and spread it evenly.
- Bake the cake in the preheated oven for 40-45 minutes or until the top turns golden brown and a toothpick inserted into the center comes out clean.

7. Make the Orange Syrup (optional):

- If using the orange syrup, while the cake is baking, combine the orange juice and granulated sugar in a small saucepan over medium heat.
- Stir until the sugar dissolves and the syrup slightly thickens. Remove from heat and stir in the orange blossom water.

8. Cool and Serve:

- Once the cake is done baking, remove it from the oven and let it cool in the pan for about 10 minutes.
- Carefully transfer the cake to a serving plate.

9. Optional Syrup Drizzle:

- If using the orange syrup, poke a few holes in the top of the cake with a toothpick or skewer.
- Drizzle the warm orange syrup over the cake, allowing it to soak in.

Nutritional Information (per serving, based on 10 servings, without syrup):
- *Calories: Approximately 300 kcal*
- *Protein: 8g*
- *Fat: 22g*
- *Carbohydrates: 21g*
- *Fiber: 2g*
- *Sugar: 18g*

Recipe Notes:
- *Orange blossom water can be found in Middle Eastern or specialty stores and adds a delicate and aromatic orange flavor to the cake.*
- *Ensure that the egg whites are whipped to stiff peaks to achieve a light and airy texture in the cake.*
- *If you prefer a more intense orange flavor, you can increase the amount of orange zest or add a few drops of orange extract to the batter.*
- *This flourless cake is naturally gluten-free and is an excellent option for those with gluten sensitivities or Celiac disease.*
- *The optional orange syrup adds a moist and citrusy touch to the cake, but the cake is delicious on its own as well.*
- *Garnish the cake with some slivered almonds and a dusting of powdered sugar for an elegant presentation.*

Indulge in the delightful flavors of Almond and Orange Blossom Flourless Cake, a perfect dessert that's both gluten-free and bursting with a citrusy twist!

Mediterranean Bread And Snacks Recipes

Whole Wheat Olive Oil Flatbread

Preparation Time: 15 minutes **Cooking Time:** 15 minutes **Total Time:** 30 minutes **Yield:** 6 flatbreads

Ingredients:
- 2 cups whole wheat flour
- 1 teaspoon baking powder
- 1/2 teaspoon salt
- 3/4 cup warm water
- 1/4 cup extra-virgin olive oil, plus extra for brushing
- 1 tablespoon honey (optional)
- 2 tablespoons chopped fresh herbs (e.g., rosemary, thyme, oregano) (optional)
- Coarse sea salt for sprinkling (optional)

Utensils Needed:
- Large mixing bowl
- Wooden spoon or spatula
- Rolling pin
- Large flat skillet or griddle
- Tongs or spatula for flipping the flatbread
- Pastry brush

Instructions:
1. In a large mixing bowl, combine the whole wheat flour, baking powder, and salt. Mix well with a wooden spoon or spatula.

2. In a separate bowl, mix the warm water, olive oil, and honey (if using) until well combined.

3. Pour the wet ingredients into the dry ingredients and stir until a dough forms. If the dough feels too dry, add a little more warm water, a tablespoon at a time, until it comes together. Conversely, if it's too sticky, add a bit more flour.

4. Lightly flour a clean surface and knead the dough for about 2-3 minutes until it becomes smooth and elastic.

5. Divide the dough into 6 equal-sized balls. Cover them with a damp cloth or plastic wrap and let them rest for 10 minutes to relax the gluten.

6. Meanwhile, heat a large flat skillet or griddle over medium heat.

7. Take one of the dough balls and, using a rolling pin, roll it out into a thin round flatbread. Aim for a thickness of about 1/8 inch (3 mm).

8. Carefully place the flatbread onto the hot skillet. Cook for about 1-2 minutes on each side until you see bubbles forming and the bread starts to puff up slightly. If your

skillet is large enough, you can cook multiple flatbreads simultaneously.

9. While the flatbread is cooking, brush the top side with a little olive oil and sprinkle some fresh herbs and coarse sea salt (if using).

10. Once both sides are lightly browned and cooked through, remove the flatbread from the skillet using tongs or a spatula and place it on a plate lined with a clean kitchen towel to keep it warm.

11. Repeat the rolling and cooking process for the remaining dough balls.

12. Serve the whole wheat olive oil flatbread warm as a side to your favorite Mediterranean dishes or use it as a base for pizzas or wraps.

Enjoy your delicious and healthy Whole Wheat Olive Oil Flatbread!

Nutritional Information (per flatbread):
- *Calories: 210 kcal*
- *Total Fat: 8g*
- *Saturated Fat: 1g*
- *Trans Fat: 0g*
- *Cholesterol: 0mg*
- *Sodium: 200mg*
- *Total Carbohydrates: 31g*
- *Dietary Fiber: 4g*
- *Sugars: 2g*
- *Protein: 5g*

Recipe Notes:
- *This flatbread recipe can be easily customized by adding various herbs and spices, such as garlic powder, cumin, or sesame seeds, to the dough.*
- *Feel free to adjust the sweetness by adding more or less honey, or omit it altogether for a savory version.*
- *The flatbreads can be stored in an airtight container at room temperature for up to 2 days, but they are best enjoyed fresh.*

Mediterranean Bruschetta

Preparation Time: 15 minutes **Cooking Time:** 5 minutes **Total Time:** 20 minutes **Yield:** Approximately 12 bruschettas

Ingredients:
- 1 French baguette or Italian ciabatta loaf, sliced into 1/2-inch thick pieces
- 3 large ripe tomatoes, diced
- 1/4 cup Kalamata olives, pitted and chopped
- 1/4 cup crumbled feta cheese
- 2 tablespoons chopped fresh basil
- 2 tablespoons chopped fresh parsley
- 1 tablespoon balsamic vinegar
- 2 tablespoons extra-virgin olive oil
- 2 cloves garlic, peeled and halved
- Salt and black pepper to taste

Utensils Needed:
- Baking sheet
- Mixing bowl
- Small whisk or fork
- Chef's knife and cutting board
- Grill pan or stovetop griddle (optional)
- Pastry brush (optional)

Instructions:
1. Preheat your oven to 375°F (190°C). If you have a grill pan or stovetop griddle, you can preheat it over medium-high heat.

2. Place the sliced bread on a baking sheet and lightly brush one side of each slice with olive oil using a pastry brush or drizzling it over the bread.

3. Toast the bread in the preheated oven for about 5 minutes or until the slices are lightly golden and crispy. Alternatively, if you're using a grill pan or griddle, toast the bread slices on each side until they have grill marks and are slightly crunchy.

4. In a mixing bowl, combine the diced tomatoes, chopped olives, crumbled feta cheese, chopped basil, chopped parsley, balsamic vinegar, and extra-virgin olive oil. Mix well with a small whisk or fork to ensure all the ingredients are coated in the dressing. Season with salt and black pepper to taste.

5. Once the bread slices are toasted, remove them from the oven or grill pan and rub one side of each slice with the halved garlic cloves. This will infuse the bread with a subtle garlic flavor.

6. Spoon a generous amount of the Mediterranean tomato mixture onto the

garlic-rubbed side of each bread slice.

7. Arrange the bruschetta on a serving platter and garnish with additional chopped herbs if desired.

8. Serve the Mediterranean Bruschetta immediately as a delightful appetizer or light snack at your next gathering or party.

Enjoy the fresh and flavorful taste of this Mediterranean Bruschetta!

Nutritional Information (per bruschetta):
- *Calories: 110 kcal*
- *Total Fat: 4.5g*
- *Saturated Fat: 1g*
- *Trans Fat: 0g*
- *Cholesterol: 5mg*
- *Sodium: 210mg*
- *Total Carbohydrates: 14g*
- *Dietary Fiber: 1g*
- *Sugars: 1g*
- *Protein: 4g*

Recipe Notes:
- *Bruschetta is best served immediately after assembly to maintain the crispy texture of the bread. However, you can prepare the tomato mixture in advance and store it in the refrigerator. Toast the bread and assemble the bruschetta just before serving.*
- *If you prefer a more intense garlic flavor, you can rub the garlic cloves directly onto the toasted bread slices instead of adding them to the tomato mixture.*
- *Feel free to customize the toppings by adding ingredients such as roasted red peppers, artichoke hearts, or capers.*

Za'atar Pita Chips

Preparation Time: 10 minutes **Cooking Time**: 10-12 minutes **Total Time**: 22 minutes
Yield: Approximately 4 servings

Ingredients:
- 4 large pita bread rounds (whole wheat or white)
- 2 tablespoons extra-virgin olive oil
- 2 tablespoons za'atar seasoning
- 1/2 teaspoon garlic powder (optional)
- 1/2 teaspoon salt (adjust to taste)

Utensils Needed:
- Baking sheet
- Pastry brush
- Chef's knife and cutting board
- Small mixing bowl

Instructions:
1. Preheat your oven to 375°F (190°C).

2. Using a sharp knife, cut each pita bread round into 8 triangular pieces, similar to tortilla chips.

3. In a small mixing bowl, combine the olive oil, za'atar seasoning, garlic powder (if using), and salt. Mix well to form a smooth paste.

4. Place the pita triangles in a single layer on a baking sheet.

5. Using a pastry brush, coat one side of each pita triangle with the za'atar and olive oil mixture. Ensure that the seasoning is evenly spread.

6. Flip the pita triangles over and brush the other side with the remaining za'atar mixture.

7. Place the baking sheet in the preheated oven and bake for 10-12 minutes or until the pita chips turn golden and crispy. Keep an eye on them to avoid overcooking.

8. Once the pita chips are done, remove them from the oven and let them cool for a few minutes.

9. Serve the Za'atar Pita Chips as a tasty and nutritious snack. They go perfectly with hummus, yogurt-based dips, or as a side to your favorite Middle Eastern dishes.

10. Store any leftover pita chips in an airtight container to maintain their crispiness for a day or two.

Enjoy the flavorful and aromatic goodness of these Za'atar Pita Chips!

Nutritional Information (per serving):
- *Calories: 180 kcal*
- *Total Fat: 7g*

- Saturated Fat: 1g
- Trans Fat: 0g
- Cholesterol: 0mg

- Sodium: 350mg
- Total Carbohydrates: 25g
- Dietary Fiber: 3g

- Sugars: 1g
- Protein: 5g

Recipe Notes:
- Za'atar is a Middle Eastern spice blend typically made from dried thyme, sumac, sesame seeds, and salt. It is easily available in most grocery stores and specialty food markets. However, you can also make your own za'atar blend if you cannot find it in your area.
- You can customize the seasoning by adding other spices such as paprika, cumin, or red pepper flakes for an extra kick.
- Be sure to keep an eye on the pita chips while baking to prevent them from burning as oven temperatures may vary.

Cucumber Yogurt Dip

Preparation Time: 15 minutes **Total Time:** 15 minutes **Yield: Approximately** 2 cups

Ingredients:
- 1 large cucumber, grated and squeezed to remove excess moisture
- 2 cups plain Greek yogurt
- 2 cloves garlic, minced
- 1 tablespoon extra-virgin olive oil
- 1 tablespoon fresh lemon juice
- 1 tablespoon chopped fresh dill (or 1 teaspoon dried dill)
- 1 tablespoon chopped fresh mint (optional)
- Salt and black pepper to taste

Utensils Needed:
- Grater
- Mixing bowl
- Garlic press or mincer
- Whisk or fork

Instructions:
1. Begin by grating the cucumber using a box grater. After grating, place the cucumber in a clean kitchen towel or cheesecloth and squeeze out as much moisture as possible. This step is crucial to prevent the dip from becoming too watery.

2. In a mixing bowl, combine the grated and squeezed cucumber, Greek yogurt, minced garlic, extra-virgin olive oil, and fresh lemon juice.

3. Add the chopped dill and mint (if using) to the mixture.

4. Use a whisk or fork to mix all the ingredients together until well combined.

5. Season the cucumber yogurt dip with salt and black pepper to taste. Start with a small amount of salt and adjust to your preference.

6. Taste the dip and adjust the flavors, adding more lemon juice or dill if desired.

7. Once you are satisfied with the taste, transfer the cucumber yogurt dip to a serving bowl.

8. Optionally, garnish the dip with a drizzle of olive oil, a sprinkle of chopped dill or mint, and a few cucumber slices for an attractive presentation.

9. Serve the Cucumber Yogurt Dip immediately with an assortment of fresh vegetables, pita bread, or as a complement to grilled meats.

Enjoy this refreshing and tangy Cucumber Yogurt Dip at your next gathering or as a healthy snack!

Nutritional Information (per serving, about 2 tablespoons):
- Calories: 25 kcal

- Total Fat: 1g
- Saturated Fat: 0g
- Trans Fat: 0g
- Cholesterol: 2mg
- Sodium: 15mg
- Total Carbohydrates: 2g

- Dietary Fiber: 0g
- Sugars: 1g
- Protein: 2g

Recipe Notes:

- This cucumber yogurt dip, also known as Tzatziki, is a refreshing and healthy option for dipping vegetables, pita bread, or as a sauce for grilled meats and falafels.
- You can use regular yogurt if you don't have Greek yogurt, but Greek yogurt provides a thicker and creamier consistency.
- For a more pronounced garlic flavor, let the dip sit in the refrigerator for an hour or two before serving.
- This dip can be refrigerated in an airtight container for up to 3 days, but it's best when served fresh.

Moroccan Almond Cookies (Ghriba)

Preparation Time: 20 minutes **Cooking Time:** 15 minutes **Total Time**: 35 minutes **Yield:** Approximately 24 cookies

Ingredients:
- 2 cups almond flour
- 1 cup powdered sugar
- 1/2 teaspoon ground cinnamon
- 1/4 teaspoon ground nutmeg
- 1/4 teaspoon salt
- Zest of 1 lemon
- 2 large egg whites
- 1 teaspoon almond extract
- 1/4 cup whole almonds, blanched (optional, for decoration)
- Powdered sugar, for dusting

Utensils Needed:
- Mixing bowl
- Wooden spoon or spatula
- Baking sheet
- Parchment paper or silicone baking mat
- Electric hand mixer (optional, but helpful for beating egg whites)
- Zester or grater
- Small spoon or cookie scoop
- Cooling rack

Instructions:
1. Preheat your oven to 350°F (175°C). Line a baking sheet with parchment paper or a silicone baking mat.

2. In a mixing bowl, combine the almond flour, powdered sugar, ground cinnamon, ground nutmeg, salt, and lemon zest. Mix well using a wooden spoon or spatula.

3. In a separate bowl, whisk the egg whites until frothy. Add the almond extract to the beaten egg whites and mix to combine.

4. Pour the beaten egg whites and almond extract mixture into the dry ingredients. Stir until a soft and sticky dough forms.

5. Using a small spoon or cookie scoop, portion the dough onto the prepared baking sheet, leaving some space between each cookie.

6. Optionally, press a blanched almond into the center of each cookie for decoration.

7. Bake the cookies in the preheated oven for about 15 minutes or until they turn lightly golden around the edges.

8. Remove the cookies from the oven and allow them to cool on the baking sheet for a few minutes.

9. Carefully transfer the cookies to a

cooling rack to cool completely.

10. Once the cookies have cooled, lightly dust them with powdered sugar for an elegant finishing touch.

11. Store the Moroccan Almond Cookies in an airtight container at room temperature for up to one week.

Enjoy these delightful Moroccan Almond Cookies with a cup of tea or coffee, and savor the rich almond flavors and enticing spices!

Nutritional Information (per cookie):
- *Calories: 80 kcal*
- *Total Fat: 5g*
- *Saturated Fat: 0.4g*
- *Trans Fat: 0g*
- *Cholesterol: 0mg*
- *Sodium: 20mg*
- *Total Carbohydrates: 8g*
- *Dietary Fiber: 1g*
- *Sugars: 6g*
- *Protein: 2g*

Recipe Notes:
- *Almond flour can be easily made by grinding blanched almonds in a food processor until finely ground. Store-bought almond flour works well too.*
- *You can adjust the level of sweetness by increasing or decreasing the amount of powdered sugar.*
- *Traditional Ghriba cookies are gluten-free, but always double-check your almond flour to ensure it's gluten-free if you have dietary restrictions.*
- *Blanched whole almonds can be placed on top of the cookies before baking for added decoration and flavor, but they are optional.*

Italian Focaccia with Rosemary and Olives

Preparation Time: 20 minutes **Rising Time:** 1 hour 30 minutes **Cooking Time:** 25 minutes **Total Time:** 2 hours 15 minutes **Yield:** 1 large focaccia (about 12 servings)

Ingredients:
- 4 cups all-purpose flour
- 1 packet (2 1/4 teaspoons) active dry yeast
- 1 1/2 cups warm water
- 1/4 cup extra-virgin olive oil, plus extra for drizzling
- 1 teaspoon sugar
- 2 teaspoons salt
- 2 tablespoons fresh rosemary leaves, chopped
- 1/2 cup pitted Kalamata olives, halved
- Coarse sea salt for sprinkling

Utensils Needed:
- Large mixing bowl
- Plastic wrap or clean kitchen towel
- Baking sheet or rectangular baking pan (approximately 9x13 inches)
- Plastic wrap or silicone dough scraper (optional)
- Pastry brush
- Plastic fork or fingers for dimpling the dough

Instructions:

1. In a small bowl, combine the warm water, sugar, and active dry yeast. Stir gently and let it sit for about 5 minutes until it becomes frothy.

2. In a large mixing bowl, add the flour and salt. Mix well.

3. Pour the yeast mixture and olive oil into the flour mixture. Stir until the dough comes together.

4. Transfer the dough onto a floured surface and knead for about 5-7 minutes until it becomes smooth and elastic. If using a stand mixer, knead the dough with the dough hook attachment for the same duration.

5. Form the dough into a ball and place it back into the mixing bowl. Cover the bowl with plastic wrap or a clean kitchen towel.

6. Let the dough rise in a warm, draft-free area for about 1 hour or until it has doubled in size.

7. Preheat your oven to 425°F (220°C). Lightly oil a baking sheet or rectangular baking pan.

8. Punch down the risen dough and transfer it to the prepared baking sheet. Gently press and stretch the dough to fit the pan.

9. Using your fingers or a plastic fork, create dimples all over the dough, pressing down slightly. This is a

traditional focaccia texture.

10. Drizzle the top of the focaccia with extra-virgin olive oil, ensuring it fills the dimples.

11. Sprinkle the chopped rosemary leaves and halved olives over the dough.

12. Finally, lightly sprinkle coarse sea salt over the top for added flavor.

13. Allow the dough to rest for an additional 15-20 minutes while the oven finishes preheating.

14. Bake the focaccia in the preheated oven for 20-25 minutes or until the top turns golden brown.

15. Remove the focaccia from the oven and let it cool slightly before cutting it into squares or wedges.

16. Serve the Italian Focaccia with Rosemary and Olives warm as a delicious appetizer, side dish, or accompaniment to salads and soups.

Enjoy the delightful flavors of this classic Italian focaccia!

Nutritional Information (per serving, based on 12 servings):
- *Calories: 230 kcal*
- *Total Fat: 8g*
- *Saturated Fat: 1g*
- *Trans Fat: 0g*
- *Cholesterol: 0mg*
- *Sodium: 490mg*
- *Total Carbohydrates: 34g*
- *Dietary Fiber: 2g*
- *Sugars: 0g*
- *Protein: 5g*

Recipe Notes:
- Focaccia is a versatile bread that can be customized with various toppings, such as cherry tomatoes, red onions, or cheese.
- The rising time may vary depending on the ambient temperature. The dough should approximately double in size during the rising process.
- The olive oil plays a crucial role in giving the focaccia its characteristic soft and chewy texture. Don't skimp on it.
- You can use either a stand mixer with a dough hook or mix the dough by hand.
- If you prefer a thinner focaccia, you can divide the dough into two portions and shape them on separate baking sheets.

Greek Pita Bread with Hummus

Preparation Time: 15 minutes **Rising Time:** 1 hour 30 minutes **Cooking Time:** 10 minutes **Total Time:** 1 hour 55 minutes **Yield:** 8 pita breads and approximately 2 cups of hummus

Ingredients for Pita Bread:
- 2 1/2 cups all-purpose flour
- 1 packet (2 1/4 teaspoons) active dry yeast
- 1 teaspoon sugar
- 1 cup warm water
- 1 tablespoon olive oil
- 1 teaspoon salt

Ingredients for Hummus:
- 1 can (15 ounces) chickpeas (garbanzo beans), drained and rinsed
- 1/4 cup tahini (sesame paste)
- 3 tablespoons fresh lemon juice
- 2 garlic cloves, minced
- 2 tablespoons extra-virgin olive oil
- 1/2 teaspoon ground cumin
- 1/4 teaspoon ground paprika
- Salt and black pepper to taste
- Water (for adjusting consistency)

Utensils Needed for Pita Bread:
- Large mixing bowl
- Plastic wrap or clean kitchen towel
- Baking sheet
- Rolling pin
- Pastry brush
- Non-stick skillet or griddle

Utensils Needed for Hummus:
- Food processor or blender
- Rubber spatula
- Serving bowl

Instructions for Pita Bread:
1. In a small bowl, combine the warm water, sugar, and active dry yeast. Stir gently and let it sit for about 5 minutes until it becomes frothy.
2. In a large mixing bowl, add the flour and salt. Mix well.
3. Pour the yeast mixture and olive oil into the flour mixture. Stir until a dough forms.
4. Transfer the dough onto a floured surface and knead for about 5-7 minutes until it becomes smooth and elastic. You can also use a stand mixer with a dough hook for this step.
5. Form the dough into a ball and place it back into the mixing bowl. Cover the bowl with plastic wrap or a clean kitchen towel.
6. Let the dough rise in a warm, draft-free area for about 1 hour or until it has doubled in size.
7. Preheat your non-stick skillet or griddle over medium-high heat.
8. Punch down the risen dough and divide it into 8 equal-sized pieces.
9. On a floured surface, roll each dough piece into a circle, about 6 inches in diameter and 1/4 inch thick.
10. Carefully place one rolled-out dough circle onto the preheated skillet or griddle. Cook for about 1-2 minutes on each side or until puffed and lightly browned.
11. Repeat the process for the remaining dough circles.

Instructions for Hummus:
1. In a food processor or blender, combine the

drained and rinsed chickpeas, tahini, lemon juice, minced garlic, extra-virgin olive oil, ground cumin, ground paprika, salt, and black pepper.

2. Blend the ingredients until smooth, scraping down the sides of the processor or blender as needed. If the hummus is too thick, add water, a tablespoon at a time, until you achieve your desired consistency.

3. Taste the hummus and adjust the seasonings to your preference. You can add more lemon juice, garlic, or spices if desired.

4. Transfer the hummus to a serving bowl.

Assembly:

1. Cut the Greek pita bread in half to form pockets.

2. Fill each pita pocket with a generous amount of homemade hummus.

3. Serve the Greek Pita Bread with Hummus as a delightful and nutritious appetizer, snack, or light lunch.

Enjoy the authentic flavors of Greece with this delicious combination of Greek pita bread and homemade hummus!

Nutritional Information (per serving, based on 1 pita bread and 1/4 cup of hummus):
- *Pita Bread:*

- *Calories: 160 kcal*
- *Total Fat: 2g*
- *Saturated Fat: 0g*
- *Trans Fat: 0g*
- *Cholesterol: 0mg*
- *Sodium: 240mg*
- *Total Carbohydrates: 31g*
- *Dietary Fiber: 1g*
- *Sugars: 0g*
- *Protein: 5g*

- *Hummus (1/4 cup):*
- *Calories: 140 kcal*
- *Total Fat: 10g*
- *Saturated Fat: 1g*
- *Trans Fat: 0g*
- *Cholesterol: 0mg*
- *Sodium: 150mg*
- *Total Carbohydrates: 9g*
- *Dietary Fiber: 3g*
- *Sugars: 0g*
- *Protein: 4g*

Recipe Notes:
- Pita bread can be made ahead of time and stored in an airtight container for up to 3 days. Hummus can also be prepared in advance and refrigerated for up to 5 days.
- Traditional Greek pita bread is typically soft and thin, making it perfect for stuffing with various fillings like hummus and veggies.
- For a creamier hummus, you can add a little more tahini or olive oil.
- Adjust the seasonings in the hummus to your taste. You can also add other ingredients like roasted red pepper or sun-dried tomatoes for additional flavor variations.

Turkish Simit

Preparation Time: 30 minutes **Rising Time:** 1 hour 30 minutes **Cooking Time:** 15 minutes **Total Time:** 2 hours 15 minutes **Yield:** Approximately 12 simit

Ingredients:
- 4 cups all-purpose flour
- 2 teaspoons active dry yeast
- 1 cup warm water
- 1/4 cup vegetable oil
- 1/4 cup plain yogurt
- 2 tablespoons granulated sugar
- 1 teaspoon salt
- 1 large egg, beaten (for egg wash)
- 1/2 cup sesame seeds

Utensils Needed:
- Large mixing bowl
- Small bowl
- Plastic wrap or clean kitchen towel
- Baking sheet
- Parchment paper or silicone baking mat
- Pastry brush
- Large shallow dish or plate (for sesame seed coating)

Instructions:
1. In a small bowl, combine the warm water, sugar, and active dry yeast. Stir gently and let it sit for about 5 minutes until it becomes frothy.

2. In a large mixing bowl, add the flour and salt. Mix well.

3. Pour the yeast mixture, vegetable oil, and plain yogurt into the flour mixture. Mix until a dough forms.

4. Transfer the dough onto a floured surface and knead for about 8-10 minutes until it becomes smooth and elastic. You can also use a stand mixer with a dough hook for this step.

5. Form the dough into a ball and place it back into the mixing bowl. Cover the bowl with plastic wrap or a clean kitchen towel.

6. Let the dough rise in a warm, draft-free area for about 1 hour or until it has doubled in size.

7. Preheat your oven to 400°F (200°C). Line a baking sheet with parchment paper or a silicone baking mat.

8. Punch down the risen dough and divide it into 12 equal-sized pieces.

9. Roll each dough piece into a long rope, about 12-14 inches in length.

10. Join the ends of each rope to form a circle and twist them together to create the classic simit shape. Press the ends firmly to seal.

11. In a large shallow dish or plate, spread the sesame seeds.

12. Dip each simit into the beaten egg, making sure it is coated all over.

13. Immediately coat the simit with sesame seeds, pressing gently to adhere the seeds to the dough.

14. Place the sesame-coated simit onto the prepared baking sheet.

15. Repeat the process for the remaining dough pieces.

16. Let the simit rest for about 10-15 minutes before baking.

17. Bake the simit in the preheated oven for 12-15 minutes or until they turn golden brown.

18. Remove the simit from the oven and let them cool slightly on a wire rack.

19. Serve the Turkish Simit warm or at room temperature, alongside Turkish tea or as a delightful snack.

Enjoy the delicious and authentic flavors of Turkish Simit!

Nutritional Information (per simit):
- *Calories: 230 kcal*
- *Total Fat: 9g*
- *Saturated Fat: 1g*
- *Trans Fat: 0g*
- *Cholesterol: 20mg*
- *Sodium: 200mg*
- *Total Carbohydrates: 31g*
- *Dietary Fiber: 1g*
- *Sugars: 3g*
- *Protein: 6g*

Recipe Notes:
- *Simit is a traditional Turkish bread, similar to a bagel, but coated in sesame seeds and typically served with tea or eaten as a snack.*
- *You can use black or white sesame seeds for coating, or a combination of both for a more visually appealing result.*
- *The egg wash gives the simit a beautiful golden color and adds shine to the sesame seed coating.*
- *Simit is best enjoyed fresh on the day of baking, but you can store any leftovers in an airtight container for up to 2 days. Reheat briefly in the oven or toaster before serving.*

Sicilian Arancini (Rice Balls)

Preparation Time: 30 minutes **Cooking Time:** 30 minutes **Total Time:** 1 hour **Yield:** Approximately 12 arancini

Ingredients:
- 2 cups Arborio rice (or any short-grain rice)
- 4 cups chicken or vegetable broth
- 1/2 cup grated Parmesan cheese
- 1/4 cup chopped fresh parsley
- 2 large eggs
- 8 ounces mozzarella cheese, cut into small cubes
- 1 cup breadcrumbs
- Vegetable oil, for frying
- Salt and black pepper to taste
- Marinara sauce, for serving (optional)

Utensils Needed:
- Large saucepan
- Wooden spoon
- Mixing bowl
- Plastic wrap or clean kitchen towel
- Deep fryer or large, deep skillet
- Slotted spoon or spider strainer
- Paper towels (for draining excess oil)

Instructions:
1. In a large saucepan, bring the chicken or vegetable broth to a simmer. Add the Arborio rice and cook according to package instructions until it's tender and the liquid is absorbed.

2. Remove the cooked rice from the heat and stir in the grated Parmesan cheese, chopped parsley, and one beaten egg. Season with salt and black pepper to taste. Let the rice cool completely.

3. Once the rice is cooled, take a handful of rice and flatten it in your palm. Place a small cube of mozzarella cheese in the center and carefully shape the rice around the cheese, forming a ball. Repeat this process to create 12 arancini.

4. In a shallow bowl, beat the remaining egg. Dip each arancino into the beaten egg, ensuring it is coated on all sides.

5. Roll the arancini in the breadcrumbs until they are evenly coated.

6. Place the breaded arancini on a baking sheet and cover them with plastic wrap or a clean kitchen towel. Chill the arancini in the refrigerator for at least 30 minutes. This step helps them hold their shape during frying.

7. In a deep fryer or large, deep skillet, heat vegetable oil to 350°F (180°C).

8. Carefully lower a few arancini into the hot oil using a slotted spoon or spider strainer. Fry them in batches to avoid overcrowding the oil.

9. Fry the arancini until they are golden brown and crispy, about 4-5 minutes per batch.

10. Using the slotted spoon or spider strainer, remove the fried arancini from the oil and place them on a plate lined with paper towels to drain excess oil.

11. Repeat the frying process for the remaining arancini.

12. Serve the Sicilian Arancini warm, optionally with marinara sauce for dipping.

Enjoy the crispy and cheesy goodness of these classic Sicilian Arancini as a delicious appetizer or snack!

Nutritional Information (per arancino):
- *Calories: 200 kcal*
- *Total Fat: 8g*
- *Saturated Fat: 3.5g*
- *Trans Fat: 0g*
- *Cholesterol: 45mg*
- *Sodium: 280mg*
- *Total Carbohydrates: 23g*
- *Dietary Fiber: 1g*
- *Sugars: 1g*
- *Protein: 9g*

Recipe Notes:
- *Arancini can be made with various fillings. The traditional filling is mozzarella and meat sauce, but you can also use other cheeses, vegetables, or even a mix of ragù and peas.*
- *Use chilled rice when shaping the arancini, as it holds its shape better and is easier to handle.*
- *Make sure the oil is hot enough before frying the arancini to achieve a crispy exterior and to prevent them from becoming too greasy.*

Spanakopita Triangles

Preparation Time: 30 minutes **Cooking Time:** 25 minutes **Total Time:** 55 minutes **Yield:** Approximately 20-24 triangles

Ingredients:
- 10 ounces frozen spinach, thawed and well-drained (or 1 pound fresh spinach, blanched and chopped)
- 1 cup crumbled feta cheese
- 1/2 cup ricotta cheese
- 1/4 cup chopped fresh dill
- 1/4 cup chopped fresh parsley
- 1/2 cup chopped green onions (or finely diced yellow onion)
- 2 large eggs, lightly beaten
- 1/4 teaspoon ground nutmeg
- Salt and black pepper to taste
- 1 package (16 ounces) phyllo dough, thawed
- 1/2 cup unsalted butter, melted

Utensils Needed:
- Large mixing bowl
- Pastry brush
- Baking sheet
- Plastic wrap or clean kitchen towel
- Chef's knife and cutting board

Instructions:
1. Preheat your oven to 375°F (190°C). Grease a baking sheet or line it with parchment paper.

2. In a large mixing bowl, combine the well-drained spinach, crumbled feta cheese, ricotta cheese, chopped dill, chopped parsley, chopped green onions, beaten eggs, ground nutmeg, salt, and black pepper. Mix well until all the ingredients are evenly distributed.

3. Unroll the phyllo dough and cover it with plastic wrap or a damp clean kitchen towel to keep it from drying out.

4. Take one sheet of phyllo dough and place it on a clean work surface. Brush the entire sheet with melted butter.

5. Place another sheet of phyllo dough on top of the first one, and brush it with butter as well. Repeat this process with 2 more sheets of phyllo dough, so you have a stack of 4 buttered sheets.

6. Cut the buttered phyllo stack lengthwise into 3 equal strips.

7. Place a spoonful of the spinach and cheese filling at the bottom of each strip, leaving a small border around the edges.

8. Fold the bottom corner of the strip over the filling to form a triangle. Continue folding the strip in a

triangular shape until you reach the top, like folding a flag. Seal the edges with a little butter to keep the triangle secure. Repeat this process with the remaining phyllo dough and filling.

9. Place the assembled spanakopita triangles on the prepared baking sheet.

10. Brush the tops of the triangles with more melted butter.

11. Bake the spanakopita triangles in the preheated oven for 20-25 minutes or until they turn golden brown and crispy.

12. Remove the triangles from the oven and let them cool for a few minutes before serving.

Serve the delicious and flaky Spanakopita Triangles as an appetizer or party snack, and enjoy the delightful taste of Greek cuisine!

Nutritional Information (per triangle, based on 24 triangles):
- *Calories: 80 kcal*
- *Total Fat: 5g*
- *Saturated Fat: 3g*
- *Trans Fat: 0g*
- *Cholesterol: 25mg*
- *Sodium: 125mg*
- *Total Carbohydrates: 6g*
- *Dietary Fiber: 1g*
- *Sugars: 0g*
- *Protein: 3g*

Recipe Notes:
- *Spanakopita triangles are a classic Greek appetizer made with layers of flaky phyllo dough filled with a savory spinach and cheese mixture.*
- *Phyllo dough is delicate and dries out quickly. Keep it covered with plastic wrap or a damp clean kitchen towel while working with it to prevent it from becoming brittle.*
- *You can use fresh or frozen spinach for this recipe. If using frozen spinach, make sure to thaw it completely and drain it well to remove excess moisture.*
- *Spanakopita triangles can be assembled in advance and frozen. To bake frozen triangles, add a few extra minutes to the baking time.*

Mediterranean Beverages Recipes

Mint Lemonade

Time to Prepare: 15 minutes **Cooking Time:** 0 minutes **Servings:** 4

Ingredients:
- 4 cups cold water
- 1 cup freshly squeezed lemon juice (about 4-5 lemons)
- 1/2 cup granulated sugar (adjust to taste)
- 1/4 cup fresh mint leaves, tightly packed
- Ice cubes, for serving
- Lemon slices and fresh mint sprigs, for garnish

Utensils Needed:
- Pitcher or large glass jar
- Citrus juicer or lemon squeezer
- Wooden spoon or muddler
- Strainer or sieve
- Tall glasses

Recipe:
1. Start by washing the lemons thoroughly under cold running water to remove any dirt or pesticides. Pat them dry with a clean towel.

2. Cut each lemon in half and use a citrus juicer or lemon squeezer to extract the juice. Pour the freshly squeezed lemon juice through a strainer to catch any seeds or pulp, into a pitcher or large glass jar.

3. In a small bowl, combine the granulated sugar and fresh mint leaves. Use a wooden spoon or muddler to gently crush the mint leaves, releasing their flavor and aroma. This step helps infuse the mint flavor into the lemonade.

4. Transfer the crushed mint and sugar mixture into the pitcher with the lemon juice.

5. Add the cold water to the pitcher as well. Stir the mixture until the sugar dissolves completely.

6. Taste the lemonade and adjust the sweetness or tartness to your liking. You can add more sugar if you prefer it sweeter or more lemon juice if you want it tangier.

7. Fill tall glasses with ice cubes and pour the mint lemonade over the ice.

8. Garnish each glass with a lemon slice and a sprig of fresh mint for a beautiful presentation.

9. Serve the mint lemonade immediately and enjoy its refreshing flavor!

Nutritional Information (per serving):
- *Calories: 85 kcal*
- *Carbohydrates: 22g*
- *Sugars: 20g*
- *Fat: 0g*
- *Protein: 0g*
- *Fiber: 1g*
- *Vitamin C: 34mg (38% DV)*
- *Iron: 0.2mg (1% DV)*

Recipe Notes:
- For a more intense mint flavor, you can let the crushed mint and sugar mixture sit in the lemon juice for about 10 minutes before adding the water. This will allow the mint to infuse even more into the lemonade.

- If you want to make the lemonade in advance, you can prepare the lemon juice, sugar, and mint mixture and keep it refrigerated. Add the cold water and ice just before serving to maintain the freshness and fizziness.

- You can customize this recipe by adding a splash of sparkling water or soda for a fizzy mint lemonade variation.

- To make it a "Mint Limeade," you can substitute lime juice for the lemon juice, following the same steps.

- The nutritional information provided is approximate and may vary based on the actual ingredients used.

Mint lemonade is a perfect refreshing drink for hot summer days, and the combination of mint and lemon makes it incredibly invigorating. Enjoy this delightful beverage with friends and family, and stay cool during the scorching weather!

Greek Frappe Coffee

Time to Prepare: 5 minutes **Cooking Time:** 0 minutes **Servings:** 1

Ingredients:
- 2 teaspoons instant coffee (preferably Greek or Nescafé)
- 2 teaspoons granulated sugar (adjust to taste)
- 2 tablespoons cold water
- 1 cup cold milk (whole or skim, depending on preference)
- Ice cubes
- Optional: 1-2 tablespoons evaporated milk or whipped cream for a creamier version

Utensils Needed:
- Tall glass (around 12-16 oz capacity)
- Cocktail shaker or handheld milk frother
- Drinking straw
- Long-handled spoon

Recipe:
1. In the tall glass, add the instant coffee and granulated sugar.

2. Pour the cold water into the glass.

3. Use a cocktail shaker or a handheld milk frother to vigorously shake or froth the coffee mixture for about 20-30 seconds. If using a frother, plunge it up and down rapidly to create a foamy consistency.

4. The coffee mixture should now have a thick, frothy foam on top. Fill the glass with ice cubes almost to the top.

5. Slowly pour the cold milk over the ice until it reaches near the brim of the glass.

6. If you prefer a creamier frappe, add 1-2 tablespoons of evaporated milk or top it off with a dollop of whipped cream.

7. Optionally, you can stir the milk and foam gently with a long-handled spoon to combine the flavors.

8. Insert a drinking straw into the glass and serve immediately.

Nutritional Information (per serving):
- *Calories: 50 kcal*
- *Carbohydrates: 8g*
- *Sugars: 8g*
- *Fat: 0g*
- *Protein: 4g*
- *Fiber: 0g*

Recipe Notes:
- *Greek frappe coffee is typically served without any additional flavorings or syrups, but you can customize it by adding a splash of vanilla or almond extract if desired.*

- Adjust the sweetness to your liking by adding more or less sugar. Some people prefer their frappe very sweet, while others enjoy a less sweet version to savor the coffee flavor.

- To make the coffee stronger, you can add an extra teaspoon of instant coffee. Likewise, for a milder taste, reduce the amount of coffee used.

- If you don't have a cocktail shaker or handheld frother, you can also achieve a frothy coffee by combining the coffee, sugar, and water in a jar with a tight-fitting lid. Shake the jar vigorously until you get a foam. Then proceed with the recipe as mentioned.

- If you're using sweetened evaporated milk or whipped cream, you may want to adjust the amount of sugar in the coffee mixture to avoid an overly sweet beverage.

- Frappe coffee is a popular summer drink in Greece and is enjoyed both indoors and outdoors. It's a great way to beat the heat and enjoy a cold, refreshing coffee.

- The nutritional information provided is approximate and may vary based on the actual ingredients used, especially if you customize the recipe with additional milk or cream.

Greek frappe coffee is a delightful and easy-to-make beverage that offers a smooth and frothy coffee experience. Whether you're a coffee enthusiast or just looking for a unique and refreshing coffee treat, the Greek frappe won't disappoint! Enjoy it in the company of friends, or as a solo pick-me-up during a warm afternoon.

Moroccan Mint Tea

Time to Prepare: 5 minutes **Cooking Time:** 10 minutes **Servings:** 4

Ingredients:
- 4 cups water
- 3-4 teaspoons loose green tea leaves (gunpowder green tea is traditional, but any green tea will work)
- 1 bunch fresh mint leaves (about 1 cup), plus extra for garnish
- 4-6 teaspoons granulated sugar (adjust to taste)
- Optional: Moroccan tea glasses or heat-resistant glass cups for serving

Utensils Needed:
- Teapot or medium-sized saucepan with a lid
- Tea strainer or fine-mesh sieve
- Teacups or glasses for serving
- Teapot warmer (optional, but helps to keep the tea warm)
- Teaspoon for stirring

Recipe:
1. In a teapot or medium-sized saucepan, bring the water to a boil over medium heat.

2. Once the water boils, remove the pot from the heat and add the loose green tea leaves to the water. Let the tea steep for about 1 minute. (If you prefer a stronger tea, you can let it steep for up to 3 minutes, but be cautious as green tea can become bitter if steeped for too long.)

3. While the tea is steeping, rinse the fresh mint leaves under cold running water to remove any impurities.

4. Add the fresh mint leaves to the pot with the steeped green tea.

5. Return the pot to the heat and bring it to a boil again.

6. Add the sugar to the pot, starting with 4 teaspoons, and stir until the sugar is completely dissolved. You can add more sugar to taste if you prefer a sweeter tea.

7. Allow the tea to boil for another 2-3 minutes to infuse the flavors of the mint.

8. Remove the pot from the heat and strain the tea using a tea strainer or fine-mesh sieve into a separate container.

9. Pour the Moroccan mint tea into teacups or heat-resistant glass cups for serving.

10. Optionally, garnish each cup with a sprig of fresh mint.

11. Serve the tea hot and enjoy its soothing and refreshing flavor!

Nutritional Information (per serving, without sugar):	- Calories: 0 kcal - Carbohydrates: 0g - Sugars: 0g - Fat: 0g	- Protein: 0g - Fiber: 0g

Recipe Notes:

- Traditionally, Moroccan mint tea is served very sweet. Feel free to adjust the amount of sugar to your taste preferences. You can also try using honey as a natural sweetener for a different flavor profile.

- While green tea is the most common base for Moroccan mint tea, you can experiment with other types of tea like white tea or even a blend of green and black tea.

- Moroccan mint tea is typically poured from a height into the cups, creating a frothy layer on top. This is done to enhance the flavor and mix the ingredients thoroughly. However, it requires some skill, so don't worry if you're not able to do it right away.

- Moroccan mint tea is often served as a symbol of hospitality and is a central part of Moroccan culture and social gatherings.

- To keep the tea warm for an extended period, you can use a teapot warmer or place the teapot on a heat-resistant surface like a trivet.

- The nutritional information provided is based on the tea without any added sugar. The calorie and carbohydrate content will vary depending on the amount of sugar you add.

Moroccan mint tea is not only a delicious beverage but also a beautiful cultural tradition. Its aromatic blend of mint and green tea is a wonderful treat to enjoy on its own or paired with Moroccan sweets and pastries. Invite friends over and immerse yourself in the Moroccan tea-drinking experience!

Red Wine Sangria

Time to Prepare: 15 minutes **Chilling Time:** 2-4 hours (or overnight) **Servings:** 6

Ingredients:
- 1 bottle (750 ml) red wine (Spanish Rioja, Merlot, or any fruity red wine)
- 1/4 cup brandy or orange liqueur (e.g., Triple Sec)
- 1/4 cup simple syrup (or more, to taste)
- 1 cup orange juice
- 1 cup apple juice or apple cider
- 1 medium orange, thinly sliced
- 1 medium lemon, thinly sliced
- 1 medium lime, thinly sliced
- 1 medium apple, cored and thinly sliced
- 1 cup mixed fresh berries (strawberries, blueberries, raspberries)
- 2-3 cups ice cubes

Utensils Needed:
- Large pitcher
- Long-handled spoon
- Wine glasses or tumblers for serving

Recipe:
1. In a large pitcher, pour the red wine, brandy or orange liqueur, simple syrup, orange juice, and apple juice or apple cider. Stir well to combine all the liquids.

2. Add the thinly sliced orange, lemon, lime, and apple to the pitcher.

3. Toss in the mixed fresh berries.

4. Stir everything together gently with a long-handled spoon to ensure the flavors are well combined.

5. Cover the pitcher with plastic wrap or a lid and place it in the refrigerator to chill for at least 2-4 hours, or ideally overnight. Chilling allows the flavors to meld and infuse, making the sangria even more delicious.

6. When you're ready to serve, add the ice cubes to the pitcher and give it a final gentle stir.

7. Pour the red wine sangria into wine glasses or tumblers filled with some ice.

8. Garnish each glass with a few fresh berries and citrus slices for an appealing presentation.

9. Sip, savor, and enjoy your refreshing homemade red wine sangria!

Nutritional Information (per serving, estimated):
(Note: The following nutritional information is approximate and may vary depending on the specific ingredients and brands used.)
- *Calories: 200 kcal*
- *Carbohydrates: 19g*
- *Sugars: 12g*
- *Fat: 0g*
- *Protein: 1g*
- *Fiber: 2g*

Recipe Notes:

- To make simple syrup, combine equal parts sugar and water in a small saucepan. Bring the mixture to a simmer over medium heat, stirring until the sugar dissolves completely. Let it cool before using. You can adjust the sweetness of the sangria by adding more or less simple syrup, depending on your preference.

- Feel free to customize your sangria with your favorite fruits. Besides the ones listed, you can add peaches, plums, kiwis, or any other fruits you enjoy.

- To add some fizz to your sangria, you can top off each glass with a splash of club soda or sparkling water just before serving.

- If you're short on time and need to serve the sangria immediately, you can use chilled red wine and serve it over plenty of ice. However, for the best flavor, allowing the sangria to chill and infuse in the refrigerator is recommended.

- The nutritional information provided is approximate and may vary based on the specific brands and quantities of ingredients used.

- This recipe can easily be doubled or halved to accommodate larger or smaller gatherings.

Red wine sangria is a delightful and fruity drink that's perfect for gatherings, parties, or even a relaxing evening at home. Its vibrant colors and refreshing taste make it a crowd-pleaser, and it's a wonderful way to enjoy the flavors of various fruits combined with a good quality red wine. Enjoy responsibly and savor the moments with friends and family!

Fresh Fruit Smoothies

Time to Prepare: 10 minutes **Cooking Time**: 0 minutes **Servings:** 2

Ingredients:
- 1 cup fresh or frozen mixed fruits (e.g., strawberries, blueberries, bananas, mangoes, peaches)
- 1 cup plain yogurt or Greek yogurt
- 1/2 cup milk (dairy or plant-based)
- 1 tablespoon honey or maple syrup (optional, adjust to taste)
- 1/2 teaspoon vanilla extract (optional, for added flavor)
- Ice cubes (if using fresh fruits)
- Fresh fruit slices, mint leaves, or chia seeds for garnish (optional)

Utensils Needed:
- Blender or smoothie maker
- Measuring cups and spoons
- Glasses or jars for serving

Recipe:
1. Wash and prepare the fresh fruits by removing any pits, stems, or peels as needed. If using frozen fruits, make sure they are thawed slightly to ease the blending process.

2. In the blender, add the mixed fruits, yogurt, milk, honey or maple syrup (if using), and vanilla extract (if using).

3. If using fresh fruits and you prefer a colder smoothie, add a few ice cubes to the blender.

4. Put the lid on the blender securely and blend the ingredients on high speed until the mixture becomes smooth and creamy. This should take about 1-2 minutes.

5. Taste the smoothie and adjust the sweetness or flavorings as desired. If it's too thick, you can add a little more milk to achieve your preferred consistency.

6. Once the smoothie is well blended and has reached your desired taste and texture, pour it into glasses or jars for serving.

7. Optionally, you can garnish each smoothie with fresh fruit slices, mint leaves, or a sprinkle of chia seeds for added visual appeal.

8. Serve the fresh fruit smoothies immediately and enjoy the delightful combination of flavors!

Nutritional Information (per serving):
(Note: The following nutritional information is approximate and may vary depending on the specific ingredients and quantities used.)
- *Calories: 150 kcal*
- *Carbohydrates: 26g*
- *Sugars: 20g*
- *Fat: 4g*
- *Protein: 7g*
- *Fiber: 3g*

Recipe Notes:

- Feel free to customize your smoothie with your favorite fruits and combinations. Berries, tropical fruits, and bananas work particularly well in smoothies.

- If you prefer a thicker smoothie, you can add more yogurt or reduce the amount of milk. On the other hand, if you like a thinner consistency, increase the milk or use more liquid.

- To make the smoothie more indulgent, you can add a scoop of vanilla or fruit-flavored ice cream, but keep in mind that it will increase the calorie content.

- For a dairy-free version, use plant-based yogurt and milk alternatives like almond milk, soy milk, or coconut milk.

- If you want to boost the nutritional value, consider adding a handful of spinach or kale to the blender. The mild flavor of the fruits will mask the taste of the greens.

- Smoothies are an excellent way to use ripe fruits, as their sweetness enhances the overall taste.

- To make the smoothies in advance, you can store them in the refrigerator for a few hours, but they are best consumed shortly after preparation to retain their freshness and nutrients.

- Get creative with the garnishes and use sliced fruits, a sprinkle of cinnamon, a dollop of yogurt, or a drizzle of honey to make your smoothies even more appealing.

Fresh fruit smoothies are not only delicious but also a nutritious way to start your day or enjoy as a refreshing snack. They are packed with vitamins, fiber, and antioxidants from the fruits and offer a creamy and satisfying treat for any time of the day. Cheers to good health and enjoyable taste!

Italian Limoncello

Time to Prepare: 30 minutes (approximately 24 servings)

Infusing Time: 7 days

Servings: Makes about 3 cups

Ingredients:
- 6-8 large lemons (organic if possible)
- 750 ml (3 cups) high-quality vodka or grain alcohol (at least 40% alcohol by volume)
- 2 cups water
- 1 1/2 cups granulated sugar

Utensils Needed:
- Vegetable peeler or zester
- Airtight glass jar or large glass container
- Fine-mesh sieve or cheesecloth
- Funnel
- Glass bottles with stoppers or caps for storing

Recipe:
1. Wash the lemons thoroughly under cold running water to remove any dirt or wax. Pat them dry with a clean towel.

2. Using a vegetable peeler or zester, carefully remove the outer yellow zest from the lemons, avoiding the white pith, which can impart bitterness. Place the zest in a large glass container or airtight jar.

3. Pour the vodka or grain alcohol over the lemon zest in the container.

4. Seal the container tightly and place it in a cool, dark place for at least 7 days, shaking it gently every day to help infuse the flavors.

5. After 7 days, the alcohol should have taken on a bright yellow color and the lemon zest should be fragrant.

6. In a saucepan, combine the water and granulated sugar. Heat the mixture over medium heat, stirring until the sugar dissolves completely. This creates a simple syrup.

7. Allow the simple syrup to cool completely to room temperature.

8. Strain the infused alcohol through a fine-mesh sieve or cheesecloth into a separate bowl or pitcher.

9. Add the cooled simple syrup to the strained lemon-infused alcohol, stirring to combine.

10. Using a funnel, carefully pour the Limoncello into clean

glass bottles with stoppers or caps for storing.

11. Seal the bottles tightly and store them in the refrigerator or freezer.

12. Serve the Limoncello well-chilled in small liqueur glasses as a delightful after-dinner digestif.

Recipe Notes:
- The quality of the lemons is crucial for a delicious Limoncello. Use organic lemons if possible, as they will be free from any chemical residues or waxes.

- You can adjust the sweetness of the Limoncello by adding more or less simple syrup. Some people prefer it sweeter, while others enjoy a more intense lemon flavor with less sweetness.

- The longer the lemon zest infuses in the alcohol, the more intense the lemon flavor will be. You can infuse it for up to a month for a stronger taste.

- Limoncello is best served well-chilled, so consider storing it in the freezer to achieve the desired temperature.

- The alcohol content of the Limoncello will vary depending on the type of alcohol used. Vodka typically has an alcohol by volume (ABV) of 40%, while grain alcohol can have a higher ABV.

- Limoncello can be stored in the refrigerator for several months or in the freezer for even longer without significant changes in flavor or quality.

- Consider using decorative glass bottles for gifting your homemade Limoncello to friends and family. Personalize the labels or add a ribbon for a special touch.

Limoncello is a popular Italian liqueur known for its bright lemon flavor and smooth finish. It's a wonderful drink to savor after a meal or to enjoy as a refreshing aperitif. With its vibrant color and citrusy taste, Limoncello captures the essence of the Mediterranean and brings a taste of Italy to any occasion. Sip and savor the authentic Italian experience!

Turkish Coffee

Time to Prepare: 5 minutes **Cooking Time:** 5 minutes **Servings:** 2

Ingredients:
- 2 cups cold water
- 2 tablespoons finely ground Turkish coffee (you can buy pre-ground Turkish coffee or grind it to a fine consistency at home)
- 2 teaspoons granulated sugar (adjust to taste, optional)
- Pinch of ground cardamom (optional, for added flavor)

Utensils Needed:
- Traditional Turkish coffee pot (cezve/ibrik) or a small saucepan
- Turkish coffee cups (small, handleless cups)
- Small spoon or coffee stirrer
- Serving tray (optional)

Recipe:
1. Measure the cold water using the Turkish coffee cups you plan to serve the coffee in. The coffee cups typically hold about 1/2 cup of liquid each.

2. Pour the cold water into the Turkish coffee pot or a small saucepan.

3. Add the finely ground Turkish coffee to the water in the pot.

4. Optionally, add the granulated sugar to the coffee mixture. Turkish coffee is traditionally served unsweetened, but you can adjust the sweetness to your preference.

5. Optionally, sprinkle a pinch of ground cardamom over the coffee for a delightful aroma and taste. Cardamom is a popular spice used in Turkish coffee, but you can omit it if you prefer.

6. Place the coffee pot or saucepan over low to medium heat.

7. Slowly heat the coffee mixture, stirring gently with a small spoon or coffee stirrer to combine the coffee with the water.

8. As the coffee heats up, you will notice a layer of foam forming on top. Be careful not to let it boil over, as Turkish coffee should not be boiled.

9. Once the coffee begins to foam and the grounds have settled at the bottom, remove the pot from the heat.

10. Allow the coffee to sit for a minute or two to allow any remaining grounds to settle.

11. Carefully pour the Turkish coffee into the small coffee cups, making sure not to disturb the settled grounds.

12. Serve the Turkish coffee immediately, along with a glass of water to cleanse your palate between sips.

Recipe Notes:

- Turkish coffee is typically served without milk. If you prefer your coffee with milk, you can add a small amount of warmed milk to the coffee cups before pouring in the coffee.

- The cardamom is optional but adds a unique and aromatic flavor to the coffee. If you don't have ground cardamom, you can crush a few cardamom pods and add them to the coffee during brewing.

- Turkish coffee is often enjoyed with a small sweet treat, such as Turkish delight or a piece of baklava.

- It's common to read the coffee grounds after drinking Turkish coffee as a form of fortune-telling. The grounds remaining at the bottom of the cup can form patterns that are believed to reveal glimpses of the future.

- Turkish coffee is an integral part of Turkish culture and is traditionally served during social gatherings and special occasions.

- When ordering Turkish coffee in a café or restaurant, you can specify how sweet you want it. The options are usually sade (unsweetened), az sekerli (a little sugar), orta sekerli (medium sugar), or çok sekerli (very sweet).

Turkish coffee is more than just a beverage; it's a cherished cultural tradition. Sip this strong and flavorful coffee slowly, and enjoy the moment as you partake in an age-old ritual that has been passed down through generations in Turkey and beyond.

Greek Iced Coffee (Frappe)

Time to Prepare: 5 minutes **Cooking Time**: 0 minutes **Servings**: 1

Ingredients:
- 2 teaspoons instant coffee (preferably Greek or Nescafé)
- 2 teaspoons granulated sugar (adjust to taste)
- 2 tablespoons cold water
- 1/2 cup cold milk (whole or skim, depending on preference)
- Ice cubes
- Optional: 1-2 tablespoons evaporated milk or whipped cream for a creamier version

Utensils Needed:
- Shaker bottle or cocktail shaker
- Drinking straw
- Tall glass

Recipe:
1. In a shaker bottle or cocktail shaker, add the instant coffee and granulated sugar.
2. Pour the cold water into the shaker.
3. Seal the shaker with the lid and shake vigorously for about 20-30 seconds. This will create a frothy coffee mixture.
4. Fill a tall glass with ice cubes.
5. Pour the frothy coffee mixture over the ice, making sure to include all the foam.
6. Add the cold milk to the glass, pouring it gently over the coffee mixture.
7. If you prefer a creamier frappe, add 1-2 tablespoons of evaporated milk or top it off with a dollop of whipped cream.
8. Insert a drinking straw into the glass.
9. Give the frappe a gentle stir to mix the coffee, milk, and foam together.
10. Serve the Greek iced coffee immediately and enjoy its creamy and refreshing taste!

Nutritional Information (per serving):
(Note: The nutritional information may vary based on the specific ingredients and quantities used.)
- *Calories: 30 kcal*
- *Carbohydrates: 5g*
- *Sugars: 5g*
- *Fat: 0g*
- *Protein: 1g*
- *Fiber: 0g*

Recipe Notes:
- Greek iced coffee, known as "Frappe," is a beloved and popular summer drink in Greece. It is typically enjoyed cold, and its frothy texture sets it apart from other iced coffee variations.

- The key to making a great frappe is to achieve a thick and creamy foam. Shaking the instant coffee and sugar with cold water is the secret behind creating the foam. The longer you shake, the more foam you'll get.

- Frappe is usually made with instant coffee, but you can also experiment with espresso if you prefer a stronger coffee flavor.

- Adjust the sweetness to your liking by adding more or less sugar. Some people enjoy a sweeter frappe, while others prefer it less sweet to taste the coffee better.

- To make a dairy-free version, you can use plant-based milk like almond milk, soy milk, or coconut milk.

- To enhance the coffee flavor, you can add a splash of coffee liqueur like Kahlúa or a drop of vanilla extract.

- For a fun twist, you can blend the coffee, ice, milk, and sugar in a blender instead of using a shaker. This method will create a slushier texture.

- Frappe is a great beverage to enjoy on a hot summer day or whenever you need a refreshing pick-me-up.

- The nutritional information provided is approximate and may vary based on the actual ingredients used, especially if you customize the recipe with additional milk or cream.

Greek iced coffee (Frappe) is an iconic and easy-to-make beverage that will transport you to the sunny shores of Greece. Its frothy and creamy texture combined with the rich coffee taste makes it an irresistible treat for coffee lovers. Sip it leisurely and let its coolness energize your day!

Spanish Sangria Blanca

Time to Prepare: 15 minutes **Chilling Time**: 2-4 hours (or overnight) **Servings:** 6

Ingredients:
- 1 bottle (750 ml) dry white wine (e.g., Sauvignon Blanc, Pinot Grigio, or Albariño)
- 1/2 cup brandy
- 1/4 cup triple sec or Cointreau
- 1/4 cup simple syrup (adjust to taste)
- 1 cup orange juice
- 1 medium lemon, thinly sliced
- 1 medium lime, thinly sliced
- 1 medium green apple, cored and thinly sliced
- 1 cup green grapes, halved
- 2-3 cups ice cubes

Utensils Needed:
- Large pitcher
- Long-handled spoon
- Wine glasses or tumblers for serving

Recipe:
1. In a large pitcher, combine the white wine, brandy, triple sec or Cointreau, simple syrup, and orange juice.

2. Add the thinly sliced lemon, lime, and green apple to the pitcher.

3. Toss in the halved green grapes.

4. Stir all the ingredients together gently with a long-handled spoon to ensure the flavors are well combined.

5. Cover the pitcher with plastic wrap or a lid and place it in the refrigerator to chill for at least 2-4 hours, or ideally overnight. Chilling allows the flavors to meld and infuse, making the sangria even more flavorful.

6. When you're ready to serve, add the ice cubes to the pitcher and give it a final gentle stir.

7. Pour the Spanish Sangria Blanca into wine glasses or tumblers filled with some ice.

8. Optionally, garnish each glass with a slice of lemon or lime or a few green grapes for an elegant presentation.

9. Serve the Sangria Blanca well-chilled and enjoy its crisp, fruity, and refreshing taste!

Nutritional Information (per serving):
(Note: The following nutritional information is approximate and may vary depending on the specific ingredients and quantities used.)
- *Calories: 230 kcal*
- *Carbohydrates: 25g*
- *Sugars: 17g*
- *Fat: 0g*
- *Protein: 1g*
- *Fiber: 1g*

Recipe Notes:

- To make simple syrup, combine equal parts sugar and water in a small saucepan. Bring the mixture to a simmer over medium heat, stirring until the sugar dissolves completely. Let it cool before using. You can adjust the amount of simple syrup to your preference for sweetness.

- Spanish Sangria Blanca is traditionally made with dry white wine, but you can experiment with other varieties to suit your taste preferences.

- For a non-alcoholic version, you can substitute the wine, brandy, and triple sec with white grape juice or apple juice. Increase the amount of orange juice to maintain the fruity flavor.

- Feel free to customize the fruit selection to your liking. You can add other fruits like white peaches, nectarines, or kiwis to enhance the taste and appearance.

- If you prefer a sweeter sangria, you can add more simple syrup or use a sweeter white wine. For a less sweet version, reduce the amount of simple syrup or use a drier white wine.

- Spanish Sangria Blanca is a delightful beverage for warm weather gatherings, parties, or any festive occasion. Its light and refreshing taste make it perfect for sipping on a sunny day.

- The nutritional information provided is approximate and may vary based on the specific ingredients and quantities used.

Spanish Sangria Blanca is a wonderful twist on the classic red sangria. With its beautiful array of fruits and a hint of citrus, it's a captivating and irresistible drink that will delight your guests and elevate any celebration. So raise your glasses and toast to the flavors of Spain!

Mint-Infused Water

Time to Prepare: 5 minutes **Chilling Time**: 1-2 hours (optional) **Servings**: 4

Ingredients:
- 4 cups water (filtered or still water)
- 1 small bunch fresh mint leaves (about 1/2 cup loosely packed)
- 1 small lemon or lime, thinly sliced (optional)
- Ice cubes

Utensils Needed:
- Pitcher or large glass container
- Long-handled spoon or muddler
- Serving glasses

Recipe:
1. Wash the fresh mint leaves thoroughly under cold running water to remove any dirt or impurities. Pat them dry with a clean towel.

2. In a pitcher or large glass container, add the fresh mint leaves.

3. If you're using lemon or lime slices, add them to the pitcher along with the mint leaves.

4. Pour the water over the mint and citrus slices in the pitcher.

5. Using a long-handled spoon or a muddler, gently press down on the mint leaves and citrus slices to release their flavors. This will help infuse the water with the refreshing taste of mint and a hint of citrus.

6. Optionally, add some ice cubes to the pitcher to chill the water and keep it cool while it infuses.

7. Cover the pitcher with a lid or plastic wrap and let the water sit at room temperature for at least 1-2 hours. This will allow the flavors of the mint and citrus to meld with the water.

8. Alternatively, if you prefer a more intense infusion or want to serve the water immediately, place the pitcher in the refrigerator for about 30 minutes.

9. When the water is sufficiently infused, give it a final stir to mix the flavors.

10. Pour the mint-infused water into serving glasses filled with ice cubes.

11. Optionally, you can garnish each glass with a fresh sprig of mint or a slice of lemon or lime.

12. Serve the mint-infused water immediately and enjoy its refreshing taste!

Recipe Notes:

- Mint-infused water is a versatile and refreshing beverage that can be enjoyed on its own or alongside meals. It's a great way to stay hydrated and add a burst of flavor to plain water without any added sugars or calories.

- You can adjust the strength of the mint flavor by using more or fewer mint leaves. If you prefer a subtle mint taste, use a smaller amount of mint; for a bolder flavor, add more leaves.

- Adding citrus slices like lemon or lime is optional, but it adds a pleasant tangy note to the water. Feel free to customize the infusion with other fruits like oranges, cucumbers, or berries.

- If you want to serve the mint-infused water immediately, you can use chilled water or add extra ice cubes to the pitcher. The longer the water sits, the more pronounced the mint and citrus flavors will become.

- You can refill the pitcher with water a couple of times before the mint loses its flavor. However, for the best taste, prepare a fresh batch of mint-infused water after a day or two.

- Mint-infused water is a wonderful base for creating various flavored water combinations. Feel free to experiment with other herbs, fruits, or even a touch of ginger or cucumber for a unique twist.

- The nutritional information provided is approximate and may vary based on the actual ingredients used and the serving size.

Mint-infused water is a delightful and healthy alternative to sugary beverages. It offers a cooling and invigorating taste that's perfect for warm days or when you need a refreshing drink. Keep a pitcher of mint-infused water in the fridge, and you'll have a delicious and thirst-quenching treat ready to enjoy at any time!

Mediterranean Appetizers And Salads Recipes

Greek Salad with Feta and Kalamata Olives

Time to Prepare: 20 minutes **Cooking Time:** 0 minutes

Ingredients:
- 3 large ripe tomatoes, diced
- 1 cucumber, peeled and diced
- 1 red onion, thinly sliced
- 1 green bell pepper, diced
- 1 cup Kalamata olives, pitted and halved
- 200g feta cheese, crumbled
- 2 tablespoons extra-virgin olive oil
- 1 tablespoon red wine vinegar
- 1 teaspoon dried oregano
- Salt and black pepper to taste
- Freshly chopped parsley for garnish (optional)

Utensils Needed:
- Large mixing bowl
- Cutting board and knife
- Whisk or fork for dressing
- Salad tongs or large spoon

Instructions:

1. Wash and prepare the vegetables:
- Wash the tomatoes, cucumber, and green bell pepper under cold running water.
- Dice the tomatoes and cucumber into bite-sized pieces and place them in a large mixing bowl.
- Thinly slice the red onion and dice the green bell pepper. Add them to the bowl.

2. Prepare the dressing:
- In a small bowl, whisk together the extra-virgin olive oil, red wine vinegar, dried oregano, salt, and black pepper until well combined. Adjust the seasoning to your liking.

3. Assemble the salad:
- Pour the dressing over the diced vegetables in the mixing bowl. Toss gently to ensure all the ingredients are coated with the dressing.

4. Add the olives and feta cheese:
- Add the Kalamata olives to the salad and gently toss them in with the vegetables.
- Crumble the feta cheese over the top of the salad.

5. Garnish and serve:
- If desired, sprinkle freshly chopped parsley on top of the salad for added freshness and color.
- Serve immediately as a refreshing appetizer, side dish, or a light main course.

Enjoy your delicious and authentic Greek Salad with Feta and

Kalamata Olives! It's a perfect accompaniment to grilled meats or as a stand-alone meal on its own.

Nutritional Information (per serving):
- *Calories: approximately 250 kcal*
- *Carbohydrates: 10g*
- *Protein: 8g*

- *Fat: 20g*
- *Fiber: 3g*
- *Vitamin C: 40mg*
- *Calcium: 200mg*
- *Iron: 2mg*

Recipe Notes:

- This Greek salad is a perfect light and refreshing dish for hot summer days or any time you crave a healthy and delicious meal.
- Feel free to adjust the quantities of ingredients to suit your taste preferences. Some people prefer more tomatoes or cucumber, while others might want extra olives or feta cheese.
- Make sure to use good quality extra-virgin olive oil and red wine vinegar as they are key components of the dressing and contribute to the authentic Greek flavor.
- If you can't find Kalamata olives, you can substitute them with any other good-quality black olives, preferably ones with a slightly tart and briny taste.
- Traditional Greek salads do not include lettuce, but if you prefer a bit of greenery, you can add some torn Romaine lettuce or mixed salad greens.

Hummus with Whole Grain Pita Bread

Time to Prepare: 15 minutes **Cooking Time:** 0 minutes

Ingredients for Hummus:

- 1 can (15 oz) chickpeas (garbanzo beans), drained and rinsed
- 1/4 cup tahini (sesame paste)
- 3 tablespoons freshly squeezed lemon juice
- 2 cloves garlic, minced
- 1/2 teaspoon ground cumin
- 1/2 teaspoon salt (adjust to taste)
- 3 tablespoons extra-virgin olive oil
- 2-3 tablespoons water (adjust for desired consistency)
- Optional toppings: drizzle of olive oil, sprinkle of paprika, chopped parsley

Ingredients for Whole Grain Pita Bread:

- 4 whole grain pita bread rounds

Utensils Needed:

- Food processor or blender
- Mixing bowl
- Spoon or spatula for serving
- Toaster or oven (optional, for warming pita bread)

Instructions:

1. Prepare the Hummus:

- In a food processor or blender, add the drained and rinsed chickpeas, tahini, freshly squeezed lemon juice, minced garlic, ground cumin, and salt.
- Process or blend until the mixture is well combined and starts to become smooth.

2. Add Olive Oil and Water:

- While the food processor or blender is running, drizzle in the extra-virgin olive oil. This will help make the hummus creamier.
- If the hummus is too thick for your liking, add 2-3 tablespoons of water, one tablespoon at a time, until you achieve the desired consistency.

3. Adjust Seasoning:

- Taste the hummus and adjust the seasoning as needed. You can add more salt, lemon juice, or garlic according to your preference.

4. Serve the Hummus:

- Transfer the hummus to a serving bowl.
- If desired, drizzle a little extra-virgin olive oil on top and sprinkle with paprika or chopped parsley for added flavor and presentation.

5. Prepare the Whole Grain Pita Bread:

- You can serve the pita bread as is or warm it up for a few minutes in a toaster or oven. Warming the pita will make it softer and more pliable for dipping.

6. Serve and Enjoy:

- Serve the hummus with the warm or room-temperature whole grain pita bread on the side.

- You can also serve the hummus with sliced veggies (carrots, cucumber, bell peppers) for a delicious and healthy snack or appetizer.

Enjoy your homemade Hummus with Whole Grain Pita Bread! It's a fantastic dip for parties, gatherings, or a delightful addition to your daily snacking routine.

Nutritional Information (per serving - hummus, based on approximately 1/4 cup):
- *Calories: 150 kcal*
- *Carbohydrates: 10g*
- *Protein: 5g*
- *Fat: 11g*
- *Fiber: 4g*

Recipe Notes:
- *Hummus is a popular Middle Eastern dip made from chickpeas, tahini, and various seasonings. It's creamy, nutritious, and incredibly versatile.*
- *You can adjust the seasonings and ingredients according to your taste preferences. Some people like to add a bit more lemon juice or garlic for extra tang and flavor.*
- *Store-bought tahini works well for this recipe, but you can also make your own by blending toasted sesame seeds and oil until smooth.*
- *Whole grain pita bread is a healthier option than regular pita bread, as it contains more fiber and nutrients.*

Caprese Salad with Fresh Basil

Time to Prepare: 10 minutes **Cooking Time:** 0 minutes

Ingredients:
- 2 large ripe tomatoes
- 200g fresh mozzarella cheese
- Fresh basil leaves
- Extra-virgin olive oil
- Balsamic glaze (optional)
- Salt and black pepper to taste

Utensils Needed:
- Sharp knife
- Cutting board
- Serving plate
- Small bowl (for optional balsamic glaze)

Instructions:

1. Wash and Slice the Tomatoes:
- Wash the tomatoes under cold running water and pat them dry with a paper towel.
- Using a sharp knife, slice the tomatoes into ¼-inch thick rounds. Try to make even and attractive slices.

2. Slice the Fresh Mozzarella:
- Similarly, slice the fresh mozzarella into ¼-inch thick rounds. Ensure they are similar in size to the tomato slices for a balanced presentation.

3. Arrange the Salad:
- On a serving plate, start by arranging a layer of tomato slices.
- Place a fresh mozzarella slice on top of each tomato slice.
- Take a fresh basil leaf and gently tear it into smaller pieces. Sprinkle the torn basil leaves over the mozzarella.

4. Season the Salad:
- Drizzle extra-virgin olive oil over the salad, ensuring it touches each tomato and mozzarella slice.
- Optionally, if using balsamic glaze, drizzle a small amount over the salad for a tangy and sweet touch.
- Sprinkle a pinch of salt and freshly ground black pepper over the salad to enhance the flavors.

5. Serve and Enjoy:
- The Caprese Salad is best served immediately after preparation to enjoy the freshness and vibrant flavors of the ingredients.
- It can be served as an appetizer, a light side dish, or even as a main course for a light lunch.

Recipe Variation:
- *For a more visually appealing presentation, you can also arrange the tomato and mozzarella slices in an alternating pattern, slightly overlapping each other in a circle on a round serving*

tuck the leaves in between the slices for a beautiful Caprese Salad wreath.

Enjoy your refreshing and delightful Caprese Salad with Fresh Basil!

It's a wonderful addition to any meal and perfect for showcasing the best of summer's bounty.

Nutritional Information (per serving):

- Calories: approximately 200 kcal
- Carbohydrates: 3g
- Protein: 15g
- Fat: 14g
- Fiber: 1g
- Calcium: 300mg
- Vitamin C: 20mg

Notes:

- Caprese Salad is a classic Italian dish that highlights the delicious combination of ripe tomatoes, fresh mozzarella cheese, and aromatic basil. It's simple, light, and bursting with flavors.
- The quality of the ingredients is crucial for the success of this dish. Use the ripest and juiciest tomatoes, high-quality fresh mozzarella, and fragrant basil leaves.
- If you can find it, use authentic Italian buffalo mozzarella (mozzarella di bufala) for an even more delightful experience.
- Balsamic glaze is a sweet and tangy reduction of balsamic vinegar. It complements the flavors of the salad but is optional. You can easily make it by reducing balsamic vinegar in a saucepan over low heat until it thickens.

Tabbouleh

Time to Prepare: 20 minutes **Cooking Time:** 0 minutes (No cooking required)

Ingredients:
- 1 cup bulgur wheat
- 1 1/2 cups boiling water
- 2 cups fresh parsley leaves, finely chopped
- 1/2 cup fresh mint leaves, finely chopped
- 2 medium tomatoes, diced
- 1/2 cucumber, diced
- 1/4 cup red onion, finely chopped
- 1/4 cup extra-virgin olive oil
- 1/4 cup freshly squeezed lemon juice
- Salt and black pepper to taste

Utensils Needed:
- Medium-sized bowl
- Fine mesh strainer
- Fork
- Knife and cutting board
- Mixing spoon
- Serving bowl

Instructions:
1. Prepare the Bulgur Wheat:
- Place the bulgur wheat in a medium-sized bowl.
- Pour the boiling water over the bulgur wheat, ensuring it is fully submerged.
- Cover the bowl with a plate or lid and let it sit for about 15 minutes to allow the bulgur to absorb the water and soften.

2. Rinse and Drain the Bulgur Wheat:
- After 15 minutes, use a fine mesh strainer to drain any excess water from the bulgur wheat.
- Use a fork to fluff the bulgur wheat and break up any clumps.

3. Chop the Fresh Herbs and Vegetables:
- Finely chop the fresh parsley and mint leaves and add them to the bulgur wheat in the bowl.
- Dice the tomatoes and cucumber and finely chop the red onion. Add them to the bowl as well.

4. Prepare the Dressing:
- In a separate small bowl, whisk together the extra-virgin olive oil, freshly squeezed lemon juice, salt, and black pepper to make the dressing.

5. Combine the Ingredients:
- Pour the dressing over the bulgur wheat and vegetable mixture in the bowl.
- Use a mixing spoon to gently toss and combine all the ingredients until well coated with the dressing.

6. Adjust Seasoning:
- Taste the tabbouleh and adjust the seasoning if

needed. Add more salt, pepper, or lemon juice according to your preference.

7. Serve and Enjoy:

- Transfer the tabbouleh to a serving bowl and garnish with additional parsley or mint leaves if desired.
- Serve immediately or refrigerate for a few hours before serving to allow the flavors to meld together.

Enjoy your delicious and refreshing Tabbouleh! It's a fantastic salad to accompany grilled meats, as a side dish, or as a light and healthy meal on its own.

Nutritional Information (per serving - based on approximately 1 cup):
- *Calories: approximately 200 kcal*
- *Carbohydrates: 28g*
- *Protein: 5g*
- *Fat: 8g*
- *Fiber: 6g*
- *Vitamin C: 45mg*
- *Iron: 2mg*

Recipe Notes:
- *Tabbouleh is a popular Middle Eastern salad made with bulgur wheat, fresh herbs, tomatoes, and other vegetables, dressed with lemon juice and olive oil. It's a refreshing and nutritious dish perfect for hot days.*
- *Traditionally, tabbouleh is heavy on the parsley and mint, so be sure to use a generous amount of these herbs for an authentic flavor.*
- *You can adjust the ingredient quantities to suit your taste preferences. Some people prefer more tomatoes or cucumber, while others may want to add a touch of garlic or green onions.*
- *For a gluten-free version, you can substitute the bulgur wheat with quinoa, millet, or finely chopped cauliflower.*

Stuffed Grape Leaves (Dolma or Dolmades)

Time to Prepare: 45 minutes **Cooking Time**: 1 hour 30 minutes

Ingredients:
- 1 jar (about 60-70) grape leaves in brine, rinsed and drained
- 1 cup long-grain white rice
- 1/2 cup finely chopped onions
- 1/4 cup finely chopped fresh dill
- 1/4 cup finely chopped fresh mint
- 1/4 cup pine nuts (optional)
- 1/4 cup extra-virgin olive oil
- 2 cups vegetable broth or water
- 1/4 cup freshly squeezed lemon juice
- Salt and black pepper to taste
- Greek yogurt or tzatziki sauce for serving (optional)

Utensils Needed:
- Large pot with a lid
- Fine mesh strainer
- Cutting board and knife
- Small mixing bowl
- Spoon or fork for mixing
- Deep oven-safe casserole dish or Dutch oven
- Plate or lid for weighing down the stuffed grape leaves during cooking

Instructions:

1. Prepare the Rice Filling:
- Rinse the rice under cold running water in a fine mesh strainer until the water runs clear.
- In a small mixing bowl, combine the rinsed rice, finely chopped onions, dill, mint, pine nuts (if using), extra-virgin olive oil, lemon juice, salt, and black pepper. Mix well until everything is evenly combined.

2. Stuff the Grape Leaves:
- Lay a grape leaf flat on the cutting board, vein side up, and remove any tough stem parts.
- Place about a teaspoon of the rice filling near the stem end of the grape leaf.
- Fold the sides of the leaf over the filling and then roll it up tightly into a small cylinder shape.
- Repeat the process with the remaining grape leaves and rice filling until everything is used up.

3. Arrange in a Cooking Pot:
- Line the bottom of the deep oven-safe casserole dish or Dutch oven with a few extra grape leaves or a thin layer of sliced onions (optional).
- Arrange the stuffed grape leaves tightly in layers, seam side down, until the

bottom of the pot is covered. Continue stacking them in layers until all the leaves are used.

4. Add Liquid and Cook:

- Pour the vegetable broth or water over the stuffed grape leaves in the pot.

- Place a plate or lid directly on top of the stuffed grape leaves to weigh them down during cooking. This helps them stay compact and prevents them from unraveling.

- Cover the pot with the lid and cook over low heat for about 1 hour and 30 minutes or until the rice is fully cooked and tender.

5. Cool and Serve:

- Once cooked, remove the stuffed grape leaves from the pot and let them cool to room temperature.

- You can serve them at room temperature or chilled from the refrigerator.

- Optionally, serve with Greek yogurt or tzatziki sauce on the side for dipping.

Enjoy your delicious Stuffed Grape Leaves (Dolma/Dolmades)! They make a delightful appetizer or side dish, and their tangy and herby flavors will impress your guests at any gathering or party.

Nutritional Information (per serving - about 3-4 stuffed grape leaves):
- *Calories: approximately 150 kcal*
- *Carbohydrates: 18g*
- *Protein: 3g*
- *Fat: 8g*
- *Fiber: 1g*
- *Vitamin C: 4mg*
- *Iron: 1mg*

Recipe Notes:
- *Stuffed grape leaves, known as dolma or dolmades in Greek and Middle Eastern cuisines, are a delightful appetizer or side dish. They are typically served cold or at room temperature, making them a great make-ahead dish for parties and gatherings.*
- *Grape leaves in brine can be found in jars at specialty stores or online. If using fresh grape leaves, blanch them in boiling water for a few seconds to soften before using.*
- *The pine nuts add a delightful crunch and flavor to the stuffing, but you can omit them if you have nut allergies or prefer a nut-free version.*

Mediterranean Quinoa Salad

Time to Prepare: 15 minutes **Cooking Time:** 20 minutes

Ingredients:
- 1 cup quinoa
- 2 cups water or vegetable broth
- 1/2 cup cherry tomatoes, halved
- 1/2 cucumber, diced
- 1/4 cup Kalamata olives, pitted and halved
- 1/4 cup red onion, finely chopped
- 1/4 cup crumbled feta cheese
- 1/4 cup fresh parsley, chopped
- 1/4 cup fresh mint, chopped
- 1/4 cup extra-virgin olive oil
- 2 tablespoons freshly squeezed lemon juice
- 1 garlic clove, minced
- Salt and black pepper to taste

Utensils Needed:
- Fine mesh strainer
- Medium-sized saucepan with a lid
- Large mixing bowl
- Cutting board and knife
- Whisk or fork for dressing

Instructions:

1. Cook the Quinoa:
- Rinse the quinoa in a fine mesh strainer under cold running water.
- In a medium-sized saucepan, bring 2 cups of water or vegetable broth to a boil.
- Add the rinsed quinoa to the boiling liquid, reduce the heat to low, cover the saucepan with a lid, and simmer for about 15-20 minutes or until the quinoa is cooked and the liquid is absorbed.
- Fluff the quinoa with a fork and let it cool to room temperature.

2. Prepare the Vegetables and Herbs:
- Wash the cherry tomatoes, cucumber, parsley, and mint under cold running water.
- Halve the cherry tomatoes, dice the cucumber, and chop the parsley and mint leaves. Finely chop the red onion.

3. Assemble the Salad:
- In a large mixing bowl, combine the cooked and cooled quinoa, halved cherry tomatoes, diced cucumber, Kalamata olives, chopped red onion, crumbled feta cheese, chopped parsley, and chopped mint.

4. Prepare the Dressing:
- In a small bowl, whisk together the extra-virgin olive oil, freshly squeezed lemon juice, minced garlic, salt, and black

pepper until well combined.

5. Dress the Salad:

- Pour the dressing over the quinoa and vegetable mixture in the large bowl.

- Use a spoon or fork to gently toss and combine all the ingredients until they are evenly coated with the dressing.

6. Adjust Seasoning:

- Taste the Mediterranean Quinoa Salad and adjust the seasoning if needed.

Add more salt, pepper, or lemon juice to your liking.

7. Chill and Serve:

- Cover the salad bowl with plastic wrap or a lid and refrigerate for at least 30 minutes before serving to allow the flavors to meld together.

- Serve the chilled Mediterranean Quinoa Salad as a refreshing and healthy dish, perfect for lunch, picnics, or as a side for grilled meats or fish.

Enjoy your delicious and nutritious Mediterranean Quinoa Salad! It's a delightful combination of textures and flavors that will surely become a favorite in your meal rotation.

Nutritional Information (per serving):
- *Calories: approximately 320 kcal*
- *Carbohydrates: 32g*
- *Protein: 8g*
- *Fat: 18g*
- *Fiber: 5g*
- *Vitamin C: 15mg*
- *Calcium: 80mg*
- *Iron: 3mg*

Recipe Notes:
- *This Mediterranean Quinoa Salad is a hearty and flavorful dish that combines the goodness of quinoa with fresh vegetables and Mediterranean flavors. It's a great option for a light lunch, a side dish, or even as a potluck contribution.*
- *You can add other ingredients to customize the salad according to your preferences, such as artichoke hearts, roasted red peppers, or chickpeas.*
- *Make sure to rinse the quinoa thoroughly before cooking to remove its natural coating called saponin, which can taste bitter if not washed off.*
- *The dressing in this recipe is a simple lemon and olive oil dressing, but you can adjust it with your favorite Mediterranean herbs and spices, like oregano or basil.*

Bruschetta with Tomatoes and Basil

Time to Prepare: 15 minutes **Cooking Time:** 5 minutes

Ingredients:
- 4 large ripe tomatoes, diced
- 1/4 cup fresh basil leaves, chopped
- 2 garlic cloves, minced
- 2 tablespoons balsamic vinegar
- 2 tablespoons extra-virgin olive oil
- 1 baguette or Italian bread, sliced
- Salt and black pepper to taste

Utensils Needed:
- Cutting board and knife
- Medium-sized mixing bowl
- Spoon or fork for mixing
- Grill pan or toaster (optional)
- Serving platter

Instructions:

1. Prepare the Tomato Basil Topping:
- Wash the tomatoes and fresh basil leaves under cold running water.
- Dice the tomatoes into small pieces and place them in a medium-sized mixing bowl.
- Finely chop the fresh basil leaves and add them to the bowl.
- Mince the garlic cloves and add them to the bowl as well.
- Drizzle the balsamic vinegar and extra-virgin olive oil over the tomato basil mixture.
- Season with salt and black pepper to taste.
- Gently toss all the ingredients together until well combined. Let the topping sit for a few minutes to allow the flavors to meld.

2. Prepare the Bread:
- Slice the baguette or Italian bread into 1/2-inch thick slices. You can cut them on a slight diagonal for a more attractive presentation.
- If you prefer the traditional method, grill the bread slices on a hot grill pan for 1-2 minutes on each side until lightly charred and toasted. Alternatively, you can toast the bread in a toaster until it becomes golden and crispy.

3. Assemble the Bruschetta:
- While the bread is still warm, rub one side of each slice with a peeled garlic clove. The warm bread will release the garlic's aroma and flavor.
- Spoon a generous amount of the tomato basil topping over the garlic-rubbed side of each bread slice.

4. Serve and Enjoy:
- Arrange the bruschettas on a serving platter and

garnish with extra basil leaves if desired.

- Serve immediately as a delightful appetizer or light snack.

Recipe Variation:
- If you prefer a creamier version, you can also add a slice of fresh mozzarella on top of the tomato basil topping before serving. Drizzle a little extra olive oil and balsamic glaze over the mozzarella for an extra touch of richness.

Enjoy your delicious Bruschetta with Tomatoes and Basil! It's a wonderful dish to enjoy during warm weather or as an appetizer for any Italian-themed meal.

Nutritional Information (per serving - approximately 2 bruschettas):
- *Calories: approximately 150 kcal*
- *Carbohydrates: 20g*
- *Protein: 3g*
- *Fat: 6g*
- *Fiber: 2g*
- *Vitamin C: 15mg*
- *Calcium: 20mg*
- *Iron: 1mg*

Recipe Notes:
- *Bruschetta is an Italian appetizer that typically consists of grilled bread rubbed with garlic and topped with fresh tomatoes, basil, and olive oil. It's a simple and flavorful dish that highlights the freshness of the ingredients.*
- *For best results, use ripe and juicy tomatoes for the topping. Roma or cherry tomatoes work well in this recipe.*
- *The balsamic vinegar adds a tangy sweetness to the topping, but you can use red wine vinegar or lemon juice if you prefer a different flavor profile.*

Eggplant Caponata

Time to Prepare: 30 minutes **Cooking Time:** 45 minutes

Ingredients:
- 2 medium eggplants, diced into 1/2-inch cubes
- 1/4 cup olive oil, divided
- 1 large onion, finely chopped
- 3 garlic cloves, minced
- 1 celery stalk, finely chopped
- 1 can (14 oz) diced tomatoes, with juices
- 1/4 cup green olives, pitted and chopped
- 2 tablespoons capers, drained
- 2 tablespoons red wine vinegar
- 2 tablespoons honey or brown sugar
- 1/4 cup chopped fresh parsley
- Salt and black pepper to taste

Utensils Needed:
- Large skillet or sauté pan with a lid
- Cutting board and knife
- Colander
- Medium-sized mixing bowl
- Wooden spoon or spatula

Instructions:
1. **Prepare the Eggplant:**
   - Wash the eggplants under cold running water and pat them dry with a paper towel.
   - Cut off the ends of the eggplants and dice them into 1/2-inch cubes.

2. **Sauté the Eggplant:**
   - In a large skillet or sauté pan, heat 2 tablespoons of olive oil over medium heat.
   - Add the diced eggplant to the pan and cook for about 8-10 minutes, stirring occasionally, until the eggplant becomes tender and lightly browned.
   - Remove the cooked eggplant from the pan and set it aside in a medium-sized mixing bowl.

3. **Sauté the Onion, Garlic, and Celery:**
   - In the same pan, add the remaining 2 tablespoons of olive oil and heat it over medium heat.
   - Add the finely chopped onion, minced garlic, and finely chopped celery to the pan.
   - Sauté the vegetables for about 5 minutes, or until the onion becomes translucent and soft.

4. **Add Tomatoes and Simmer:**
   - Pour the can of diced tomatoes with their juices into the pan with the sautéed onion, garlic, and celery.
   - Stir well to combine the ingredients.

- Reduce the heat to low, cover the pan with a lid, and let the mixture simmer for about 10 minutes, allowing the flavors to meld together.

5. Combine Eggplant with Tomato Mixture:

- Add the cooked eggplant back into the pan with the tomato mixture.
- Stir in the chopped green olives, drained capers, red wine vinegar, and honey or brown sugar.
- Season with salt and black pepper to taste.

6. Simmer and Finish:

- Continue simmering the eggplant caponata uncovered for another 15-20 minutes, or until the mixture thickens and the flavors intensify.
- Stir occasionally to prevent sticking.

7. Garnish and Serve:

- Remove the pan from the heat and let the caponata cool slightly.
- Stir in the chopped fresh parsley.
- Serve the Eggplant Caponata warm or at room temperature as a delicious and savory appetizer or side dish.

Enjoy your flavorful and delicious Eggplant Caponata! It's a versatile dish that pairs well with crusty bread, grilled meats, or as a topping for various dishes.

Nutritional Information (per serving - approximately 1 cup):
- *Calories: approximately 180 kcal*
- *Carbohydrates: 22g*
- *Protein: 3g*
- *Fat: 10g*
- *Fiber: 5g*
- *Vitamin C: 10mg*
- *Calcium: 40mg*
- *Iron: 1mg*

Recipe Notes:
- Eggplant Caponata is a traditional Sicilian sweet and sour dish that combines eggplant with tomatoes, olives, capers, and a touch of sweetness from honey or brown sugar. It can be served as an appetizer, side dish, or even as a topping for bruschetta or crostini.
- To reduce the bitterness of the eggplant, you can optionally salt the diced eggplant and let it sit in a colander for about 20 minutes before cooking. Rinse the eggplant thoroughly and pat it dry before using.
- If you prefer a more intense flavor, you can add a splash of red wine to the caponata while cooking.

Spanakopita (Greek Spinach Pie)

Time to Prepare: 45 minutes **Cooking Time:** 45 minutes

Ingredients:
- 1 pound fresh spinach, washed and chopped (you can also use frozen spinach, thawed and drained)
- 1 cup crumbled feta cheese
- 1/2 cup ricotta cheese
- 1/2 cup grated Parmesan cheese
- 1 small onion, finely chopped
- 2 garlic cloves, minced
- 2 tablespoons olive oil
- 1/4 cup chopped fresh dill
- 1/4 cup chopped fresh parsley
- 1/2 teaspoon ground nutmeg
- Salt and black pepper to taste
- 1 package (16 ounces) phyllo dough, thawed
- 1/2 cup (1 stick) unsalted butter, melted
- Sesame seeds for sprinkling (optional)

Utensils Needed:
- Large sauté pan or skillet
- Cutting board and knife
- Mixing bowl
- Pastry brush
- 9x13-inch baking dish

Instructions:

1. Prepare the Spinach Filling:
- In a large sauté pan or skillet, heat the olive oil over medium heat.
- Add the chopped onion and minced garlic to the pan and sauté until the onion becomes translucent and the garlic is fragrant.
- Add the chopped spinach to the pan and cook for a few minutes until it wilts and reduces in volume.
- Remove the pan from the heat and let the spinach mixture cool slightly.

2. Mix the Cheese and Herbs:
- In a mixing bowl, combine the crumbled feta cheese, ricotta cheese, grated Parmesan cheese, chopped dill, chopped parsley, ground nutmeg, salt, and black pepper.
- Add the slightly cooled spinach mixture to the cheese and herb mixture. Mix everything together until well combined.

3. Prepare the Phyllo Dough:
- Preheat the oven to 375°F (190°C).
- Brush the bottom of a 9x13-inch baking dish with melted butter.

4. Layer the Spanakopita:
- Lay one sheet of phyllo dough in the buttered baking dish, allowing the excess to hang over the sides.
- Brush the phyllo sheet with melted butter. Repeat this process, layering and buttering each sheet, until you have about 8 sheets layered.

5. Add the Filling:
- Spread the spinach and cheese filling evenly over the phyllo dough in the baking dish.

6. Finish Layering the Phyllo:
- Layer and butter the remaining sheets of

phyllo dough over the filling, again allowing the excess to hang over the sides.

- Brush the top sheet with melted butter.

7. Fold and Seal:

- Gather the excess phyllo dough from the sides and fold it over the top layer to create a border or crust for the spanakopita.

- Brush the folded edges with melted butter to seal the pie.

8. Score and Sprinkle:

- Using a sharp knife, score the top of the spanakopita into serving-sized pieces.

- Sprinkle sesame seeds over the top for added texture and flavor (optional).

9. Bake:

- Place the baking dish in the preheated oven and bake for about 40-45 minutes or until the spanakopita is golden brown and crispy.

10. Serve:

- Remove the spanakopita from the oven and let it cool for a few minutes before slicing and serving.

- Enjoy your delicious and savory Spanakopita either warm or at room temperature.

Recipe Variation:
- For a vegan version, you can substitute the cheese with vegan alternatives like dairy-free feta or tofu and use plant-based butter or oil for brushing the phyllo dough.

Nutritional Information (per serving - based on 1 slice, assuming 12 slices):
- Calories: approximately 250 kcal
- Carbohydrates: 16g
- Protein: 8g
- Fat: 17g
- Fiber: 2g
- Calcium: 230mg
- Iron: 3mg

Recipe Notes:
- Spanakopita is a classic Greek dish made with layers of crispy phyllo dough filled with a flavorful spinach and cheese mixture. It's a popular appetizer or vegetarian main course option.
- Phyllo dough can be found in the frozen section of most grocery stores. Make sure to thaw it in the refrigerator overnight before using, and keep it covered with a damp cloth while working with it to prevent it from drying out.
- You can customize the filling by adding other ingredients like chopped onions or scallions, pine nuts, or raisins.

Artichoke and Roasted Red Pepper Dip

Time to Prepare: 15 minutes **Cooking Time:** 25 minutes

Ingredients:
- 1 can (14 oz) artichoke hearts, drained and chopped
- 1 cup roasted red peppers (from a jar or homemade), drained and chopped
- 1 cup grated Parmesan cheese
- 1 cup mayonnaise
- 1/2 cup sour cream
- 2 cloves garlic, minced
- 1 tablespoon lemon juice
- 1/2 teaspoon dried thyme
- 1/2 teaspoon dried oregano
- 1/4 teaspoon crushed red pepper flakes (optional, for a hint of heat)
- Salt and black pepper to taste
- Fresh parsley or chives for garnish (optional)

Utensils Needed:
- Oven or toaster oven
- Baking sheet
- Food processor or blender (optional, for a smoother dip)
- Mixing bowl
- Spoon or spatula for mixing
- Serving bowl

Instructions:

1. Roast the Red Peppers (if using fresh):
- Preheat the oven to 425°F (220°C).
- Place the whole red bell peppers on a baking sheet and roast them in the oven for about 20-25 minutes, turning them occasionally, until the skin is charred and blistered.
- Remove the peppers from the oven and transfer them to a sealed plastic bag to steam for about 10 minutes.
- Peel off the skin, remove the seeds, and chop the roasted red peppers. Set them aside.

2. Prepare the Dip:
- In a mixing bowl, combine the chopped artichoke hearts, chopped roasted red peppers, grated Parmesan cheese, mayonnaise, sour cream, minced garlic, lemon juice, dried thyme, dried oregano, crushed red pepper flakes (if using), salt, and black pepper.
- Mix all the ingredients together until well combined.

3. Optional Smooth Texture:
- If you prefer a smoother texture, transfer the mixture to a food processor or blender and blend until you achieve the desired consistency.

4. Adjust Seasoning:
- Taste the dip and adjust the seasoning if needed. Add more salt, black pepper, or

lemon juice according to your preference.

5. Chill and Garnish:

- Cover the dip bowl with plastic wrap or a lid and refrigerate for at least 30 minutes before serving to allow the flavors to meld together.
- Optionally, garnish the dip with fresh parsley or chives for a pop of color.

6. Serve and Enjoy:

- Serve the Artichoke and Roasted Red Pepper Dip with your choice of dippers, such as pita chips, tortilla chips, crackers, or fresh vegetables.

Enjoy your delicious and creamy Artichoke and Roasted Red Pepper Dip! It's a fantastic addition to any party or gathering, and its Mediterranean flavors will be a hit with your guests.

Nutritional Information (per serving - based on approximately 2 tablespoons):
- *Calories: approximately 90 kcal*
- *Carbohydrates: 2g*
- *Protein: 3g*
- *Fat: 7g*
- *Fiber: 1g*
- *Vitamin C: 8mg*
- *Calcium: 90mg*
- *Iron: 0.5mg*

Recipe Notes:
- *This Artichoke and Roasted Red Pepper Dip is a creamy and flavorful appetizer that's perfect for parties, gatherings, or even a simple snack. It pairs well with pita chips, tortilla chips, crackers, or fresh vegetables for dipping.*
- *If you prefer a smoother consistency, you can use a food processor or blender to blend the ingredients until smooth. However, some people enjoy a chunkier texture, so you can simply mix the ingredients by hand for a more rustic dip.*
- *You can use either marinated or plain artichoke hearts for this recipe. If using marinated artichokes, be sure to drain them well to avoid an overly oily dip.*
- *For homemade roasted red peppers, you can char whole red bell peppers over an open flame (gas stove) or under the broiler until blackened, then place them in a sealed plastic bag to steam for a few minutes. Peel off the skin, remove the seeds, and chop the roasted peppers.*

What To Do From Here

Congratulations!

As we reach the concluding pages of this enchanting Mediterranean recipe book, we invite you to take a moment to savor the memories and flavors you've discovered throughout this epicurean journey. From the sun-kissed shores of Greece to the aromatic spice markets of Morocco, you've embarked on a culinary adventure like no other. But fear not, dear reader, for this is not the end – it's merely the beginning of a lifelong love affair with the Mediterranean way of life.

With each recipe, you've experienced the magic of the Mediterranean Diet, not as a mere diet plan but as a celebration of life and flavors. You've delved into the world of wholesome ingredients, nourishing your body and soul with every sumptuous bite. But more than that, you've tasted the joy of simplicity, the pleasure of savoring each meal, and the art of conviviality that brings friends and family together around a table laden with love and delectable delights.

So, dear culinary explorer, as we bid you farewell from the pages of this recipe book, know that your journey has just begun. The Mediterranean way of life is not confined to these recipes; it's a tapestry of flavors, traditions, and wisdom that will enrich your life in myriad ways.

With a heart filled with gratitude and anticipation, set forth on this culinary adventure, carrying the spirit of the Mediterranean with you in every culinary creation. From the shores of the Mediterranean to your kitchen, let the love for wholesome, flavorful food guide you, and may your days be filled with the joy of savoring life's abundant blessings. Please do well to leave an awesome feedback on the review page of this book because this helps others discover this book. Also, check out my author page and follow me for more awesome books. Thank you!

Bon appétit, adventurer! Your Mediterranean Adventure Awaits!

Printed in Great Britain
by Amazon

26633410R00126